REVIEW 5

REVIEW

Volume   5   1983

Edited by

James O. Hoge and
James L. W. West III

University Press of Virginia
Charlottesville

Major funding for *Review* is provided by a grant from the Research Division and the College of Arts and Sciences at Virginia Polytechnic Institute and State University.

This journal is a member of CELJ the Conference of Editors of Learned Journals

THE UNIVERSITY PRESS OF VIRGINIA
Copyright © 1983 by the Rector and Visitors of the University of Virginia

First published 1983

ISSN 0190-3233
ISBN 0-8139-1005-6

Printed in the United States of America

The *Review* Association

Financial support for the first five volumes of *Review* has been provided by The *Review* Association, a group of major universities which support the aims and purposes of the journal. *Review* is now successfully launched, and the five-year commitments of these universities have been fulfilled. The editors wish to express sincere gratitude to these universities for their initial financial support and for their continuing interest and approval.

Columbia University
Duke University
University of Minnesota
Pennsylvania State University
Princeton University
University of Virginia

Contents

In Happy Consort, in Dubious Battle: The State of   1
Milton (and Renaissance) Criticism
  by Joseph Wittreich
    Review of Stanley Fish, ed., *ELH: A Renaissance Issue in Honor of Arnold Stein;* Michael Lieb, *Poetics of the Holy: A Reading of* Paradise Lost; John T. Shawcross, *With Mortal Voice: The Creation of* Paradise Lost

Making It Alone   17
  by Quentin Anderson
    Review of John C. Broderick, General Editor. The Writings of Henry D. Thoreau, *Journal,* vol. I, 1837–1844, ed. Elizabeth Hall Witherell, William L. Howarth, Robert Sattelmeyer, and Thomas Blanding

Critical Myths and Historical Realities; or,   31
How American Was the American Renaissance?
  by Michael Kramer
    Review of Martin Bickman, *The Unsounded Centre: Jungian Studies in American Romanticism;* Michael Davitt Bell, *The Development of American Romance: The Sacrifice of Relation*

A Definitive Edition of Browning's Poems   41
  by Jacob Korg
    Review of *Robert Browning: The Poems*, ed. John Pettigrew, Supplemented and Completed by Thomas J. Collins

The Growth of Poe Texts   49
  by Kent Ljungquist
    Review of *Collected Works of Edgar Allan Poe,* vols. I-III, ed. Thomas Ollive Mabbott; *Collected Writings of Edgar Allan Poe,* vol. I, ed. Burton R. Pollin

Yeats's Politics 59
  by Richard J. Finneran
    Review of Grattan Freyer, *W. B. Yeats and the Anti-Democratic Tradition;* Bernard G. Krimm, *W. B. Yeats and the Emergence of the Irish Free State, 1918-1939: Living in the Explosion;* Elizabeth Cullingford, *Yeats, Ireland and Fascism*

Nick Adams in the Round 69
  by Scott Donaldson
    Review of Joseph M. Flora, *Hemingway's Nick Adams*

The Continuing Relevance of William Morris 73
  by Gary L. Aho
    Review of Peter Faulkner, *Against the Age: An Introduction to William Morris;* Peter Faulkner, *Wilfrid Scawen Blunt and the Morrises;* Mary Lago, ed., *Burne-Jones Talking: His Conversations, 1895-1898, Preserved by His Studio Assistant, Thomas Rooke;* Margaret A. Lourie, ed., *William Morris: The Defence of Guenevere, and Other Poems;* Carole Silver, ed., *The Golden Chain: Essays on William Morris and Pre-Raphaelitism; William Morris and Kelmscott;* Duncan Robinson and Stephen Wildman, *Morris and Company in Cambridge;* Oliver Fairclough and Emmeline Leary, *Textiles by William Morris and Company, 1861-1940; A Book of Verse by William Morris;* John J. Walsdorf, ed., *Printers on Morris;* Florence Boos, ed., *Socialist Diary by William Morris;* Penelope Fitzgerald, ed., *The Novel on Blue Paper by William Morris*

After Strange Gods 119
  by Christian K. Messenger
    Review of Robert J. Higgs, *Laurel and Thorn: The Athlete in American Literature*

Those Blessed Structures 125
  by Maurice English
    Review of John Hollander, *Rhyme's Reason: A Guide to English Verse*

Contents ix

Two on the Aisle — More or Less 131
   by John A. Williams
      Review of Tony Buttitta and Barry Witham, *Uncle Sam Presents: A Memoir of the Federal Theatre, 1935–1939*; E. Quita Craig, *Black Drama of the Federal Theatre Era: Beyond the Formal Horizons*

"To Make Yee All Blithe": Recent Studies in John Skelton 137
   by Ian Lancashire
      Review of Robert S. Kinsman, *John Skelton, Early Tudor Laureate: An Annotated Bibliography c. 1488–1977*; John Skelton, *Magnificence*, ed. Paula Neuss; *Skelton: The Critical Heritage*, ed. Anthony S. G. Edwards

Flannery O'Connor's *Via Extrema et Negativa* 149
   by Melvin J. Friedman
      Review of Frederick Asals, *Flannery O'Connor: The Imagination of Extremity*

The Regensburg *Morte Arthure* 155
   by Mary Hamel
      Review of Karl Heinz Göller, ed., *The Alliterative Morte Arthure: A Reassessment of the Poem*

The Deterioration of Early Nineteenth-Century Book Paper 183
   by Paul S. Koda
      Review of John Murray, *Practical Remarks on Modern Paper*

Emily Dickinson's Workshop 195
   by Jerome Loving
      Review of *The Manuscript Books of Emily Dickinson*, ed. R. W. Franklin

Biographical Decoding: Gissing's Life and Work 203
  by Robert L. Selig
    Review of John Halperin, *Gissing: A Life in Books*

Crime on Their Hands 211
  by George Grella
    Review of Dennis Porter, *The Pursuit of Crime: Art and Ideology in Detective Fiction*; Robin W. Winks, *Modus Operandi: An Excursion into Detective Fiction*

Contributors 223

Editorial Board

Felicia Bonaparte
City College, CUNY

Jerome H. Buckley
Harvard University

Paul Connolly
Yeshiva University

A. S. G. Edwards
University of Victoria

Ian Jack
Cambridge University

Robert Kellogg
University of Virginia

James R. Kincaid
University of Colorado

Cecil Y. Lang
University of Virginia

James B. Meriwether
University of South Carolina

Hershel Parker
University of Delaware

Martin Roth
University of Minnesota

George Stade
Columbia University

John L. Sharpe III
Duke University

G. Thomas Tanselle
*John Simon Guggenheim
Memorial Foundation*

Stanley Weintraub
Pennsylvania State University

In Happy Consort, in Dubious Battle: The State of Milton (and Renaissance) Criticism

Joseph Wittreich

Stanley Fish, ed. *ELH: A Renaissance Issue in Honor of Arnold Stein.* Baltimore: Johns Hopkins University Press, 1982. Special issue, vol. 49, no. 2, pp. 287-542.

Michael Lieb. *Poetics of the Holy: A Reading of* Paradise Lost. Chapel Hill: University of North Carolina Press, 1981. xxi, 442 pp.

John T. Shawcross. *With Mortal Voice: The Creation of* Paradise Lost. Lexington: University Press of Kentucky, 1982. x, 198 pp.

As the days get shorter, narrowing in on the winter solstice, some stories appear that seem to take on the coloration and menace of the gathering darkness and to raise grim questions. . . . But questions like these have something to do with why I find myself reading "Paradise Lost" at about this time of the year. Because Milton helps me understand things. . . . That old epic is not "irrelevant" to those who need some "why" to go with the who, what, where and when.

— Dick Danby, *The Washington Post*

As we turn to the high place accorded Milton, and especially *Paradise Lost*, by academe, it is well to remember the considerable role he continues to play in our popular culture. Malcolm X can read Milton's epic in prison, Frank Reynolds can distribute copies of the poem to initiates of Hell's Angels, Anita Bryant can read from Milton's divorce tracts at her own trial, and Dick Danby can see in Milton's epic a reflection of the whys of Iran and even use it as a guidebook to current events. At the same time, voices can be heard from academe lamenting that studies of Milton have too often been unconcerned with literature and urging that his epic be given "the kind of dignity and serious attention that modern criticism has long accorded fiction, drama, or lyric."[1] Milton continues to live at this hour, it appears in two cultures simultaneously, and for different reasons. Criticism has yet to explore the role Milton has played in the popular culture of this, and the last, century. In studies such as those provided by John Shawcross and Michael Lieb, however, criticism reveals the whys and wherefores of the role he now plays in academe as the center of our literature and as a transmitter of our cultural baggage. Both Shawcross and Lieb mark an advance in criticism, and both also reveal that criticism has much advancing yet to do.

Historically, Milton criticism has been a fairly reliable barometer to the state of Renaissance studies generally—has been an indicator of its current capacities and concerns, of what its horizons are and are soon to be. It is a place to locate trouble when trouble is brewing and, because of its very elevation, a place from which to take a prospect on activities that may imperil it, especially from the outside. Increasingly, Milton criticism has come to center its attention on *Paradise Lost*—on matters literary and aesthetic and on the central book of that epic as both chief crux and climax of the poem. John Shawcross's *With Mortal Voice* and Michael Lieb's *Poetics of the Holy* ride the same critical wave and reveal where it is cresting, not on the political world as Christopher Hill and Fredric Jameson might have wished, but still very close to the boundaries of that world—on its very verge.

Like Louis Martz's *The Poet of Exile*, Shawcross's book is a consolidation of previously presented insights, many of them now more finely honed; and the essays that comprise his book, their materials now redistributed and in some instances their premises reconceived, are handsomely integrated with one another and within an overarching structure. The subtitle of *With Mortal Voice*, "The Creation of *Paradise Lost*," implies both the book's thesis and its concerns. Crediting Tasso's claim that only God and the poets are creators, their poems literary microcosms, Shawcross shows Milton creating in his epic "a similitude of God's creation" (p. 2; cf. p. 94): *Paradise Lost* is a poem of various forms and styles, of correspondences and symmetries—as Andrew Marvell observed long ago, it is a poetic universe founded upon number, weight, and measure. Shawcross's concerns are resolutely with Milton's poem as "an artistic creation" and hence with its "literary achievement" studied and eventually assessed through a wide range of "literary approaches" (p. vii): rhetorical and novelistic, generic and stylistic, structural and mythic. The book, Shawcross himself says, "is not an introduction to the poem but an introduction to ways to approach the poem—not all ways, but the literary ways" (p. 156).

There are no surprises here. The book's principal insights are those we have already come to credit to Shawcross: the interplay of the biblical myths of exodus and return and of their opposing philosophies of history; the layers of metaphoric meaning produced by imagistic and structural patterning; the intricacies of that patterning, often numerological, and of the large structure, marked by balances and parallelisms. *With Mortal Voice* easily meets its author's goal of presenting not "a mere collection of essays but, rather, a total view of the poem" (p. x). It is a superb literary study.

Shawcross's manner is polemical: he would like to diminish "the antagonism . . . in criticism (particularly in Milton criticism) toward structural, numerological, and psychological studies" (p. 1) and to rid this criticism of the Satanist heresy that still blights it; he deplores the notion "that nothing much happens between the thought or emotion of the author and its presentation as art form" (p. 1), as well as the tendency to identify Milton's sources, often by way of indicating his (or worse, a critic's) breadth of reading, without delving into the significance of those sources. As with *Samson Agonistes* so with *Paradise Lost*: the problems of criticism are owing to *its* failures, not Milton's, and this holds true for Shawcross's book as well.

It is written with too severe an economy; its arguments are frustratingly abbreviated and abridged, with the result that some intriguing analogies and, more important, certain crucial observations are neither amplified nor explained. The analogies involving Faulkner and Nathanael West, for example, however cogent, are undeveloped and undifferentiated; and the accompanying claim that Milton does not use myth "to expound a contemporary analogy" but rather presents that "central myth" from which all others are derived (p. 32) might better have been formulated not as an either/or predicament but instead as a both/and hypothesis, the *and* in the hypothesis investigating the extent to which Milton is not only a syncretist of myth but also a reviser of it. We are told that *Paradise Lost* is a dream vision without being alerted to the swerve that poem makes from the conventions of such poetry. Shawcross urges upon us the idea that *Paradise Lost* is "an epic, but an epic with a difference" (p. 90), "is epical but far from traditional" (p. 95); that the poem employs all the elements of epic but not in mere imitation (p. 98) and without ever twisting those elements into anything so modish as an antiepic. In the same breath Shawcross says that "the fusion of genres and the fusion of styles created a new genre and a new style. . . . Milton has gone beyond the more simple mixtures . . . and created . . . *something new*" (p. 107; my emphasis). We expect particularization, elucidation, and definition, even perhaps a naming of the *new* creation, but unexpectedly are only reminded that "*Paradise Lost* is an epic and in epical style" (p. 107). We may also expect elaboration of a statement like the following one: "The traditions of epic that are broken in *Paradise Lost* include the nature of the mixture of genres and the treatment of each kind" (p. 186). Especially here, because Shawcross's instincts are so right, his book needs to touch base with literary theory—with conceptions of containing or subsuming form, of genre and countergenre, and with notions of the cohabitation and contention of forms, with the ways in which literary forms commingle or are disjunctive. If, as Fredric Jameson proposes, genres "are essentially literary *institutions*, or social contracts between a writer and a specific public," we need to know the terms of those contracts and Milton's motives in breaking them.[2] And Jameson is relevant here, since Shawcross comes very close to saying with him that "all generic categories, even the most time hallowed and traditional, are ultimately to be understood [at least as Milton uses them] . . . as mere ad hoc, experimental constructs, derived from a specific textual occasion and abandoned like so much scaffolding when the analysis has done its work."[3] These are quibbles, though, with a richly rewarding book marked not by its failures but by its considerable critical successes.

This study contains impressive applications of the work of S. K. Heninger, Jr., on Renaissance poetics and of Georg Lukács on the novel; it offers important elaborations of, and extensions to, the work of Allan Gilbert, Isabel MacCaffrey, Joseph Summers, and Stanley Fish, along with a forceful refutation of the controlling thesis of A. J. A. Waldock's book. In his excellent eighth chapter, Shawcross provides a dazzling demonstration of how to use the cobweb of variorum annotation: Thomas Newton's citations of the *Iliad* and the *Aeneid*, of Ezekiel and the Wisdom of Solomon, for example, and Todd's of Giles Fletcher. And various chapters, especially those on the poem's structure and numerological relations, along with those on its genre, hero, and appropriation of the myth of exodus, support Shawcross's insistence upon "the importance of the Son and the Son as Man to the whole of *Paradise Lost*" (p. 15). For Shawcross, Book VI is the center of Milton's structural scheme; and the climax of that book "is structurally the highest point of the poem; it deserves the highest emotional response as theological drama; and it is the turning point of the action" (p. 26). The realization that the conclusion of this book rather than the Fall in Book IX is "the focal point of the poem," moreover, leads to the attendant recognition that Milton "is really concerned with man in the Christian world, a world which will end with Judgment Day and the resurrection of the dead. . . . Yet it is man's action in the contemporary world that worries Milton. The apocalyptic view is everywhere in the poem, and we remember the belief that the millennium would come to pass in the mid-seventeenth century" (p. 28).

We are reminded insistently here of the apocalyptic promise that the tears will be wiped forever from our eyes and of the apocalyptic strategy, which is also Milton's, of presenting Christ as Providence, of pitting cyclical and linear conceptions of history against one another and of transcending the potentially tragic in human existence by privileging the comic mode. Nor are we allowed to forget, though this is never made the horizon of Shawcross's interpretation as it will become in Lieb's, that Milton's epic, like Saint John's Revelation, "is as much a political poem as a philosophic one" (p. 10). It is a tribute to Shawcross, certainly, that the suppositions behind his own book provide the formative influence for Michael Lieb's *Poetics of the Holy*, that much only hinted at by Shawcross is brought out of concealment by Lieb in a book bulkier than Shawcross's, and more difficult, but no less fine. When their two books are placed together, we are reminded of Jameson's proposition that "the most vital exchange of energies inevitably takes place between the poles of the psychoanalytic and the theological."[4]

If, as Shawcross says, a part of the problem with Milton criticism is its "misfocus on Book IX rather than on the whole poem and specifically on Book VI as climax of the poem" (p. 146), Lieb obviates that problem by including the whole of Milton's epic within his purview and by centering his interpretative efforts in its sixth book: "*Paradise Lost* is in conception theocentric and finally Christocentric: its vision of holiness places the theocentric in the most prominent position; all else radiates from that" (p. 80). Deeply rooted in the historical point of view, as Shawcross's book is not, and aspiring to the ecumenicalism that marks the studies of Rudolf Otto and Mircea Eliade, Lieb's study takes its place within the broad field of religion and literature—is concerned with "the universality of certain religious phenomena" and, at the same time, conscious of "the parochializing tendencies of all who would 'tame' Milton by subjecting him to that tyranny of paradigm" (pp. xvii-xviii).

Poetics of the Holy is presented in three parts: the first investigates the concept of the holy, its Greco-Roman as well as Judeo-Christian contexts; the second explores the aesthetic dimension of that concept, particularly through such complex renderings of it as one finds in the Renaissance and especially in Milton's writings; and the third initiates discussion of *Paradise Lost* "as a sacral document" (p. xx). Such a perspective on the poem, as Lieb acknowledges, places it "in that body of devotional poetry that deliberately conceived of itself as a verbal representation of the sanctuary" and makes of the poem a "vehicle of worship" that presents "a vision of the holy in full resplendency" (pp. 84–85). For Lieb, Milton is no star who dwelt apart from the main literary and cultural currents of his era.

As in Shawcross's book, there are lapses here, most of which attend upon the risk of relating traditions to poem without sufficient regard for the extent to which the poem not only represents but re-presents those traditions — is a transformation of them. It may be, as Lieb argues, that Milton conjoins the roles of prophet and priest early on and that indeed he is so represented in Plate 16 of Blake's *Milton* (reproduced by Lieb as fig. 1); but it is also true that Blake sees Milton, as Milton in old age might have seen himself, as divesting himself of the priestly in order to enhance his prophetic office and mission. That, presumably, is why Blake depicts Milton stripped naked, his left foot trampling his own priestly garments. There is a question of whether Milton is "collapsing the distinctions between poet and prophet" (p. 46) in order to identify, or to distinguish those roles: are the roles, as Milton *eventually* conceives of them, complementary or opposed to one another? These roles may indeed "find consummate expression in the figure of Moses" (p. 50), and initially in *Paradise Lost* Milton may identify himself with Moses; but identifications are slippery in this poem where ultimately Milton identifies himself with the prophetic figure of John on Patmos and, as Shawcross notes, shares the prophetic office with Raphael and Michael. Is *Paradise Lost*, more than just another rendering of the prophetic tradition, a complicated criticism of it: a poem that is perhaps like the Book of Revelation in its Christocentric design and yet in certain ways resistant to John's theology and even his politics as they came to be understood in the seventeenth century?

My dispute is not with Lieb's insistence upon "the fundamentally hierophantic-oracular basis of Milton's poetics" (p. 63) but with what he sees as Milton's essentially uncritical posture toward those traditions and with his tendency to foreground what Milton, with considerable point, marginalizes in his poetry. There are, consequently, some interpretive distortions here as when Lieb represents Milton's elegies, *Lycidas* among them, as "hagiographies . . . celebrat[ing] the life of the sanctus" (p. 65), or Samson as "a saint in his own right" (p. 79), or Jesus' temptation on the pinnacle as a symbolic crucifixion "in a scene that epitomizes his passion, death, and, finally, ascension" (p. 72). It is fashionable to talk about what poets, writing under the pressure of censorship, are forced to marginalize — and one must talk about that with Milton too, but also about what Milton deliberately marginalizes in order to devalue or silence.

A series of chapters entitled "Fruit," "Place," "Mount," "Name," "Light," "Presence," and "Rest" develop Lieb's thesis and attest to its efficacy. Yet among all these *res sacrae*, the one most important to Milton's poem, and thus to Lieb's book, is "War." Lieb's own treatment of that subject is complementary to Stella Revard's and contrary to James Freeman's, or perhaps more exactly credits Revard with unraveling the mystery of Book VI while acknowledging the bearing that Freeman's conception of warfare has on the final books of Milton's epic.[5] Lieb's chapter on war is the longest in his book, but also the most provocative and, in some ways, problematical. Yet it is here that we see best both the strengths and weakness of Lieb's approach, and here too, I suspect, that the richest dialogue with Lieb's book will occur. In his discussion of warfare, especially in Book VI, Lieb assimilates to his own reading the important perceptions not just of Revard and Turner but also of Austin Dobbins, William B. Hunter, Jr., and Arnold Stein (the accommodation of Stein's perspective is, however, strained). Out of this array of interpretations, Lieb has forged a brilliant (but potentially controversial) reading of his own.

It is the Bible, Lieb posits, that authorizes the notion of war as a sacral event: it provides a compendium of holy war ideology and, at the same time, presents the entire history of Israel as a holy war with the conquest of the Promised Land figuring forth *the* holy war. The idea of holy war, according to this argument, reverberates through Jewish apocalyptic and finds consummate expression in the Christian Apocalypse of Saint John, where "holy war takes on a cosmic, cultic, and finally apocalyptic bearing, as history becomes myth" (p.

251). In the Protestant militancy of the sixteenth and seventeenth centuries, this holy war ideology is brought to the fore; and in *Paradise Lost* "the full range of meanings implicit in the ideology of holy war" is gathered into focus (p. 274).

The celestial battle of Book VI is said to conform to a holy war ideology, while laying bare its political ramifications especially in terms of the Civil War; and the early warfare of the epic's concluding books is seen completing Milton's conformation to this ideology by presenting spiritual warfare waged on earth as holy war par excellence. Lieb's argument is both neat and compelling, especially so inasmuch as he builds his argument around the Book of Revelation, a political work supplying *Paradise Lost* with a political context and a war manual teaching the rudiments of both carnal and spiritual battle. Direct lines of continuity are drawn between John's Apocalypse, Renaissance interpretations of it, and Milton's poems, not just *Paradise Lost* but *Samson Agonistes* as well, where Milton's commitment to the holy war ideology seems to Lieb abundantly evident. But not enough is said here of the disputatious nature of the vast body of biblical commentary produced during the Renaissance. Nothing much is said of *Paradise Regained*, where Jesus lashes out at the whole ideology that Milton's earlier epic might seem to support. And while Joseph Mede is cited throughout Lieb's study, and especially in this chapter, now for his description of the Apocalypse as a celestial theater, there is no mention of his being credited in his own time with solving the mystery of Revelation 12 by interpreting it as a spiritual battle. Nor is attention given the fact that many of Revelation's commentators pointed to the framing of that battle by the stories of the witnesses slain in the streets (an allegory of the crucifixion) and of the woman fleeing into the wilderness (an allegory of the wilderness temptation) to support their contention that Saint John, instead of harmonizing physical and spiritual warfare (as Lieb sees Milton doing), would transcend mortal fight by evolving a wholly new ideology of spiritual warfare. Lieb's strategy is to syncretize existing (and often contending) interpretations; Milton's, I think, is to represent them but also to value them differently. Here, more than anywhere else, one feels the subversive thrust of Milton's epic venture.

By turning his attention so steadfastly to the subject of warfaring in *Paradise Lost*, Lieb raises the sort of questions, spoken by Dick Danby, that bring Milton into the modern world and explain *why* we continue to read his poetry. Inadvertently perhaps, Lieb has also delimited the battleground for criticism that is likely to ensue, wherein we are apt to behold competing ideologies hoping to wrestle one another down. There is nothing dubious about this sort of critical warfare, or of the sort waged, let's say, by Paul Alpers against Stanley Fish (see below), where the issues are sharply defined and the stakes for criticism high. But coming on to the battlefield, it appears, is another kind of soldier — of the sort reviled by Shelley — for whom the issues of literary criticism have become personalized and who is responding to a cry for contention for contention's sake rather than as a necessary part of critical collaboration.

Dear Ann Landers: The wife of a Fortune 500 workaholic who said she wished she had married a professor made me laugh. Please inform her that the ivory tower is made up of millions of sharp teeth that bite. — Just Illinois, No City, Please

Dear Just: Ivy is just another form of grass — on the other side of the fence.
— Ann Landers, *The Washington Post*

For the purpose of celebration, Stephen Orgel, the senior editor of *ELH*, has turned over a rein of his journal to Stanley Fish who, in turn, has gathered an eclectic but still highly distinguished group of essays and presented them under the title *ELH: A Renaissance Issue in Honor of Arnold Stein.* The essays range widely — from Elizabethan romance to Civil War politics to Restoration drama, from prose fiction to sonnet sequences, with individual essays fixing attention on Peele, Shakespeare, Herrick, and especially Milton. Of these, Jackson Cope's is the most strikingly written and, along with Arthur Marotti's, the most innovative in conception and in statement. The editorial oversights are few: there are just two — sins of "commission" as it were. D. J. Gordon's occasional remarks on the Leonardo legend (written for the Leonardo quincentenary in 1952) not only disrupt the strong lines of connection between A. C. Hamilton's essay and Cope's, but now some thirty years later are patently without occasion, or even much interest. More seriously disruptive to the volume as a whole are the roars and whispers of Jonathan Goldberg's "The Politics of Renaissance Literature: A Review Essay," the first section of which is addressed to Miltonists and the last, it would seem, to our profession at large. More properly this coda to the volume might have been called "The Politics of Literary Criticism" and, more accurately, might have been subtitled "An Essay in Discipleship." I will return to it later.

Three of the essays in the Stein festschrift—Paul Alpers's on *Lycidas*, Thomas Kranidas's on *Of Reformation*, and the jointly written piece, by Stephen Booth and Jordan Flyer, on Sonnet VII—form an island in the volume to which Miltonists might retire to contemplate the state and at times the disarray, of their discipline. The three essays are a throwback, as it were, to the era of New Criticism; and yet each, in strikingly different fashion, provides testimony to the continuing vitality of an older, but not outmoded, critical methodology: Kranidas's concerns are imagistic and structural, and those of Alpers, Booth, and Flyer, contextual, linguistic, and syntactical. All three essays offer close readings, and yet evident in two of them is a curious obtuseness over where Milton studies have been leading us, even over who its leaders are.

In fairness to Alpers, the issue for him is one of critical resistance and exclusion: remarkably little of value has been written on Milton's elegy since 1961, when C. A. Patrides consolidated the best of what Alpers regards as finally undistinguished criticism. In his words, "It is remarkable how little of value has been written about *Lycidas*, and it is even more remarkable that it has been the occasion of less than good essays by very good critics . . ., most recently Stanley Fish" (pp. 468-69). Only two essays on the poem, for Alpers, are undeserving of rebuke, those by Rosemond Tuve and Berkeley colleague Donald Friedman: "Tuve['s] . . . essay on *Lycidas* is the only one that matches Friedman's in depth and subtle intelligence" (p. 480). Alpers's silences here are curious. His proposition is that pastoral—that convention—is "enabling" to *Lycidas*, especially if we follow Milton's lead and allow his Virgilian model to define the convention for us (p. 469). We hear nothing here of Edward Tayler and Louis Martz, two of a number of critics of the 1970s whose insights this essay, instead of advancing upon, in many instances merely approaches.

The magisterial tone and range of citation in Alpers's essay protect its author from the charge of critical innocence. Silence here is presumably judgmental. On the other hand, Booth and Flyer write in a different tone: "Try not to become nervous about what we are saying" (p. 463); and they leave themselves open to the very charges from which Alpers protects himself: "Evidence that Milton associated the parables with the poem [Sonnet VII] does not, of course, inform the poem, and—at least in the case of the parable of the vineyard— editors and commentators have persistently failed to recognize any such association in 'How soon hath time.' The association, however, is active in the poem and would be audible even if Milton's drafts of 'Letter to a Friend' had not survived" (p. 454). Aside from the seeming contradiction of the first and last statements in this quotation, there is a notable ignorance of Milton's editors and commentators standing naked at its center. Here is what the Columbia Variorum commentators say about the parable and the poem: "Lines 9-12 echo the parable of the vineyard in a reversed way. . . . [The entire sonnet] 'breathes the spirit of it.' "[6]

No less than Alpers's essay, this one raises the question of whether criticism is to be regarded as a cooperative — or a coterie — effort; but unlike the Booth and Flyer essay, so tedious in its presentation and so strained in its readings, Alpers's is marked throughout by a careful probing of the tissue of Milton's poem, which yields important diagnostic results. Alpers's supposition is that "somewhere in the course of the poem, the shepherd-speaker emerges"; his strategy, to "begin at the beginning and trace his emergence" in order to reveal "what kind of poem *Lycidas* is and how Milton can make new the conventions that enable it" (p. 471). While there are moments of deafness here — Alpers never hears the prophetic voice in the opening lines or in the first lines of the second verse paragraph — there is a fine intelligence everywhere evident that moves us into, then through, the depths of Milton's poem: Saint Peter's invective, for instance, and even more strikingly the flower passage in *Lycidas*. Alpers makes the point deftly, emphatically, that this is a poem written for the living, not the dead, and that it takes its bearings finally in the world of time and earthly existence. This essay, and especially the rush of eloquence in Kranidas's, brings the celebration of Arnold Stein to an impressive crescendo.

This is where closure should have been achieved, or at least cloture invoked. Unfortunately, however, yet another celebrant takes the stage, tunes the earlier and weightier festivities to another key, and issues a diatribe against certain Marxist tendencies in some recent Milton criticism. Goldberg's diatribe is moderated by fulsome praise of Stanley Fish and Stephen Orgel. The impulse to commend both is understandable, although, besides seeming out of place in *ELH*, the compliment paid to each is ill-conceived and clumsy, especially the one paid to Orgel for being able to do everything Stephen Greenblatt can do, but doing it better (p. 537).

We are justly warned by Goldberg that ideology produces closures as well as reductions in literary criticism, thereby alerting us to those damaging and condescending glances at others in Fredric Jameson's work. In what follows, though, Goldberg becomes a practitioner of what he claims to abhor. Of Christopher Hill's *Milton and the English Revolution*, Goldberg writes: "The book is full of cheap shots" (p. 523); what Hill presents as biographical commentary, Goldberg charges, is actually "autobiographical" (p. 524). Later in the review, we read gratuitously of Barbara Lewalski's "vacuous lumping" (p. 540) and of Annabel Patterson's "old historicism" (p. 541).[7] These comments, abridged to the point of insult, come upon the heels of a scorching attack on Gary Schmidgall's *Shakespeare and the Courtly Aesthetic* (1981). In the course of that attack, we hear of Schmidgall's lacking "the slightest ability to read texts" (p. 540), of his presenting for critical discussion issues "one would have thought any undergraduate knew" (p. 539), of his writing a brand of criticism without "the vitality and intelligence and moral seriousness . . . of Helen Gardner" and, finally, of Schmidgall's offering "no illumination of either historical or literary matters" (p. 538). We are hearing here of the same book recently reviewed by J. L. Styan as "one of the richest pieces of primary research of the year . . . a fine example of a 'milieu' study" and one that places *The Tempest* "squarely in its period."[8] When these decidedly different estimates are placed side by side, we are set to wondering, by the tone of Goldberg's review, about its own ideology and motives, its targets and judgments. We may remember as well the complaint of Paul Alpers, who speaks earlier in the volume, of that "melancholy indication of what ideological confrontation has done to critical discourse" (p. 473) and may feel obliged to remark upon what such confrontation, when unmonitored, can do to our profession.

More than any other piece I have read in this genre, Goldberg's review, especially its third part, raises serious questions about the politics of reviewing and the code of ethics governing the reviewing process. For that reason, but also because Goldberg's review presumes to chart another course for Milton criticism, and for Renaissance criticism generally, and thereby raises questions about the ethics of interpretation itself, I dwell on it here.

Goldberg's complaint that "Jameson wants to locate Milton's text in the context of Iran" (p. 517) is best countered by Barbara Herrnstein Smith's contention that "whatever historical investigations *can* determine, they cannot determine the historically indeterminate meanings of a poem."[9] To privilege such interpretations, as Goldberg would do — to confine interpretative activity to the determination of historical meanings—is both to devalue literary works and to diminish literary criticism. A poem like *Paradise Lost* survives into our own time by virtue of what Smith would call its *"emergent* meanings"; while it recovers the past for the present, equally it provides "metaphors and parables of an unpredictable future" and thus possesses "meanings independent of the particular context that occasioned . . . [its] composition."[10] It may be better to widen the girth of criticism than to pinch it in, and it is certainly preferable to avoid critical encounters that eventuate in the privileging of one methodology and the scuttling of another.

Goldberg's review engages "the heavies" of our profession—Jameson and Hill, Greenblatt and Orgel, Lewalski and Patterson. Still, in Part I, the shots are all from the hip; in Part II, there is too much bowing and scraping. Most disconcerting, in Part III, amidst its fulminations, an assistant professor appears in this august company only to be positioned for assault. Why he should appear here is mysterious. If Goldberg's objective was to broaden his field of inquiry by looking beyond nondramatic to dramatic literature of the Renaissance and then fixing his attention on Shakespeare, there was an obvious choice—one whose concerns are like Goldberg's political and not like Schmidgall's aesthetic: *Shakespeare as a Political Thinker*, edited by John Alvis and Thomas G. West. There would have been plenty of grist for Goldberg's mill here: Robert Heilman sounds the keynote for the volume in the opening sentence of his essay: "Political subject matter is everywhere in Shakespeare's tragedies and histories."[11] Heilman is exactly right, and ripe, for inclusion in this review. He is of the generation of Christopher Hill; he is also a New Critic here turned historicist.

If the appearance of Schmidgall's book in this review seems unaccountable by the premises Goldberg establishes for his other choices, the appearance of Goldberg's review in the setting provided by this special issue of *ELH* is more puzzling still. *ELH* does not normally publish reviews, and reviews are not *normally* featured in festschriften. One is left to wonder by whose influence it was that this hitherto obscure young man, who was neither a student nor a colleague of Arnold Stein, gained access to this volume. Given the parochialism of its praise and the undiscriminating character of its censure, why insinuate this review into a festschrift where it redounds to no one's credit and contributes to no one's honor—not Arnold Stein's certainly (he is deserving of better and so are we all) and not Stanley Fish's (the potential embarrassment to an editor who must balance so many delicacies is considerable).

More important than such political speculations, however, is the effect of Goldberg's review upon the volume as a whole. Here there is an upside-downing of all the topoi traditionally associated with festschriften. The spirit of feting, celebrating, honoring now lies mute. This is one reason for bewilderment and displeasure, because most of the earlier pages, expertly edited and arranged by Fish, in consort define the genre of festschriften nobly; Goldberg's pages, on the other hand, define the countergenre, the antigenre. As masque turns into antimasque, the academic tradition of honoring some modulates into another sort of activity, that of dishonoring others. Those earlier pages, written in the "quieter and more reflective tone" that Avrom Fleishman attributes so appropriately to Stein himself, are now replaced by pages of acrimony relieved only by the amusing hit-and-run tactics of the concluding paragraph. This is disheartening. For Stein's achievements are immense, and his scholarly eminence has always been accompanied by courtesy in dealing with his compeers and by sensitivity especially for those whose careers and reputations are still in the making.

It would not bear remarking, were the principle not so flagrantly violated, that contributions to festschriften generally involve a taking stock of another's achievement and even sometimes are an occasion for building upon it. The celebrated is the usual point of reference in such volumes. In Goldberg's essay though, the tendencies of most festschriften are reversed: the celebrants become the celebrated, theirs is the work being taken stock of, the turns and counterturns of their careers the issue. The essay is a classic in its "kind"—what Herbert Lindenberger calls the "All Outer" which, in its positive form, is "a paean of praise . . . emanating from one of the author's friends" (see Section II of Goldberg's review) and which, in its negative form, is "an uncompromising denunciation" of books that are now no more than a vehicle through which a reviewer can "vent whatever rage he can verbally emit" (see Sections I and III of Goldberg's review).[12]

The self-absorption of this review disallows for a sense of others and hence for a simple extension of courtesies. Doubtless, we have all felt the impulse to launch into a negative "All-Outer" even as most of us, with Lindenberger, remain "fully conscious of what power personal considerations can exert": "I made sure the author was of tenure-level rank and thus cleared myself of any possible guilt for helping kick still another young academic out on the street!"[13] Goldberg's review, never achieving the finer tones because never aspiring to these finer considerations, is antithetical to the whole reviewing process. As well as anyone, Wayne Booth describes the minimal expectations of a review and defines the reviewing standards that, when they go unobserved, "Do Nobody Any Good": one function of a review is to give a ready-made reader an accurate report and clear appraisal; another is to lure the indifferent or hostile reader into the enterprise; and yet another is to advance the critical inquiry by vexing others, including the book's author, into thought.[14] As authors are displaced by reviewers and as rancor replaces reason, assessments lose their balance, are turned askew, and harden into judgments rendered as final and decisive. Criticism, however, has not yet advanced to the point that it is ready for a Last Judgment (especially one pronounced by a novice); both those who pronounce such judgments and those who sponsor them might reflect upon the wisdom of Paul Ricoeur when he writes, "Neither in literary criticism or in the social sciences is there such a last word. Or, if there is any, we call that violence."[15]

Only in a negative sense are the consequences of Goldberg's review likely to be salutary. Some may be devastated by it; all of us should be unsettled by it. The current standards for advancement in our profession are rigorous, and competition is keen. Reviewers, in turn, bear an enormous burden of responsibility: what they put into print goes before their peers in other institutions and is scrutinized by personnel committees, deans, provosts, even college and university presidents. It is proper that what they scrutinize should not be inscrutable, that the contexts in which they find judgments levied should not be bizarre, and that, however severe, those judgments be equitable. "There *is*," as Barbara Smith's book affirms, "an ethics of interpretation" that governs, or should govern, the behavior of interpreters toward their audience (which includes fellow interpreters): "The fundamental imperative for all speakers is that they mean what they say and take responsibility for having said it."[16] It is not easy to defend to anybody what is wholly dismissive and categorically negative. If Goldberg's tendency to privilege one critical methodology over another is impoverishing of literature, his penchant for rhetorical abuse and the unmoderated judgment is imperiling to criticism; it frustrates the reviewing process itself.

It is not a happy situation for anyone when reviewers, instead of books, require reviewing. Then the whole profession goes on trial and its processes of evaluation are subjected to serious cross-examination. Such a situation may nevertheless serve to remind *all of us* engaged in the reviewing process that with the judgment we pronounce we shall be judged—and of a corollary: the judgment is likely to be without mercy for those who have shown no mercy.

Notes

1. John T. Shawcross, "The Chronology of Milton's Major Poems," *PMLA*, 76 (1961), 345.

2. Fredric Jameson, *The Political Unconscious: Narrative as a Socially Symbolic Act* (Ithaca: Cornell Univ. Press, 1981), p. 106.

3. Ibid., p. 145.

4. Ibid., p. 69.

5. See Stella Revard's *The War in Heaven* (Ithaca: Cornell Univ. Press, 1980) and James Freeman's *Milton and the Martial Muse* (Princeton: Princeton Univ. Press, 1980).

6. *A Variorum Commentary on the Poems of John Milton*, ed. Douglas Bush et al. (New York: Columbia Univ. Press, 1970), II, 367-68.

7. Goldberg addresses himself to the following works (those by Hill and Lewalski, prize-winning efforts): Fredric Jameson, "Religion and Ideology," in *1642: Literature and Power in the Seventeenth Century*, ed. Frances Barker et al. (Univ. of Essex, 1981); Christopher Hill, *Milton and the English Revolution* (New York: Viking Press, 1978); Barbara Lewalski, *Protestant Poetics and the Seventeenth-Century Religious Lyric* (Princeton: Princeton Univ. Press, 1979); and Annabel Patterson, *Marvell and the Civic Crown* (Princeton: Princeton Univ. Press, 1978).

8. J. L. Styan, "Recent Studies in Elizabethan and Jacobean Drama," *SEL*, 22 (1982), 341-42.

9. Barbara Herrnstein Smith, *On the Margins of Discourse: The Relation of Literature to Language* (Chicago: Univ. of Chicago Press, 1978), p. 154.

10. Ibid., p.151.

11. Robert Heilman, "Shakepearean Comedy and Tragicomedy: Implicit Political Analogies," *Shakespeare as a Political Thinker*, ed. John Alvin and Thomas G. West (Durham: Carolina Academic Press, 1981), p. 27.

12. Herbert Lindenberger, "Re-viewing the Reviews of *Historical Drama*," in *The Horizon of Literature*, ed. Paul Hernadi (Lincoln: Univ. of Nebraska Press, 1982), p. 283.

13. Ibid., p. 296.

14. Wayne Booth, "Three Functions of Reviewing at the Present Time," *The Horizon of Literature*, pp. 265-67.

15. Paul Ricoeur, "The Model of the Text: Meaningful Action Considered as a Text," *New Literary History*, 5 (Autumn 1973), 110.

16. Smith, *On the Margins of Discourse*, p. 151.

Making It Alone

Quentin Anderson

John C. Broderick, General Editor. The Writings of Henry D. Thoreau. *Journal*, Vol. I, 1837–1844. Ed. Elizabeth Hall Witherell, William L. Howarth, Robert Sattelmeyer, and Thomas Blanding. Princeton: Princeton University Press, 1981. 702 pp.

Many Americans, when led to consider what sort of culture surrounds them, tap a reservoir of scorn laced with self-hatred for a society saturated with considerations of profit, while at the same time tacitly conceding that they can no more escape it than they can avoid drawing breath. They appear to assume while reading Emerson and Thoreau that they can enter fully into the efforts to escape imaginative enclosure by a commercial society which characterize the work of these classic Americans. But we don't in fact undertake what Emerson and Thoreau did. They proposed to strike for intellectual and imaginative freedom as individuals; they carried to an extreme the still current presumption that what Americans had won was personal freedom.

Emerson's declaration of intellectual independence was not, after all, made in behalf of the nation but of the individuals who composed it. He, almost alone, reached an awareness of the limiting conditions of the freedom we had won, and it was that awareness that Thoreau came to share. Having stepped outside a church he found spiritually empty, Emerson also scented an illusory air in the institutions of Massachusetts and the Union; they failed to expand his personal freedom, the only purpose that could justify their existence. To the thoroughgoing individualist, the difference between the me and the not-me is that the first catches up all the consciousness there is. To the degree that one becomes this ample subject, the rest of the world becomes one's object. The claim of society forestalls that more inclusive grasp of the world which has what Emerson called "nature" as its object. The organized human community must be rejected because it fractures its members by inciting them to get theirs, to break off pieces of the world for their own, or to claim a superior status for themselves and diminish others.

By muting the astonishing extravagance of the demands Emerson and Thoreau made for the individual, we have hidden the extremity of the situation they believed they were facing. I do not think it over the mark to say that these provincials were uncannily right; they found the root of our modern social despair long ago. The American scene was far more subject to impersonal conditions than any other we can name. Another way of putting this is to say that traditional grounds for securing identity were unprecedentedly scarce. It has taken a long while to come to an understanding of the fact because facts so pervasive are, as Fernand Braudel maintains, the hardest to detect.

Why did individualism of this order not appear in Europe? Or, to put the same question in a narrower context, why is it misleading to call Emerson and Thoreau romantics? The answer is deceivingly simple: they founded their assertion of individual freedom on a timeless order to which the individual alone had access. (The fact that this conviction clearly derives from Christianity should not lead us to think of it as a mere inheritance; it was present reality in their eyes.) Unlike English romantics, who sought the liberty of the subject by engaging in a dialectical struggle with elements in their culture—preserving a dramatic relation to its past or present institutions, values, or tendencies—Emerson and Thoreau founded their claim for the individual on an all-inclusive order. Their individualism was necessarily more absolute because the conditions they opposed, while far less dramatic or overtly compelling, worked, as Tocqueville saw, to further an internalized despotism. The result was that the individualism of these two was forced to make a far wider claim on reality than the European romantic could possibly sustain, since the society he was faced by in Europe appeared a stage for contending powers. The romantic engaged by the coming of the French Revolution and its sequel necessarily found himself caught in temporal transformations that Emerson saw as incidental distractions from the individual's perception of a general condition.

In this respect the logic of the situation as Emerson and his young follower appear to have felt it is clear: a cultural scene informed by money, exchange, and mensuration in general does not present itself as subject to transformations in the eyes of these individualists. Other writers, who, like Washington Irving, were more deeply immersed in the cultural moment, saw such social ills as the panic of 1837 as consequences of a fever of speculation; for them those who were greedy and foolish were doing harm to others. Effectual human agency lay within the society. For Emerson such concessions to mere temporal process defeated the effort to see the large whole which lay behind it.

Hindsight suggests that the greater impersonality of the social condition in this country was the consequence of democracy and what democracy opened the way to, a society in which commercial considerations came closer to ruling the roost than elsewhere. In the absence of the variety of social options Europe afforded, the individual whom we had endowed with rights enjoyed a lonely freedom, a freedom in which he was more alone with money, with the world constituted by exchange, than were other westerners.

What Emerson and Thoreau proposed in their most assertive early phase was that their society, organized as a commercial republic, was in every important respect an imprisoning and distorting screen that hid what was truly to be fostered and cherished in each of us. They had no intention of founding a movement; to do so would have belied their largest intention, that of freeing others from their assumption that social or familial ties came first. Church, state, family, associations of all sorts were composed of persons who had not grasped their native powers, who had fractured themselves. Since they were absorbed in social roles, they were likely to believe that organized society constituted reality. Awareness of a capacity for a total vision was not available to them.

In most of our encounters with others we are forced to adopt partial guises; we must fragment ourselves. Such are the ties to family, town, and state. The high alternative was friendship, or what Emerson called "the union ideal in actual individualism." It is an exalted condition. The claim that the right perception of all existence is open only to individuals doesn't amount to saying that that perception is now being enjoyed by any particular person but rather that it can be sought and enjoyed in no other way.

What is missing in most discussions of this "transcendental" claim is an examination of its direct bearing on attitudes toward others and the society at large. The obvious danger of being impersonal to combat a condition you have defined as impersonal is that it will lead you to make an impersonal response—lead, that is, to an impoverished conception of humanity. The world seen as the destined object of the individual was one in which history, drama, and fiction became peripheral and you found yourself alone as proprietor of a vision for which you claimed a total sufficiency. That vision might conceivably be shared by a "friend," but the person so called would have, like your best self, no character save his sense of the whole of things. Emerson was well aware that he could not maintain such an inclusive perception of existence, and glimpsed it only at moments. He often deplored his divided state. But he remained persuaded that his and our only hope lay in our unique access to universality, the "one mind" which informed everything.

This exorbitant claim was supported by an intense emotion that must be called religious. The spiritual exercises of Emerson and his young convert look, from our distance, like a kind of spiritual claim-jumping; where the god of the churches had once been, let Emerson or Thoreau, or whoever answered to the indwelling spirit as they did, now be. Yet if they were announcing their possession of quasi-divine powers of vision and creation, they were also acknowledging internal divisions; they were possessed by a vision at odds with their familial and social selves. By playing down the personal stresses that Emerson and Thoreau explicitly admitted, by softening their fierceness toward public pieties, and by shunting them off into a literary realm that did not exist when they were alive, we have diffused and domesticated their disruptive force. These two were both more stressed by inner struggle *and* more radical than their present-day interpreters admit.

This general statement of a position Thoreau found congenial must not be taken to suggest that he remained a disciple. He found that the stance Emerson outlined jibed with feelings of his own; it became a part of the furnishing of his mind, but he thereafter acted on the basis of his own perceptions. For example the mature Thoreau could not, like Emerson, think of nature as grandly representative of humanity because he found it so immediately exemplary of the right way to go about being himself. Emerson set the stage for him, but his own life, his attempt to root himself in his experience of Concord, was what filled it. It is interesting and significant that his commencement speech on his graduation from Harvard in 1837 embraced a position that Emerson's address of the following day, "The American Scholar," undermined. Thoreau was one of three who spoke on the topic "The Commercial Spirit of Modern Times Considered in Its Influence on the Political, Moral and Literary Character of a Nation." Thoreau framed his address with the conventional notion of an inevitable progress, and this takes the sting out of his denunciation of the "commercial spirit." He learned from Emerson (either the next day or soon thereafter) to abandon any collective social hope and to pin his hope on the "perfect freedom" he had called "characteristic of our epoch" in his speech. His address gives vent to a playful unorthodoxy in his proposal for reform of our selfishness: "The order of things should be somewhat reversed, — the seventh should be man's day of toil, wherein to earn his living by the sweat of his brow, and the other six his sabbath of the affections and the soul, in which to range this widespread garden, and drink in the soft influences and sublime revelations of Nature." Clearly, the aspect of Emerson that counted most for the young graduate is found in the third paragraph of "The American Scholar" in which Emerson speaks of "the *divided* or social state" as disastrous to our sense of ourselves.

The use Emerson made of his extraordinary extrapolation of individual powers was clearly dazzling to Thoreau. The mind, once aware of itself and its relation to the supreme order apparent in nature, could confidently conclude that the nation was for the individual, and could thereafter be its own legislator, its own moral and spiritual guide. Most important of all, individuals were not simply the unique perceivers of the truth of things; they alone could create. Emerson puts this with aphoristic concision: "Perception makes."

The present-day reader is likely to miss the emphasis here. For Thoreau, as well as for Emerson and Whitman, it falls on the individual's power to create rather than on the things made. To create from within outward, to be, in Thoreau's phrasings, one who "is earnestly building up a life," or attempting to "build up a self," is to be creative as a tree is of its leaves or a plant its flowers. Thoreau's need for an assurance that he had this power was urgent. Emerson could tacitly profit by the classic Christian division between body and spirit. He put his body to socially sanctioned uses while his spirit went its way and proclaimed its self-sufficiency. Thoreau had to contend actively with the implication of his body with the species and society. He was, as has been emphasized, the last male Thoreau; he had to conceive of himself as having some effectual agency in his world even though he was not lover, husband, father. His family ties were all end-stopped; he was son, brother, nephew only. The possession of male genitals compromised his desire to think of himself as a self-sufficing creative source, possessed of both stamens and pistils like a flower. Masturbation and nocturnal emissions — his term is "impurity" — were discomforting reminders of incompleteness, which he defied by speaking of himself as flowering when he wrote, a usage not unconnected with his adoption of Emerson's term *publish* which, as Matthiessen used to say, was a term for an individual action —

rather, I would put it, than a commercial transaction.

The need I have spoken of to find nature exemplary, to root his aspirations in what he saw and touched, encountered another difficulty in the primary physiological necessities, eating and defecating, which ran together in his mind with generation and conception. Stephen Railton has explored Thoreau's long struggle in the journals to reconcile himself to the fact that the exquisite lilies of his river grew out of mud, and the articles of Michael West have detailed an unresting concern with both his own involement in an excrementitious world and with the way in which words, like lilies, may be thought of as arising out of the matter of existence. In short, Thoreau was beset both as a piece of nature and as a social being. The body threatened to fragment and disperse your energies unless you could discipline it properly, just as the society around you threatened to fragment your attention to the whole of nature and lead you to focus on discrete possessions or claims to status. No removal, to Walden Pond or elsewhere, was ever to lessen the need to make sentences which were sinewy enough to withstand the challenges from the very body that sustained him or the town that both nurtured and threatened him.

The brilliant youngster who began to keep a journal in the year of his graduation (he was twenty years old), did so at Emerson's prompting, and in doing so rose to the imperative posed in "The American Scholar": "Man hopes, genius creates. Whatever talents may be, if the man create not the pure efflux of the Deity is not his; — cinders and smoke there may be, but not yet flame."

This first volume of the new edition of Thoreau's journals is first of all a record of Thoreau's leap into the arena: he would be nothing less than what Emerson demanded, at once thinker, poet, and utterly self-reliant seer and seeker. The content of the volume is uneven; it is sometimes even feeble, but overall it is a highly impressive start.

This edition of the journals will supplant that of 1907, which ran to fourteen volumes, and has twice been reprinted. It is published with the seal of the Center for Editions of American Authors. An extensive scholarly apparatus follows the text, which is uncluttered except for notations which refer to physical details, such as blank, torn out, or partial pages. Of the forty-seven bound notebooks comprising the original journal, seven appear in this volume together with such fragments as the editors have assigned to the years 1837–1844. As they point out, the journal underwent changes in character over the years; this first volume is what they describe as a "writer's workbook," rather than a record of activities and reflections from day to day. There is a good deal of verse, many scraps of translation together with comments on the classics and on an extensive reading in the English poets. Drafts of essays and critical pieces are scattered throughout. In short the volume seems atypical when contrasted with Thoreau's later practice. Yet it is striking how many of Thoreau's most familiar themes and preoccupations are to be found toward the beginning of these five hundred pages of text.

I offer a rough itemization of some twenty pages (48-69). These begin with verses addressed to Walden Pond, dated 3 June 1838. There follows a paragraph in which it is noted that in "the domains of trade" our ties to others are pared down to "brotherhood by law." Then comes one of many passages in the early journals which are devoted to the themes of heroism and bravery — virtues demanded by the writer's stressed personal situation. In a following passage we find it said that truth is no other than falsehood "until it come and utter itself by my side," an instance of the rhetorical overstatement Thoreau later speaks of as necessary if one is to awaken others to their situation in the world, and in accord with a basic premise: what is known is what is directly encountered. On page 50 we find a piece of metaphysical bravado:

If with closed ears and eyes I consult consciousness for a moment — immediately are all walls and barriers dissipated — earth rolls from under me, and I float, by the impetus derived from the earth and the system — a subjective — heavily laden thought, in the midst of an unknown & infinite sea, or else heave and swell like a vast ocean of thought — without rock or headland. Where are all riddles solved, all straight lines making there their two ends to meet — eternity and space gambolling familiarly through my depths. I am from the beginning — knowing no end, no aim. No sun illumines me, — for I dissolve all lesser lights in my own intenser and steadier light — I am a restful kernel in the magazine of the universe.

The next entry rejects all the schemes he is offered as "solutions of the universe," and speaks of an unending search for an anchor within it; he is at this moment not a "restful kernel." Six days later he muses on the sound of church bells which are suggestive "of many catechisms and religious books twanging a canting peal round the world," and of an Egyptian temple, of alligators, storks, Moses in the bulrushes, and of the "beating of gongs in a Hindoo subterranean temple." In the middle of this passage on the dull and heavy interaction of an archaic religiosity, Thoreau inserts a countering reference: "Not so these larks and pewees of Musquetaquid"—employing the Indian name of Concord's river. Characteristically, he finds an anchor or a place to stand when he hears the larks and pewees along his river; he repels a shared communion, a mythos which involves a story and other characters—a Pharaoh's daughter perhaps, to rescue an infant Concord Moses. His solution of the universe is to be found here and now. He begins to become the Thoreau we know, conforming to the Emersonian injunction to start afresh; he will not answer to any authority not derived from a moment of perception. Two days later, under the heading "Holy War," he recurs to the inward struggle with "passion and appetite," once more in military terms. On the following day a passage headed "Scripture" describes Homer, the Zendavesta, and Confucius as "a strain of music wafted down to us on the breeze of time," apparently as immediate as the song of pewees and larks, "by its very nobleness it is near and audible to us." Another familiar theme appears four days later, that of the power of distance to make otherwise discordant human sounds welcome to the ear; this is followed by a visual parallel in the entry for 29 August 1838, in which the structures men build, ugly up close, assume grace and fitness when viewed from a distant hilltop. The theme is varied and generalized on 2 September under a heading used earlier and repeated here, "Sphere Music." After some notes I neglect there is a copy of verses on Fair Haven (a spot at which the Concord broadens) and various passages for a projected essay, "Sound and Silence," in which Thoreau makes a characteristic reduction of the sublime—it does not bring terror or awe, but enables us to realize ourselves: "The thunder is only our signal gun, that we may know what communion awaits us—Not its dull sound, but the infinite expansion of our being which ensues we praise—and unanimously name sublime." I skip some passages, chiefly of verse, and end my sample with this entry for March 1839, headed "The Poet" which is, for good reason, often quoted: "He must be something more than natural—even supernatural. Nature will not speak through him but along with him. His voice will not proceed from her midst, but breathing on her, will make her the expression of his thought. He then poetizes, when he takes a fact out of nature into spirit—he speaks without reference to time or place. His thought is one world, hers another. He is another nature—Nature's brother."

Since Thoreau rewrote the entries in much of this volume, and we don't have the manuscript on which he drew, it is not possible to call these passages his first fruits. But even if the present wording is that of 1842, it is hard to believe that *Walden* is more than a decade off, since so much of what occupies Thoreau in the published book is to be found here. What is essentially different is of course the quality of the prose. The comparative laxity of the writing in this volume would not have satisfied the Thoreau who, as James L. Shanley has demonstrated, made no fewer than eight revisions of the *Walden* manuscript. To take one of the most obvious indices, puns aren't frequent in this volume; one may be sure that as the weight of each word began to count for more, puns, which amplified and resonated with his intention, were likely to become more numerous; they are but one of the signs that words grew increasingly alive for Thoreau as he moved toward and through *A Week on the Concord and Merrimack Rivers* and the successive drafts of *Walden*. Stiff, cranky, forever drawing up bills of divorcement from the preoccupations of others, Thoreau nevertheless became more and more fibrously social in his use of the common tongue. His sense of himself, beset as he was from within and without, lodged more and more in the power to make sentences that rang like fine crystal under a testing tap.

His contemporaries found him prickly, but he breathes at the shoulder of any reader who takes his pleasure in the resources of the language. Such readers are so absorbed by Thoreau's flowering that they overlook the signs that he wrote for dear life; his tense effort to transform the muddy world as nature did becomes a separable delight. Of course this is what it means to say that his language is "social": like the early Whitman he woos us all because he is incapable of loving any one of us. Both isolate and universal in his appeal, he becomes a type of American individualism.

The power of such a voice works like an undertow in the world of literary scholarship. Most of Thoreau's academic readers lose their identities when they read him; they are mastered by his figured presumptions about himself; they write from within his work. For such commentators Thoreau's literary practice is a governing context; they quite forget that they have a responsibility to make judgments of Thoreau from whatever perspective they themselves enjoy.

Among those who have attempted such judgments, Mark Van Doren deserves mention because he asked as early as 1916 how what he called a "pure expansion of the pure self" could be an answer to any human problem. More wide ranging and adventurous attempts to encounter Thoreau appear in the late 1950s and the 1960s in the work of Leo Stoller and Perry Miller. Stoller is not wholly successful in placing the writer in his time and articulating the stance from which he spoke to Americans, but he does succeed in showing us what Thoreau found problematic in his society. Stoller's somewhat muted Marxism reveals the depth of Thoreau's own animus against what he had once called the commercial spirit. It lets Stoller down when he tries to show that Thoreau's Walden experiment — which he thinks of as an attempt to show that it was possible to live a life that effectually countered the stifling environment created by a capitalist culture — was succeeded by a capitulation to bourgeois values on the part of a Thoreau who became a commercially minded surveyor and forester. No such dramatic change overtook this American individualist. His struggle with the impulse to possession, like his struggle with his sexual impulses, had been internalized long before he went to Walden to live. Just as the only context Thoreau had for the discussion of heroism was his struggle with himself, since there was no other public he could respect or belong to, so he was incapable of changing his mind about a social world which he had all along said was factitious, illusory, a widely shared delusion that diverted individuals from the order of things which alone demanded their attention. Stoller's error reveals something about Thoreau studies: any analysis that overlooks his individualism is inadequate. It also points to a characteristic disability of American individualism.[1]

The claim for the unique authority of an individual vision of the whole precludes the admission that there are compelling social forces. If one person can start afresh, it follows that all can. If the present alone counts, history becomes merely illustrative or representative of aspects of the present. Since a "social" body implies the fragmentation of those who assert its existence, it cannot be anything more than an aggregation of persons who share a delusion. This solution of the relation of the particular to the universal develops out of the assumption of egalitarianism and the sentiment that we are all equal in God's eye. Its demand that each exhibit the power to embrace the totality of things makes it impossible to concede authority or relevance to any view of things less extensive than one's own widest perception; it follows that there is no room for a conception of the polity as such. When Thoreau writes that his thoughts are "murder to the state," he is using a figure of speech to refer to those who delude themselves about the significance of the actions of John Brown. Stoller doesn't simply fail to see that this is Thoreau's basic position; he also fails to see that it is a widely representative one against which all Marxist lances break in this country. Academics have failed to locate Thoreau historically because they have not taken American individualism seriously. It doesn't matter whether individualism was a delusion or not; the point is that it had consequences. Our culture has long bred individuals who expand the self to such a degree as to cancel the significance of their particular psychic development and their engagement in history. The loving celebrants of Thoreau are often people who accept his claim that political activity is itself the fruit of mass delusion since only individual assertion counts.

Stoller is important because he exposed Thoreau's focus on the fragmentation of each of us in a society in which money and exchange are imaginatively ascendant. Equally important is the long essay Perry Miller published in 1958 as a preface to Thoreau's "lost journal," *Consciousness in Concord*.[2] Lacerating to pious Thoreauvians, this essay emphasizes Thoreau's "delirium of self-consciousness." One has the impression in reading it that Miller, perhaps alerted by what he had learned of Raymond Gozzi's able psychoanalytic dissertation (N.Y.U. 1957), is confronted by something he finds repellent and difficult to discuss with his accustomed assurance and sagacity.

He describes the journals as a whole as a carefully constructed artifact of an exquisitely self-conscious kind. Thoreau's transcendentalism is on this occasion described simply in terms of its effects on Thoreau's relation to other people. It appears that Thoreau's aggressiveness boils down to a defense of his cherished self. Although Miller elsewhere speaks very highly of *Walden*, the reader of this account of the journals may wonder how such a man could have written anything of substance. Miller thinks it is plain—here my sense of Thoreau coincides with his—that Thoreau's impulse to write is a way of coping with the threat of death. But in describing his relation to human others in a chapter subtitled "Woman and Man" in which Miller discusses the almost ridiculously elevated conceptions of friendship in Thoreau, Emerson, and others, he fudges to avoid outright statement and fails to see what is at stake for Thoreau. His most explicit sentence runs: "The reader can hardly help concluding, to put it crudely, that he is confronted with a hunger which dreads satisfaction more than it suffers from deprivation" (p. 93). A bit earlier, commenting on journal passages on friendship, Miller says, "These entries are variations, depressingly slight variations, on the motif that friendship is a threat to the integrity of Henry Thoreau. And yet by their insistence they seem to be pleading for the dreaded invasion" (p. 90).

It is, I think, very hard to read the journals through without being aware that Thoreau longed for erotic experience with another man. But in denying himself that experience, as in denying himself the ownership of a farm or other ties to the world around him, Thoreau is scrapping to preserve his sense of himself; he fears splitting his outlook on the world and the loss of his creative voice. Like Lambert Strether in *The Ambassadors*—who in this instance speaks for James more directly than any other of his characters—he must accept nothing for himself, his selfish self, for if he did he would lose his sense of the whole affair—in Thoreau's case his relation to nature itself.

Miller, incurably social and passionate, carries on a lively quarrel with his isolato which comes closer to opening Thoreau to public inspection than anything else I know. As in the case of Stoller, both his rightness and his wrongness are helpful in pointing to what Thoreau was up to. In a journal passage for 30 January 1852, Thoreau speaks of the energy of love as a necessity in writing well: "There must be the copulating and generating force of love behind every effort destined to be successful. The cold resolve gives birth to, begets nothing. The theme seeks me, not I it. The poet's relation to his theme is the relation of lovers." Miller suggests that Thoreau "beholds in the objects which produce his entries those which make love to him," and that this gives us "a glimmering of what the art of composition had become to him" (p. 93). He goes on:

The successive moments of realization which the *Journal* is—or which he tried to make it become—are efforts to sustain this passion. For this reason among others, the inferior passions of human intercourse, love and friendship, are *required* to prove abortive!

It would be trite to say that the *Journal* is in any sense a "sublimation" of inhibited loves, or a "compensation" for a ghastly sense of inferiority, or a neurotic defense against a fear of humiliation. (All of which, in so far as literature can be, it is.) Supposing that the elements in the drama can be so isolated, we have to insist that these are only factors in a complex of forces which focused the total being of Henry Thoreau upon realizing—to the point of exquisite torture—the delirium of self-consciousness. By 1858 he could say it straight-out; "Genius is inspired by its own works; it is hermaphroditic." The one release from his compulsion, as well as the one control over it was incessant writing. Out of such dark soil flowers the clarity and simplicity, the oratory, of his prose. Within the strict confines of a stringently limited knowledge of life, Thoreau did contrive to become an artist. [pp. 94-95]

Miller comes close to the mark though he also misses it when he quotes Thoreau on genius as hermaphroditic. This use of the idea of a single creator is not the result of Thoreau's self-absorption; it is an assertion—we may call it desperate if we wish—of the agency and powers of the individual creator made over against a world which Thoreau saw, as did Emerson and Whitman, as imaginatively enslaved by acquisitiveness. Emerson too speaks of our highest state as hermaphroditic. The very existence of two sexes ties us to a world of reciprocal exchanges. Thoreau did not of course "contrive" to become an artist; he survived by becoming an artist, and in this way coped both with his own inner stresses and a society he saw as inhabited by those who, in splitting the world into pieces they could acquire, had also split themselves. Sentences might convey a sense of what it was to be whole and to see the world as a whole. Only by becoming a writer, by becoming "Henry David Thoreau," could he survive in his own eyes. Thoreau was not of course turning inward in answer to a compulsion; he had, in fact, no conception of art as separate from direct address to others—Miller's word *oratory* suggests an awareness of this—and Miller is therefore wrong to suggest that Thoreau's writing was not directed to the world. Yet in the sense that Thoreau is limiting his audience it may be argued that he was right. Thoreau addresses us in the degree that we feel ourselves as solitary as he did, and invites us to possess the world as he did, by ourselves. When John Brown forced him to modify that position, it appeared that he could do so only by identifying himself with Brown's total view.

Although it is difficult to keep up with the spate of Thoreau discussion, I have the impression that at the moment there are at least two Thoreaus in the field—I set Stanley Cavell's version aside; he alone seems wholly taken up by Thoreau's encounter with his own solitariness. The Thoreaus I am thinking of are on the one side the cherished dweller at Walden, celebrated in Sherman Paul's *Shores of America* and in many other places, and on other side the hag-ridden Thoreau, submerged in a welter of loneliness, anxiety, and doubt who has been exhibited in a rather gingerly way in Richard Bridgman's *Dark Thoreau*. Richard Lebeaux's *Young Man Thoreau* has exposed something of the effects of sibling rivalry and guilt following the death of John Thoreau; Raymond Gozzi long ago showed that Thoreau was tied to his mother's apron strings, and urged plausibly enough that the phallic power of the father who conferred life was daunting to the man who could only make sentences. Despite Walter Harding's labors, it isn't yet the case that Thoreau is now a firmly established figure of known and indubitable qualities.[3]

It seems clear that we needed Thoreau and those with whom he has the closest affinities, Emerson and Whitman, to construct our American pantheon. We needed them so much that we detached them from history and generic circumstances and are now, rather awkwardly in Thoreau's case, trying to reinsert them in the human fix from which we tried to spring them earlier. They have most to teach us when we admit that they were in that fix all along, and that what they achieved is all the more admirable for that. Moreover, we will get some instruction about our culture if we admit that they tried to make it alone because they were faced by a society they could find no other way of dealing with. The neglected term *individualism* will have to come back into currency if we wish to face up to what we have in common with Thoreau and the other two. It is the very fact that all three were beset in the same way that will enable us to understand that when we look at the world impersonally, as they did, we use the same desperate device to counter what we most dislike in our society and ourselves—the money firmament under which we walk. It doesn't work to say that we can make it alone. It was a noble but unsuccessful try, and we had better find other ways to go to work.

Notes

1. Leo Stoller, *After* Walden: *Thoreau's Changing Views on Economic Man* (Stanford: Stanford Univ. Press, 1966).

2. Boston: Houghton Mifflin, 1958. Subsequent page references are cited parenthetically in the text.

3. Sherman Paul, *Shores of America: Thoreau's Inward Exploration* (Champaign: Univ. of Illinois Press, 1958); Richard Bridgman, *Dark Thoreau* (Lincoln: Univ. of Nebraska Press, 1982); Richard Lebeaux, *Young Man Thoreau* (Amherst: Univ. of Massachusetts Press, 1977).

Critical Myths and Historical Realities; or, How American Was the American Renaissance?

Michael Kramer

Martin Bickman. *The Unsounded Centre: Jungian Studies in American Romanticism.* Chapel Hill: University of North Carolina Press, 1981. ix, 182 pp.

Michael Davitt Bell. *The Development of American Romance: The Sacrifice of Relation.* Chicago: University of Chicago Press, 1981. xiv, 291 pp.

From D. H. Lawrence's resuscitation of our "classic" works to Sacvan Bercovitch's revaluation of their Puritan origins, our best critics have sought to discover the links between American literature and culture. How is American writing different from European writing, they ask, and what about American culture can account for the difference? For some, style is central—romance, symbolism, the struggle with traditional forms. Others look to pervasive themes—to frontier motifs, say, or Adamic myths. Still others analyze notions of selfhood ("imperial," "corporeal") or systems of thought (Calvinist, democratic). Every publishing season brings new versions of the question and new variations on the answers. It is a tradition: homage is paid to predecessors, and their work is elaborated upon or revised. Voices may now and again be raised in opposition; they find in this less of a tradition and more of a habit (and a bad one at that). Still, the issue of "American-ness" looms large over the nation's literary heritage. An impressive body of criticism that cannot easily be swept aside presents itself to every new scholar. In very different ways, and with strikingly different results, these studies by Martin Bickman and Michael Bell begin with this confrontation.[1]

The critical tradition is so imposing, I think, because it strikes at the core of the literature itself. From the very beginning, American writers were obsessed with the question of uniqueness. After the Revolution and especially during the period of buoyant and anxious nationalism that followed the War of 1812, Americans felt the pressing need to establish the new nation's literary credentials. It was seen by many as a necessary extension of the struggle for political liberty from Britain. They could not be "free indeed" until they developed their own way of expressing themselves as a nation. They could not continue to imitate Old World models. These sentiments are what F. O. Matthiessen had in mind when he called his book *American Renaissance:* the literature of the mid-nineteenth century was a sign of America's "coming to its first maturity and affirming its rightful heritage in the whole expanse of art and culture." Antebellum writers had "felt it was incumbent upon their generation to give fulfillment to the potentialities freed by the Revolution, to provide a culture commensurate with America's political opportunity."[2]

By lending support to this literary project, the writers and theorists were not only pledging their allegiance to America but also to the belief that literature received (in Longfellow's formulation) "distinguishing features . . . from the spirit of a nation, — from its scenery and climate, its historic recollections, its Government, its various institutions — from all those national peculiarities, which are the result of no positive institutions, and, in a word, from the thousand external circumstances, which either directly or indirectly exert an influence."[3] This theory is not particularly American; it formed the foundation of Herder's *The Spirit of Hebrew Poetry,* Madame de Staël's *Of Germany,* as well as Tocqueville's *Democracy in America.* But for the Europeans the theory of literary relativity was primarily a mode of historical and cultural analysis. Ancient Hebrew literature could be held up against ancient Israelite society, and connections could be made. The same could be done for Germany, France, or England; wherever a literature and a society existed, links could be ascertained and conclusions drawn. But for the Americans, there was as yet no literature — some even said no society — to provide the raw materials for critical analysis. So literary relativity became primarily a mode of critical prescription. Because the literature of a nation *must* bear an essential relation to its culture, the argument ran, so American literature *should* bear an essential relation to its culture.[4]

To investigate the "American-ness" of classic American literature is to study it on its own terms. But if the material itself offers a historical justification for a particular method of study, it also issues its own note of caution. For the literary Americanists were less concerned with cultural mimesis than with the dissemination of myth. Whereas Tocqueville could expect that American literature would bear the impress of the democracy's more mundane features, the Americans were more apt to separate the country they saw from the nation they envisioned. They could turn from the marketplace and the political arena to the Revolutionary past that inspired them or to the vast virgin wilderness that beckoned them. In so doing they obscured the broader social and literary contexts of the works they advocated and created. It is one thing to declare cultural independence and another to achieve it.

Early in *The Unsounded Centre* Martin Bickman pays homage to the classic critical studies of American literature and culture but then rejects their cisatlantic perspective in favor of a more broadly historical and transcultural view. He argues that significant "convergences" exist between American Romanticism (Emerson, Poe, Whitman, and Dickinson) and the analytical psychology of Carl Gustav Jung. This is not, he claims, just another volume of psychoanalytic criticism. For in this study "the psychology itself is viewed as another formulation, however powerful and useful, of the confluence of traditions that shaped American Romanticism" (p. 5). In other words, Bickman intends *The Unsounded Centre* to be read, in part at least, as an exercise in intellectual history, one that promises to modify prevailing notions of the uniqueness of America's literary heritage.

The historical connections between twentieth-century psychology and nineteenth-century romanticism are certainly not new. Freud himself readily acknowledged the important discoveries regarding the unconscious made by the poets and philosophers who preceded him. Jung's German-romantic roots have also been traced. The traffic between German and American romanticism, though yet to be discussed in a comprehensive manner, has long been noted by scholars.[4] But Bickman is not interested in drawing these lines of influence; his concerns are at once broader and more limited. Instead of providing substantial discussions of those figures who link Jung and the Americans historically — Kant, Goethe, Schiller, the Schlegels, Fichte, and perhaps most importantly, Coleridge — Bickman chooses to refer the reader to "a broad matrix of thought stretching across the centuries, from which both Romanticism and Jungian psychology arise" (p. 47), an occult tradition that extends from Heraclitus and Plato through Böhme and Swedenborg to Harold Bloom. Those writers and thinkers (Jung would have called them "visionaries") share a predilection for symbolic language and "unity-division-reintegration" patterns of thought. The various occult discourses fall into a discernible pattern of historical development, that the author terms "the progressive self-discovery of the psyche" (p. 147). American romanticism occupies an important stage in that process whereby occult concepts "are divested of much of their philosophical and theological status and reattached to the original conditions, feelings, aspirations from which they were abstracted." (p. 52). In this scheme "Jungian psychology completes the movement of American Romanticism to turn metaphysics into a phenomenology of consciousness" (p. 39).

Bickman's is a unique brand of intellectual history. He has not chosen to write the sort of systematic and comprehensive study that might convince us of the validity of his historical thesis. On the contrary, he believes "that a critical hypothesis should not have to cover any and all applications" and has crafted his study "to be suggestive rather than comprehensive" (p. 148). In this he has ingeniously attempted to fashion his methodology from his subject matter. He develops his "mythodology" as an analogue to Jungian hermeneutics, in which a patient's symbolic dreams or fantasies are related to other symbolic material to *suggest* the profound and enigmatic truth that language strains to articulate. Bickman finds that hermeneutical amplification "converges" with romantic theories of language that treat symbolism, with its ambiguity and paradox, as "a way of knowing and speaking that in some areas of human experience has more ontological validity than any other" (p. 8). *The Unsounded Centre* " uses Jungian psychology . . . as the new symbol or set of symbols in a configuration that arises primarily from American Romanticism itself" (pp. 15-16). By "amplifying" one with the other, Bickman hopes "to lure others further and deeper into unexplored spaces" and to "provide ways of encountering a literature that is always in danger of becoming too familiar to us" (pp. 148, 16).

Often in this slim volume Bickman shows himself an articulate and perceptive critic. His opening chapter on symbolic language offers a useful introduction to a topic of renewed interest to critics of the American Renaissnace.[5] Readers are sure to find throughout helpful explanations of unwieldy texts. But those not predisposed to Jungian studies will find much of *The Unsounded Centre* neither suggestive nor alluring. Bickman's progressive view of history, his insistence that Jungian psychology somehow "completes" American romanticism, gives to Jung's ideas a conceptual priority that makes Bickman sound at times like those less judicious psychoanalytical critics from whom he disassociates himself.

More importantly, *The Unsounded Centre* obscures the distinctive elements in the two discourses. Jung himself believed that literature responded to a particular culture's psychic ailments, but Bickman's methodology leaves little room for these considerations.[6] Despite repeated disclaimers as to the "culture-bound and historically shaped components of Jung's own system" (p. 149), the author makes no effort to elucidate them. And only briefly in the afterword does he suggest the cultural factors to which the American writers were responding. ("The Delphic injunction to know oneself becomes a radical and immediate venture in a land perceived as the embodiment of the unknown" [p. 147].) Bickman's comparative approach may prompt us to question the uniqueness of American symbolism, but it also calls us back finally to the Americanist enterprise. Had he tried to be less innovative in his critical method, had he looked for difference as well as "convergences," he might have made a more substantial contribution to the study of American literature and culture.

In *The Development of American Romance,* on the other hand, Michael Bell's major concern is with the question that Bickman leaves unanswered: what are the distinctive features of the American literary tradition? His focus is narrower: making no claims for American romanticism, he assumes the mantle of Trilling, Chase, and Perry Miller and turns his attention to the romance—the narrative form identified by many as quintessentially American. In fact, Bell's focus is still more limited: his interest is in a particular sort of romance, something he terms *the experimental tradition*—specifically, the fiction of Charles Brockden Brown, Washington Irving, Edgar Allan Poe, Nathaniel Hawthorne, and Herman Melville. (Cooper and the other American Scotts are conspicuously absent.) By narrowing his focus, Bell manages to give his work a degree of depth and specificity that Bickman has sacrificed for breadth and suggestiveness.

Sidestepping the controversy over the precise generic distinctions between the American "romance" and the English "novel," Bell begins judiciously with a simple historical observation. However we may label them today, his five authors did call their works romances. It would be best, he suggests, to discover what the term meant in nineteenth-century critical discourse. What he finds is that *romance* was used more often in opposition to "reality" than to the "novel." Romance was synonymous with fiction; its primary characteristic was its "sacrifice of relation" to the real world. By using the term, Bell suggests, the romancers implicated themselves in the complex social process by which the republic was trying to define its corporate identity and to come to terms with its Revolutionary heritage.

In essence, Bell controverts Trilling's well-known thesis: it was not the lack of social texture, the absence of that "hum and buzz of implication" that comes with a fixed social structure, that led writers to produce romances, but the imposing and repressive character of "orthodox" American opinion. Americans may not have had any manners, as Trilling argued, but they did have morals—and it was the rationalistic moralism of American critics that determined the peculiar nature of American romance.[7] Grounding their strictures in Scottish Common Sense psychology, political and religious leaders condemned romances as figments of their authors' "heated" imaginations and, as such, potentially subversive. Reason was the faculty which ordered society; imagination threatened to dissolve it. Drawing upon the social psychology of sociologists Kai Erikson and Howard Becker, Bell argues that to call oneself a romancer was tantamount to labeling oneself a deviant. Brown, Irving, Poe, Hawthorne, and Melville aspired to the role of romancer precisely because of its deviancy, although, at the same time, they remained deeply ambivalent about their "sacrifice of relation" to American society. Out of this ambivalence sprang a particularly American brand of romance, imaginative works written in a language that at once expresses and represses the author's hostility to American society.

To be sure, we have known of the duplicity in American romance for some time, at least since D. H. Lawrence admonished us to trust the tale and not the teller. And, since Feidelson, we have been aware of the American writer's intense interest in language and symbolism. Bell's contribution is to have recognized a connection between the stylistic accomplishments of our major writers and the psychocultural tensions generated by the Revolution, between, as it were, American language and American liberty. Doing so, he draws together two major critical traditions. In the series of sparkling essays that comprise most of the book, the author demonstrates how the sacrifice of the romancer's relation to American society was translated into an exploration of the sacrifice of relation between statement and intention, language and meaning, words and things. Within this framework Bell charts the "development" of the "experimental" romance in America, a "neurotic" tradition that draws its narrative power from the psychological dislocation of the authors from mainstream American society. Brown's thematic interest in ventriloquism and other kinds of aural deception and his stylistic experiments with unreliable narrators run together with the ambivalence that underlies his political journey from radicalism to Federalism and his abandonment of romantic fiction. Irving, hemmed in by his inability to reconcile his own imaginative drives with an overriding conformism, produced gothic tales that at once suggest psychological horrors and cover them with a pleasing veneer of urbane humor. Rejecting out of hand the Common Sense restrictions imposed upon imaginative writers, Poe dared to create a literature effectually divorced from reality, a literature whose "pure" language never *means* anything, whose purpose is to achieve an "effect," not to explore "truth." Hawthorne and Melville could not go so far as Poe: their works are self-reflexive romances whose primary stylistic intention was to explore the relation between language and meaning and whose political aim was to investigate America's sacrifice of relation to its Revolutionary ideals, of its promise of liberation to the exigencies of social stability. In their best works (*The Scarlet Letter, Moby-Dick*) we find the culmination of the experimental tradition. And in Melville's later works, especially *The Confidence Man*, we see its dissolution.

A brief summary of this sort cannot suggest the intricacy and force of Bell's individual analyses, but the general outline of his thesis, I hope, remains clear: American romance issues from the interaction of the imaginative writer with the concrete, repressive condition of his society, from the displacement of the writer's guilt and aggression onto the level of aesthetics. The validity of Bell's thesis rests finally on his analysis of American society, and here it needs to be questioned. Despite his efforts to ground his analysis in respectable sociological thought, Bell may have oversimplified the dynamics of antebellum culture. As soon as we step outside the enclosed arena of "orthodox" opinion that Bell constructs, the force of his argument begins to abate. The monolith of Common Sense psychology did not prevent the flourishing of transcendentalism in New England or Methodism in the West. By midcentury, when Hawthorne and Melville wrote their masterpieces of experimental romance, even more conservative, antirevivalist theologians like James Marsh and Horace Bushnell had adopted the ideas of European romanticism and had given increased importance to the imagination. When one considers further the numerous sources of tension in antebellum society—the political battles between whigs and democrats and the continual realignment of allegiances, the sectional hostility, the changing demographic patterns brought about by immigration and economic and geographic mobility—one realizes that Bell reconstructs only a limited model of the culture. Further still, when one realizes that a host of "deviants" then populated the United States—communists, anarchists, advocates of celibacy, promoters of free love, utopians, vegetarians, millenarians—one begins to wonder just how deviant Bell's five romancers could have felt. It was a time, too, when society was developing new attitudes toward deviants (the criminal, the poor, the insane).[8] Could the opprobrium heaped upon the romancers have been as debilitating as Bell suggests?

Perhaps. Bell's readings are always intriguing, often persuasive, and his critical impulse is sound. But too many questions are left unanswered. When we look at the broader cultural picture, Bell's American tradition reads too much like an American myth: oppressed writers struggling to liberate themselves from the tyranny of a repressive society. American literature may have been born of myth, but Americanist criticism should not be. The fascinating enigma of American uniqueness still looms large. And, as evidenced by *The Development of American Romance,* it continues to attract bold and creative minds. However, to get at the American-ness of the American Renaissance, we must first understand American culture, the rhetoric and the reality. That is a formidable venture, one that demands the cooperation of hosts of scholars from various disciplines. But it is a promising one.

Notes

1. See D. H. Lawrence, *Studies in Classic American Literature* (1923;rpt. New York: Viking, 1964); Sacvan Bercovitch, *The Puritan Origins of the American Self* (New Haven: Yale Univ. Press, 1975) and *The American Jeremiad* (Madison: Univ. of Wisconsin Press, 1978). On style, e.g., Lionel Trilling, "Manners, Morals, and the Novel" (1948) in *The Liberal Imagination* (Harmondsworth: Peregrine, 1970), pp. 208-23; Richard Chase, *The American Novel and Its Tradition* (New York: Anchor, 1957); Perry Miller, "The Romance and the Novel" (1956), in *Nature's Nation* (Cambridge: Harvard Univ. Press, 1966), pp. 241-78; Joel Porte, *The Romance in America* (Middletown: Wesleyan Univ. Press, 1969); Charles Feidelson, *Symbolism and American Literature* (Chicago: Univ. of Chicago Press, 1953); and Richard Poirier, *A World Elsewhere: The Place of Style in American Literature* (New York: Oxford Univ. Press, 1966). On themes, e.g. Henry Nash Smith, *Virgin Land* (Cambridge: Harvard Univ. Press, 1950); R. W. B. Lewis, *The American Adam* (Chicago: Univ. of Chicago Press, 1955); Leo Marx, *The Machine in the Garden* (New York: Oxford Univ. Press, 1964); Leslie Fiedler, *Love

and Death in the American Novel (New York: Stein and Day, 1960, 1966); Richard Slotkin, *Regeneration through Violence* (Middletown: Wesleyan Univ. Press, 1975); Bernard Rosenthal, *City of Nature* (Newark: Univ. of Delaware Press, 1980). On selfhood, e.g., Quentin Anderson, *The Imperial Self* (New York: Knopf, 1972); Sharon Cameron, *The Corporeal Self* (Baltimore: Johns Hopkins Univ. Press, 1981). On systems of thought, e.g., Michael Gilmore, *The Middle Way* (New Brunswick: Rutgers Univ. Press, 1977); Harold Kaplan, *Democratic Humanism and American Literature* (Chicago: Univ. of Chicago Press, 1972); Robert Penn Warren, *Democracy and Poetry* (Cambridge: Harvard Univ. Press, 1975); Henry Nash Smith, *Democracy and the Novel* (New York: Oxford Univ. Press, 1979); and Larzer Ziff, *Literary Democracy* (New York: Viking, 1981). Dissenting voices include Nicholas Mills, *American and English Fiction in the Nineteenth Century* (Bloomington: Indiana Univ. Press, 1973) and Edward Eigner, *The Metaphysical Novel in England and America* (Berkeley and Los Angeles: Univ. of California Press, 1978). For an overview of literary Americanism to 1965, see Howard Mumford Jones, *The Theory of American Literature* (Ithaca: Cornell Univ. Press, 1966).

2. F. O. Matthiessen, *American Renaissance* (New York: Oxford Univ. Press, 1941) pp. vii, xv. On literary nationalism see Benjamin Spencer, *The Quest for Nationality* (Syracuse: Syracuse Univ. Press, 1957) and Jones, *Theory of American Literature*, pp. 18-78.

3. [Henry Wadsworth Longfellow], "Defence of Poetry," *North American Review*, 34 (1832), 70.

4. See Lionel Trilling, "Freud and Literature," in *The Liberal Imagination*, pp. 47-68; Henri Ellenberger, *The Discovery of the Unconscious* (New York: Basic Books, 1970); René Wellek, *Confrontations* (Princeton: Princeton Univ. Press, 1965); and Carl Diehl, *Americans and German Scholarship 1770-1870* (New Haven: Yale Univ. Press, 1978).

5. See, e.g., Philip F. Gura, *The Wisdom of Words* (Middletown: Wesleyan Univ. Press, 1981), and John Irwin, *American Hieroglyphics* (New Haven: Yale Univ. Press, 1980).

6. Jung writes: "Every period has its bias, its particular prejudice and its psychic ailment. An epoch is like an individual; it has its own limitations of conscious outlook, and therefore requires a compensatory adjustment. This is effected by the collective unconscious in that a poet, a seer, or a leader allows himself to be guided by the unexpressed desire of his times and shows the way, by word or deed, to the attainment of that which everyone blindly craves and expects." (Jung, "Psychology and Literature," in *20th Century Literary Criticism: A Reader*, ed. David Lodge [London: Longman, 1972], p. 184).

7. Trilling, "Manners, Morals, and the Novel," p. 209.

8. Well-known works which provide perspectives on American culture different from Bell's include Alice Felt Tyler, *Freedom's Ferment* (1944; rpt. New York: Harper & Row, 1962); Arthur M. Schlesinger, Jr., *The Age of Jackson* (Boston: Little, Brown, 1945); Oscar Handlin, *Boston's Immigrants* (1959; rpt. New York: Atheneum, 1968); and David J. Rothman, *The Discovery of the Asylum* (Boston: Little, Brown, 1971).

A Definitive Edition of Browning's Poems

Jacob Korg

Robert Browning: The Poems. Ed. John Pettigrew. Supplemented and Completed by Thomas J. Collins. New Haven: Yale University Press, 1981. 2 vols. xxxiii, 1190 pp.; xxxviii, 1167 pp.

This superb edition is a part of the series of Penguin English Poets produced under the general editorship of Christopher Ricks that are distributed in North America as reprints by the Yale University Press. It is also a salvo in a small battle of the books that has been raging over the question of editing Browning since 1969. In that year the Ohio University Press brought out the first volume of a projected thirteen-volume edition of the *Complete Works of Robert Browning* that was intended to be a definitive edition with an extensive apparatus including a textual analysis based on manuscripts and all significant publications of Browning's work antecedent to the copy-text. But it was attacked as seriously deficient in a variety of ways, the editors were forced to admit that it contained many errors, the editorial board was reconstituted, and publication was suspended—though not discontinued—after the fourth volume appeared in 1973. The Penguin-Yale edition is the work of two of the most vigorous critics of the Ohio edition, and has now appeared to compete with it.

These two volumes, together with Richard D. Altick's edition of *The Ring and the Book*, published in the same format in 1971 (1981 in the U.S.), complete an edition of Browning's poems. It includes thirty-seven pages of uncollected verse and the text of the "Essay on Shelley" as an appendix to Volume 1, but is not a *Complete Works*, as the Ohio edition was supposed to be. As the preface acknowledges, certain scraps of minor verse unavailable for publication and the "Browning version" of the *Agamemnon* have been omitted. More materially, Browning's five plays written for stage presentation and the "Essay on Chatterton" (all included in the Ohio edition) have been excluded. The two volumes, each over a thousand pages, are cumbersome; and it is regrettable that the material could not have been distributed over three or even four volumes.

Apart from these obvious and perhaps unavoidable limitations, this edition seems beyond criticism. Its merits can perhaps best be appreciated against the background of the controversy surrounding the Ohio edition. The introduction to the latter offered some new principles of editing. The copy-text, the collected edition of 1888-1889, was regarded as authoritative and unalterable (except for obvious misprints) on the grounds that Browning had full control of the editorial decisions involved in it and that editorial functions, especially in the case of an author who took so active a part in them as Browning, should be considered a part of authorship. All variants from manuscripts and four earlier texts were recorded in footnotes; the innumerable changes Browning had made in puncuation through the years were included, on the ground that puncuation is not an accidental, as it has traditionally been regarded, but is crucial to the meaning of a text.

The attack on the Ohio edition was opened in 1970 by Thomas J. Collins in a survey of the year's research on Browning in the *Browning Newsletter* and a review in *Victorian Studies*.[1] He argued that the editors' unconditional acceptance of their copy-text was not supported by evidence that Browning had control of it, and that their editorial policy prevented them from amending it on the basis of evidence from other sources, in accordance with established methods. He was also critical of their policy of recording all variants without distinguishing between accidentals and substantives, whether they were meaningful or not, and of the confusing method of textual annotation. One of the editors of the Ohio edition, Morse Peckham, replied in the following number of *Newsletter*, reaffirming the need for new procedures in the editing of nineteenth-century publications; in the Spring 1971 number, William Peterson defended the choice of the 1888-1889 edition as copy-text, and Michael Hancher offered evidence that Browning had exercised close editorial control over it, while Collins answered Peckham by again supporting conventional editing methods. The battle was continued in the third volume of the edition, which responded to the critics by restating and defending the original position. In a judicious review of the situation in *Studies in Browning* in 1972, Peter Davison conceded that the Ohio editors had raised valid questions about traditional editing practices, but argued that they should nevertheless have distinguished between editorial and authorial functions, undertaken emendations, and made a selection of variants, thus supporting most of Collins's original objections.[2]

The Definitive Browning

In the meantime, John Pettigrew, who was to edit the Penguin-Yale edition, opened a new front in his review of Volumes 1 and 2 in *Essays in Criticism* by pointing out that the text contained numerous misprints, and that the notes were guilty of errors of fact and judgment. A reply from Roma A. King, Jr., the General Editor of the Ohio edition, only brought an even more emphatic charge of inaccuracy from Pettigrew.[3] In a later article he stated that he had come across "many hundreds" of errors in the notes and text of the Ohio *Sordello* while working on his own edition.[4] His sampling of errata, which include misspellings of Italian and Latin names, wrong numbers for lines and dates, inaccurate geographical and historical information, careless glosses and ordinary misprints, was especially damaging.

When the fourth volume of the troubled edition appeared in 1973, something like a capitulation took place, for the part of the preface called "Choice of Text" was rewritten to acknowledge that the text ought to draw on all available evidence, and that "in cases where conflicting readings result it becomes the responsibility of the editors to make a choice." Consequently, the practice of amending the text and referring to emendations in the notes was to be introduced in Volume 4 (such emendations do, in fact, appear), and the next volume would contain an appendix listing emendations to the first three volumes. In the meantime, another effort to improve editorial procedures retroactively was made by publishing lists of errata in some of the journals.

In the Spring 1974 number of *Victorian Poetry*, Donald H. Reiman offered a more balanced assessment of the Ohio edition by sorting out its merits and deficiencies.[5] His most severe criticism was the charge that the editors had not located all the relevant manuscript materials, as they said they had. He acknowledged that the text was far from perfect, citing a letter from Morse Peckham which stated that over half the pages in Volume 1 and a third of the pages in Volume 2 contained errors, and that there were as many as 800 errors in the text (as distinguished from the notes), thus confirming Pettigrew's criticism. Peckham added that he had resigned from the editorial board, that the edition had lost its value, and that it ought to be abandoned. Reiman, however, took a more realistic view of the situation, pointing out that a reputable edition of Shelley has five to twenty errors on each page, and that the text of the *Prelude*, after much correction, is still imperfect. "In my opinion," he said, "the percentage of errors in the Ohio Browning is low enough to make it above the average quality of editions of nineteenth-century English poets presently available" (Reiman, p. 95). He praised the notes (which are thorough and extensive, if not entirely reliable) and recommended that the edition be completed at a pace which would allow a greater degree of editorial accuracy.

If the Ohio edition is carried forward, its sponsors will have to face the dismal fact that it has been anticipated by the much better Penguin-Yale edition. The Ohio edition was produced by a large editorial committee, but the new edition is the work of a single diligent and gifted editor, who unfortunately died of leukemia in April 1977 at the age of forty-seven, before his manuscript went to press. Pettigrew requested that the task of bringing the edition to publication be carried out by Thomas J. Collins, who reviewed the copy and proofs repeatedly and brought the bibliographical and prefatory materials up to date, a time-consuming and exacting labor that resulted in a long but fully justified delay in publication. The preface describes the editorial principles that have been followed, characterizing them as "conservative," and tells how certain problems have been resolved. (This material is reprinted as front matter in the second volume.) The apparatus includes a useful table of dates, suggestions for further reading that constitute a selective bibliography, and, of course, textual and explanatory notes. The accuracy of the text is impossible to gauge without long familiarity, but Pettigrew's critique of the Ohio notes to *Sordello*, which shows that he was capable of enormous patience in checking such things as variant spellings of foreign names and page and line numbers, earns credibility for the accuracy of his text, though it does not, of course, guarantee it.

In his textual notes Pettigrew has naturally not repeated the Ohio edition's practice of recording all variants in punctuation, which had a tendency to swamp the substantive ones in the Ohio footnotes (the proportion being about ten to one), but he has recorded a "generous selection" of substantive variants from manuscripts, earlier editions, and other sources in conventional form, making it possible to follow the revisions with ease. Manuscript readings that differ from printed ones are recorded; and where revisions are known to be due to the suggestions of Elizabeth Barrett or some other person, the evidence is given.

But the special strength of this edition is in the explanatory notes, which reflect a tireless energy in the accumulation of facts together with imagination and sensitivity. An obituary article on Pettigrew says of his work on the Browning edition: "His labours here were immense, including numerous visits to American and British libraries to consult Browning manuscripts, and on-the-spot checking in Italy. . . . He had the true scholar's passion for fact, and would cheerfully spend his days digging about to verify (and often to correct) the work of earlier editors."[6] The notes make it not only easy but necessary to believe this characterization. They constitute an achievement that could not have been accomplished without a heroic, dedicated, protracted effort. The notes for each poem begin with an account of its publishing history, then give information about the manuscript, composition, and sources, and finally provide a carefully selected bibliography of critical books and articles relevant to the poem. Taken as a whole, this information functions as a very good up-to-date substitute for the *Browning Handbook*, which it sometimes corrects and augments. As the preface observes, the amount of knowledge needed to annotate Browning properly is beyond the capacity of most mortals, so that the editor was compelled to carry out his task by consulting and verifying the findings of earlier scholars. He cites the latest (and no doubt final) explanation of "Hy, Zy, Hine" and passes on the *OED* account of how the unprintable word got in *Pippa Passes*. The article identifying "Pictor Ignotus" as the Renaissance painter Fra Bartolommeo leads Pettigrew to relate the striking line "Shrinking, as from the soldiery a nun" to the episode in which the painter was caught up in a savage battle between the enemies and supporters of Savonarola. Besides supplying more copious information than any other of the Browning handbooks or editions (except for the Ohio edition, whose notes are also ample, if less reliable), these notes establish important relationships between the texts and Browning's other poems, letters, and similar sources, ranging widely to offer illuminating interpretations and allusions. A good example is the headnote to the entry on the short poem "Development," which is worth quoting in full: "Browning was always devoted to Homer, but the poem is about much more than reading Homer, alluding as it does to the Biblical (as well as classical) Higher Criticism and its 'unsettling one's belief' and reminding one of much in 'A Death in the Desert,' especially in its stress on the need to conceive of man as developing animal; and again bearing on educational theory, on the theme of 'Transcendentalism,' and on the relation of fiction and fancy to fact . . . in a way that recalls Browning statements in *The Ring and the Book* in particular" (p. 1129). There are also some entertaining reflections of the annotator's personality. "Bubble and squeak," which appears as a kind of interjection in "Holy-Cross Day," is Johnsonianly defined as "a mixture of meat and cabbage which, in England, masquerades as food" (p. 1139).

Since Browning's vocabulary presents many difficulties, this edition aims to be "fully glossed," and the text is often surprisingly illuminated by turning the full light of the *OED* on it. (The *OED* and the Bible, seem, to judge from the notes, to be the two aids most necessary for a reading of Browning.) Readers who have been stumped by such words as *tweedle, argute, ellops,* and *kottabos* (all from *Aristophanes' Apology*) will find the *OED* definitions of them in the notes. In Sebald's description of Ottima's "morbid olive faultless shoulder-blades" in *Pippa Passes,* "morbid" seems no better than acceptable. The note illuminates the precisions of Browning's intention by directing us to the *OED* third meaning for the word, "flesh-like." This has its source in the Italian "morbidezza" or "morbido," which alludes to the softness of wax or butter. The note leads not only to an obviously correct meaning which Browning knew and most of his readers don't but also to an indispensible connotative background.

The glosses suggest the extent of Browning's originality in his use of English, for they note a number of usages and forms not found in the *OED*, such as "impressment" in the sense of "impression" (*Red Cotton Night-Cap Country*), "fiddlepin" ("The Two Poets of Croisic"), and "frontleted" (*Balaustion's Adventure*). Even more significantly, they show that Browning is of some importance as a contributor of new forms, for there are many instances in which his use of a word is the initial or only recorded one. Among the examples are "rede" in the sense of "interpretation" and "dabster" for "know-it-all" (*Prince Hohenstiel-Schwangau*), "stubbed" meaning "filled with stubble" ("Childe Roland to the Dark Tower Came"), "myrrhy" ("Waring"), "exalt" as an adjective, "falsish" and "febricity" (all from *Aristophanes' Apology*).

There is authoritative information about the few places where ambiguities cannot be resolved, or where Browning's grasp of the facts slipped, as it did from time to time. It is good to see definitely stated what has been hinted from time to time: that the church of Santa Prassede, which is the original of the one in "The Bishop Orders His Tomb," does not correspond at all to the description in the poem; the "Baldassaro" in the first line of "A Toccata of Galuppi's" is simply an uncorrected error for "Baldassare," and that the mountain named "Calvano" mentioned in "The Englishman in Italy" does not exist.

In "Fra Lippo Lippi," Browning quoted the motto on the scroll in Fra Lippo's painting "The Coronation of the Virgin" as reading "Iste Perfecit Opus." The notes correct Browning by observing that the scroll says "Is," not "Iste." (Browning's misreading was probably caused by a fold in the scroll which he must have taken for further lettering.) In the same poem, "hot cockles" is an innocent childish game; but the notes assert, probably with full justification, that Browning thought it was a euphemism for erotic by-play. They observe that the last line of "Bishop Blougram's Apology," which says that Gigadibs has "studied his last chapter of Saint John," has never been satisfactorily explained, and offer several of the more plausible (and mutually inconsistent) interpretations.

Browning's texts being what they are, it is not likely that any set of notes will fully satisfy all comers, and if Pettigrew's notes, excellent though they may be, are subjected to the sort of close scrutiny that he gave to the Ohio notes for *Sordello*, a critical reader can find some room for improvement in odd places. One wonders, for example, what authority exists for omitting the second "o" in "Pollaiuolo" as it appears in the notes to "Old Pictures in Florence," or the apostrophe from such names as Cosimo de' Medici ("The Statue and the Bust"). In the notes to the latter poem, the prize of a "dram" is defined as "a very light weight, that is, a trifling stake." What Puritanical compunction prevented Pettigrew from giving the more obvious and perfectly appropriate meaning "drink"? The Brownings are said to have lived in a house "near Lucca" in 1853; actually it was in the quite separate town of Bagni di Lucca, seventeen miles away. The note on page 1090 to "Jochanan Hakkadosh" that identifies "Tsaddik" as Browning's invention ("his name means 'righteous'") is not as clear as it might be; Browning is simply using the Hebrew word for a saintly, righteous person. Oddly, the Hebrew lines in "The Melon Seller" are not identified as a quotation from Job 2:10, though the fact is not a secret. In an edition so fully annotated, it does seem necessary to explain that when "Pictor Ignotus" dreams of having his pictures carried in processions "Through old streets named afresh from the event," he is alluding to Vasari's apocryphal statement that the Florentine street called "Borgo Allegri," or "street of joy," was given that name after Cimabue's *Madonna and Child Enthroned* had been carried through it. This omission, though minor, is especially unfortunate, since the cover design for the Penguin edition of Volume 2 shows a fine detail from Lord Leighton's painting of this very scene.

In taking its place as the best presentation of Browning's poems, the edition produced by Pettigrew and Collins has the ironic effect of granting a measure of vindication to the rival edition they criticized so severely. There is, of course, no justification for the numerous proofreading errors in the Ohio edition, or for the misspelling of names, but the human capacity for accuracy in these matters is limited. And the policy of giving final authority to the collected-edition copy-text (a policy that has been changed, as I have noted), was, it now appears, not as damaging as one might expect, however perverse it may have been in principle. According to Pettigrew's preface, the differences between Browning's text and his own are "few," setting aside obvious misprints and, presumably, such matters of style as quotation marks. It follows that there were "few" opportunities for exercising the editorial discretion the Ohio editors were accused of shirking or for making improvements in the copy-text.

Notes

1. Thomas J. Collins, "Review of the Year's Research," *Browning Newsletter*, 4 (1970), 14-17, and *Victorian Studies*, 13 (1970), 441-44.

2. Morse Peckham, "The Collins Review of the Browning Edition," *Browning Newsletter*, 5 (1970), 3-5; William Peterson, "Review of the Year's Research," *Browning Newsletter*, 6 (1971), 3-20; Michael Hancher, "Browning and the *Poetical Works* of 1888-1889," *Browning Newsletter*, 6 (1971), 25-27; Thomas J. Collins, "The Peckham Reply to the Collins Review of the Browning Edition: A Reply," *Browning Newsletter*, 6 (1971), 21-24; Peter Davison, "Science, Method and the Textual Critic," *Studies in Browning*, 25 (1972), 1-28.

3. John Pettigrew, "Back to His Book Then," *Essays in Criticism*, 22 (1972), 436-41; Roma A. King, Jr., "The Ohio *Browning,*" *Essays in Criticism*, 24 (1974), 317-19; Pettigrew, "The Ohio *Browning*," 25 (1975), 480-83.

4. John Pettigrew, "For 'Flute' Read 'Lute': or, Notes on the 'Notes' on *Sordello* in the Ohio Edition," *The Library*, 33 (1978), 162-69.

5. Donald H. Reiman, *Victorian Poetry*, 12 (1974), 86-96.

6. Robert D. Chambers, "John Stewart Pettigrew," *Journal of Canadian Studies*, 12 (1977), 113.

The Growth of Poe Texts

Kent Ljungquist

Collected Works of Edgar Allan Poe. Ed. Thomas Ollive Mabbott. Vol. I, *Poems.* Cambridge: Belknap Press of Harvard University Press, 1969. xxx, 627 pp.

Collected Works of Edgar Allan Poe. Ed. Thomas Ollive Mabbott. Vol. II, *Tales and Sketches, 1831–1842.* Cambridge: Belknap Press of Harvard University Press, 1978. xxxii, 713 pp.

Collected Works of Edgar Allan Poe. Ed. Thomas Ollive Mabbott. Vol. III, *Tales and Sketches, 1843–1849.* Cambridge: Belknap Press of Harvard University Press, 1978. vii, 736 pp.

Collected Writings of Edgar Allan Poe. Ed. Burton R. Pollin. Vol. I, *The Imaginary Voyages.* Boston: G. K. Hall, 1981. xix, 667 pp.

In the inaugural issue of the *Poe Newsletter* (1968), J. Albert Robbins addressed what he termed the sorry state of Poe scholarship and underscored the pressing need for an "edition which meets modern standards."[1] In the same issue, a list of editorial notes included an announcement by Thomas Ollive Mabbott that his edition of the prose tales was forthcoming from Harvard University Press. Those who follow the projected schedules of scholarly editions know that they arrive with the speed and punctuality of mass transit lines in metropolitan areas. The Harvard Poe was no exception. Fifteen years after Robbin's call for action, *Poe Studies,* the heir to the *Poe Newsletter,* includes an announcement that submissions should be matched to a crazy quilt of frequently cited texts of Poe's writings. Poetic citations are to be keyed to Mabbott's old-fashioned, variorum-style *Poems,* or to the less fully annotated compilation by Floyd Stovall (1965); fictional passages to the two-volume *Tales and Sketches,* edited by Mabbott with the assistance of Eleanor Kewer and Maureen Cobb Mabbott; and criticism to *The Complete Works of Edgar Allan Poe,* edited by James A. Harrison, an edition which contains several reviews that Poe did not compose and which omits others that are clearly his.[2]

One expects that quotations from *The Narrative of Arthur Gordon Pym,* "Hans Pfaall," and "The Journal of Julius Rodman" shall now be keyed to *The Imaginary Voyages,* edited by Burton R. Pollin, the first in a projected series of volumes that purportedly sustain Mabbott's "spirit and methods" (p. v).

Despite a variety of separate editions and despite considerable time between the appearance of *Poems* and the volumes of fiction, the state of Poe texts has advanced since Robbins offered his estimate. Mabbott's edition of the poems constitutes a major scholarly achievement; it includes juvenilia, miscellaneous lyrics, and verse epigrams in addition to major poetic texts. Mabbott prints alternative versions of significantly revised poems and records selectively other substantive variants. The poems are copiously annotated, reflecting the wide learning and erudition that students of Poe came to expect from Mabbott. The long-awaited *Tales and Sketches* displayed a similar immersion in sources, analogues, and contemporaneous parallels. The two volumes have won plaudits for inclusiveness (even trifles like "Theatrical Rats" appear) and for common sense — Mabbott prints coupled versions of heavily revised pieces: "A Decided Loss" and "Loss of Breath," "The Bargain Lost" and "Bon-Bon," "The Landscape Garden" and "The Domain of Arnheim."

Mabbott's idiosyncratic textual principles have, however, garnered severe criticism from the Greg-Bowers school of textual editing.[3] His life-consuming labors on behalf of Poe began before the Center for Editions of American Authors initiated its monumental quest for reliable texts. He also had the temerity to piece together an edition on his own, initially without an army of collators and without foundation or government support. His one-man operation did not require the machinery to inspect multiple copies for silent emendations during production or reprinting. His edition of the *Tales* ignored principles established by the CEAA and the Center for Scholarly Editions; it also avoided the studious impersonality of editions that have won the CSE imprimateur.

Textual experts have singled out for criticism Mabbott's admittedly inexplicable selection of the Griswold edition as copy-text for forty-one tales. Mabbott offered only this somewhat casual justification: "Careful study of the variants shows that Griswold had for some tales obviously superior readings, improvements that must have come from Poe. For these it may be assumed that Griswold had clippings with revisions in Poe's hands" (p. xxvii). In the face of Griswold's known forgeries of Poe's letters and misrepresentation of other documents, Mabbott's assumption seems dangerous at best. His belief that Griswold *must* have had revisions directly from Poe is offered without supporting evidence. His claim that all revisions constitute improvements begs the question of Poe's craftsmanship and ignores the exigencies of house styling and copyediting. Most significantly, his reliance on Griswold for copy-text shifts focus to the printed form farthest from the author's hand, a practice that flies in the face of editing principles adhered to by the Center for Scholarly Editions. Mabbott's procedure forecloses any opportunity to approximate Poe's practices for accidental variants, an editing strategy particularly unfortunate in cases where manuscripts exist. The reader can piece together the pattern of Poe's revisions for substantive variants by scrutinizing Mabbott's bottom-of-the page notes, but such a task serves to distance one from Poe's original conceptions rather than to chart the stages of his texts from their original states. Following Mabbott's notes for variants is like tracing steps on a path that has long been cold.

For his edition of Poe's longer narratives, Burton R. Pollin had the luxury of monitoring the critical reception of the "Mabbott Poe," as well as CSE editions, as they came off the presses. *Poe's Imaginary Voyages* follows all too closely the spirit of Mabbott's edition in mixing painstaking scholarship with questionable textual work.

The format of the edition is similar, but not identical, to Mabbott's in style. After a general introduction on "Aims and Methods," Pollin regales the reader with a thorough survey of Poe's sources in *Pym*. Pollin scrutinizes *Pym* within the context of the bantering, satirical style of Poe's earliest prose. Anomalies and inconsistencies in plotting, Pollin argues, reflect reliance on and parody of three categories of sources: juvenile sea tales, mariners' chronicles, and travel books. Suggesting that slack plotting and indifferent style mark Poe's satirical intent, Pollin contends that any attempt to impose a serious thematic framework on *Pym* would be mistaken. For Pollin, parody amounts to imitation, close paraphrase, direct borrowing, or parallelism of action. He scants any more sophisticated discussion of literary parody.

While Pollin follows Mabbott in making *Poe's Imaginary Voyages* essentially a one-man operation, he includes a seven-page essay by Joseph V. Ridgely on "The Growth of the Text." Ridgely acknowledges that his own 1966 essay on *Pym* requires modification.[4] He traces four stages in the evolution of *Pym*: (1) installments in the *Southern Literary Messenger,* (2) chapters in the vein of sea narratives, (3) material influenced by Benjamin Morrell's *Narrative of Four Voyages,* and (4) material influenced by J. L. Stephen's *Incidents of Travel* and Alexander Keith's *Evidence of Prophecy.* Pollin's and Ridgely's fixing of interpretation so close to sources may be sound for a work so derivative, but their approach invites as many questions as it answers. Ridgely asks two good ones in his discussion of the growth of the text: Did Poe present Harpers with a scenario inducing them to publish the book? And did Poe turn in material in segments, a process of composition that may account for many of the book's inconsistencies? To Ridgely's list of queries one might add the following: Is Pollin's dogmatic insistence that *Pym* resists allegorical interpretation consistent with Ridgely's assertion that its conclusion provides "some ultimate revelation of man's history and his fate"? (p. 35). Does the alleged banter in *Pym* comport with its publication, according to Ridgely, "during one the darkest periods in Poe's literary career"? (p. 29). Pollin's ruling out of thematic implications runs counter to symbolic, psychological, and sociological readings of *Pym*. Many of the most fascinating "interpretations" of *Pym* have been advanced by creative writers like W. H. Auden and Jules Verne. Most of those "creative" responses receive just dues from Pollin; others are ignored, such as the fugitive comments by Jorge Luis Borges and Vladimir Nabokov, John Gardner's *The King's Indian* (1974), and, on a lesser level, the clever *Pym*-pastiche by Steven Utley and Howard Waldrop.[5] Perhaps more than any other work by Poe, *Pym* marks a sharp discrepancy between the views of academic critics who score it for its disunity, sloppy plotting, and careless style, and creative writers who have found in its conclusion a palimpsest to be read according to subjective predilection.[6] In light of Pollin's repudiation of allegorical readings, the more "creative" responses to *Pym* receive scant attention, a stance inconsistent with Poe's own comment on Hawthorne that the "deepest allegory, as allegory, is a very imperfectly satisfied sense of the writer's ingenuity in overcoming a difficulty we should have preferred his not having attempted to overcome."[7] Pollin's literal-minded approach downplays Poe's call to decipher, even in the face of difficult and ingenious mysteries like the ending of *Pym*, the meaning of riddling allegories.[8] For all its copiously detailed and authoritative notes, Pollin's edition of *Pym* may serve to limit rather than to broaden interpretation of Poe's enigmatic narrative.

For copy-text Pollin uses the 1838 first edition, an almost inevitable choice since it was the sole authorized text during Poe's lifetime. He employs a slightly more complicated system of annotation than Mabbott in *Tales and Sketches*. Mabbott lists substantive variants at the bottoms of pages, a format that allows easy access to Poe's revisions. Pollin includes a complete list (separate from the 1838 text) of substantive and accidental variants from the *Southern Literary Messenger*. From this list and from Ridgely's discussion, one can see that Poe changed the ages of Pym and Augustus and modified dates when he transformed *Messenger* material into book form. The listing of all accidentals is of dubious value since much of the *Messenger* punctuation apparently resulted from house styling rather than Poe's wishes. From this list and Pollin's explanatory apparatus, one wonders whether all errors and inconsistencies in spelling, punctuation, or grammar result from Poe's slack writing or from compositorial error. Pollin waffles on modernized spelling, hyphenated compounds, and various adverbs, suggesting that forms such as "afterward" (changed from "afterwards") and "farther" (from "further") reflect house styling that received Poe's approval. Changes in punctuation, such as the replacement of dashes by semicolons, tighten the narrative, Pollin argues, but these modifications result from house styling sanctioned by Poe. On the authority of the 1838 text, Pollin accepts "above board," but calls it an error since it means "without artifice" rather than "on the main deck," as Poe may have intended. Of the nine "clear or probable errors" in the copy-text, Pollin corrects five in punctuation, all of which could have been corrected on the basis of Poe's common practice. Of the remaining four substantive "errors," Pollin allows three to stand on the authority of the 1838 text, even though two of the *Messenger* forms provide superior readings. As for other inconsistencies, Pollin suggests that Poe's poor copying led to the printing of "wings" for the "rings" of sea slugs, that he miswrote "pelicans" for "penguins," that he miscopied the spelling of "gastropeda," that other misspellings of proper names resulted from his miscopying from sources. Although all these errors need not be ascribed to Poe, Pollin allows them to stand on the authority of the 1838 text. When errors in spelling occur in the *Messenger* installments, Pollin lists them along with other variants and then adds an italicized comment: *error* or *probable error*. Except for nine changes that are inconsistently handled, Pollin's *Pym* follows the 1838 text, including two sub-divisions marked "Chapter 23." Poe intended a late insertion at Chapter 23 and apparently expected the copy editor to change subsequent chapter numbering. In his strict adherence to the 1838 text, Pollin chooses not to emend even at this point, a procedure also followed by Griswold in his 1856 edition. Pollin's edition thus contains a chapter marked by the editor as Chapter 23^A and one marked Chapter 23bis. With his reluctance to emend, Pollin's *Pym* amounts to reproduction of the 1838 text, including its errors, attended by a separate collation of the *Messenger* installments. His textual principles could be termed "conservative" or "idiosyncratic"; they certainly do not follow Greg-Bowers, the Center for Scholarly Editions, or any other standard editing practice. Inasmuch as he does not emend, he must annotate copiously, taking space for explanation of small errors and changes that could have been resolved rather simply had a common-sense system of emendation been established. The result is an "edition" with 153 pages of text, 152 pages of variants and notes, and 48 pages of introductory material.

Pollin's selection of copy-text was based on the sole authorized text during Poe's lifetime, one that may not have been faithful to Poe's accidentals, or to cite Pollin more precisely, one that may have included accidentals to which Poe gave tacit approval. In light of his choice for *Pym,* it is surprising that for "Hans Pfaall" Pollin selects for copy-text the Griswold edition of 1850. Pollin has, in essence, emulated Mabbott by choosing the text farthest from Poe's original conception, an unfortunate practice since a fair copy manuscript of "Hans Pfaall" survives. In the case of Poe's narrative of lunar exploration, Pollin has therefore forfeited an opportunity to recover Poe's accidentals.

The fair copy manuscript of "Hans Pfaall" was used for its appearance in the *Southern Literary Messenger* in 1835, but Poe had no opportunity to check its accuracy since he was in Baltimore. The story subsequently underwent fairly rigorous revision. According to Pollin, Poe gave his tacit approval to changes incorporated into its appearance in the 1839 *Tales.* Pollin assumes that Poe gave Lea and Blanchard a marked copy of the story but offers no evidence for this assumption. Two more sets of revisions occurred after 1840: for the tale's projected appearance in *Phantasy-Pieces* (1842) and for its printing in *Tales* (1845). "Hans Pfaall," then, reflects one of Poe's heaviest, if intermittent, stints of revising; he added, in fact, an entire appendix for the 1839 edition. In light of these significant changes, Pollin prints the Griswold text, arguing that revisions therein are ascribable solely to Poe. His choice contradicts accepted copy-text practice; in addition, he acknowledges that the text Griswold used for the 1850 edition has been destroyed. "Hans Pfaall" thus appears in the form farthest from Poe's hand with revisions accepted on the basis of Griswold's editorial judgment, without the text that Griswold purportedly edited.

Other irregularities attend Pollin's treatment of the text of "Hans Pfaall." Unlike his handling of *Pym,* in which all accidentals are listed, Pollin here records variants in commas and semicolons only for substantive changes. Changes that indicate substantial deletions from earlier states are repeated at the bottoms of pages and also appear in the official list of variants. For variants that change or expand a single or a double word, a slash is used to accompany superscript letters. Rather than the clear text appearing in the Harrison edition with notes at the ends of volumes, Pollin presents the text with an array of superscript letters, a distracting format for a text as heavily revised as "Hans Pfaall." A brief sample will suffice to show a textual format that may become a nuisance to some readers:

But, if this point were even attained, I could dispense with ballast and other weight to the amount of nearly 300 pounds.^{oC} In the meantime, the force of gravitation would be constantly diminishing, in proportion to the squares of the distances, and so,^{p} with a velocity prodigiously accelerating,$^{p'}$ I should at length arrive in those distant regions where the force^q of the earth's attraction$^{q'}$ would be superseded by ^{r}that of the moon.^{rD}

There was ^{s}another difficulty, however,^{s} which occasioned me some little disquietude. It has been observed, that, in^t balloon ascensions^u to any considerable height, besides the pain attending respiration, great uneasiness is^v experienced about the head and body, often accompanied with bleeding at the nose, and other symptoms of an alarming kind,^{A} and growing more and more inconvenient in proportion to the altitude attained.^{*w}

Fewer problems attend Pollin's presentation of the text of "The Journal of Julius Rodman." He follows the version in *Burton's Gentleman's Magazine,* January to June 1840. The narrative was published there anonymously, and Pollin provides the interesting tidbit that Lewis Gaylord Clark had guessed Poe's authorship in an April 1840 issue of the *Knickerbocker.* Scholars ignored Clark's inference until J. H. Ingram's 1877 discovery of Poe's letter to William Burton that offered reasons for noncompletion.

Pollin's choice of the *Burton's* text is inevitable, since it was the sole authorized version during Poe's lifetime. Like the Grabhorn Press edition of 1947, Pollin's edition offers a faithful printing of the *Burton's* installments but ascribes various forms rather casually to Poe's "intentions." In the absence of a manuscript Pollin properly adheres to the *Burton's* text, but he ascribes all forms to Poe's wishes: the inconsistent use of compounds like "any-thing," "birch-bark", and "flower-garden"; the misspelling of "alter" for "altar"; the intentional misspelling of proper names for satirical effect ("Amateaza" for "Ahmateaza"); inconsistent plural forms for animals ("beavers" and "beaver," "buffaloes" and "buffalo," "elks" and "elk"). Pollin cites these anomolies to suggest Poe's indifferent attitude toward his tale of western exploration. They could as easily result from house styling, compositorial misreading, or copy editor's error. Despite these quibbles, one welcomes a reliable text as well as Pollin's useful work in adducing sources, analogues, and cross-references.

In sum, the Harvard and G. K. Hall Poe editions mark significant strides in our knowledge of Poe's sources and practices. They disappoint, however, in their idiosyncratic textual work: Mabbott's in his excessive reliance on Griswold for copy-text, Pollin's in that no consistent policy can be inferred from his practices. For typographical accuracy, Mabbott's is superior. Typographical errors mar Pollin's commentary: Mr. Pym is called "Dr. Pym" (p. 10); Donald Ringe's name is misspelled "Ring" (p. 27); Eleanor Kewer's first name is misspelled "Elinor" (p. v); and Iola Haverstick's surname is misspelled "Havistock" (p. 339). Such errors are particularly ironic in an edition in which Pollin so scrupulously monitors Poe's orthography. Despite these flaws, *The Imaginary Voyages* supersedes other editions for *The Narrative of Arthur Gordon Pym* and "The Journal of Julius Rodman." But for the reasons cited above, this reviewer must demur on "The Unparalleled Adventure of one Hans Pfaall."

Finally, one must regard as a mixed blessing a situation in which Poe's works have been brought to the scholarly public by so many different hands and by different presses. Mabbott's death prevented him from completing the heroic task of editing Poe's works, and his labors were "finished" by able and well-meaning assistants. Nevertheless, the bracketed insertions in the Harvard Poe, provided by Mrs. Mabbott and Ms. Kewer, detract from the smoothness of the already complicated annotations. Their completion of Mabbott's work undermines the view that editing according to modern standards can be done by one person. Both Mabbott's and Pollin's editions suffer from lack of machine collation, a lamentable oversight since the Griswold copy-text endured one or more accidents to its type after 1853, imperfections that affect the typography of "Hans Pfaall" and other tales. Machine inspection might have revealed other defects that seldom surface during sight collation, but neither Mabbott nor Pollin chose to contract mechanical assistance. Rather, they collated by sight, edited according to subjective practice, and annotated, according to their wide but sometimes pedantic scholarship; their volumes, as a result, bear the stamps of their personalities. But Poe scholars still do not have a complete, consistently edited, uniformly annotated edition of his writings. The poetry and fiction are all in print, but the G. K. Hall volume follows quite a different format from the Harvard Poe. The serious student of Poe faces a multiplicity of Poe texts, a situation rendered even more complicated by the University Press of Virginia's publication of the *Marginalia* and by Pollin's projection of other G. K. Hall volumes that will compete with already existing texts. The pressing need enunciated by Professor Robbins in 1968 has yet to be met.

Notes

1. J. Albert Robbins, "The State of Poe Studies," *Poe Newsletter,* 1 (1968), 1-2.

2. See J. Lasley Dameron's overview, "Thomas Ollive Mabbott on the Canon of Poe's Reviews," *Poe Studies,* 5 (1972), 56-57.

3. Reservations have been registered by Thomas Philbrick in his untitled review, *Nineteenth-Century Fiction,* 33 (1978), 403-5; by Joseph J. Moldenhauer, "Mabbott's Poe and the Question of Copy-Text," *Poe Studies,* 11 (1978), 41-46; and by J. Albert Robbins in his untitled review, *Resources for American Literary Study,* 8 (1978), 211-15. John E. Reilly strikes a more complimentary note in his untitled review, *Mississippi Quarterly,* 33 (1978-79), 96-99.

4. See J. V. Ridgely and Iola S. Haverstick, "Chartless Voyage: The Many Narratives of Arthur Gordon Pym," *Texas Studies in Literature and Language,* 6 (1966), 63-80.

5. Nabokov's response is noted by Richard Kopley, "The Secret of *Arthur Gordon Pym:* The Text and the Source," *Studies in American Fiction,* 8 (1980), 203-18. Borges's response is recorded by Paul Theroux, *The Old Patagonian Express: By Train through the Americas* (New York: Houghton Mifflin, 1979). See also Steven Utley and Howard Waldrop, "Black as a Pit, from Pole to Pole," in *Year's Finest Fantasy,* ed. Terry Carr (New York: Berkley Publishing Company, 1978), pp. 71-112, reprinted from *New Directions,* 7 (1977).

6. A representative academic perspective, characteristically negative, is found in Stuart Levine, *Edgar Poe: Seer and Craftsman* (Deland: Everett Edwards, 1972).

7. *The Complete Works of Edgar Allan Poe,* ed. James A. Harrison (New York: Thomas Y. Crowell, 1902), XIII, 148.

8. I make this point more fully in "Descent of the Titans: The Sublime Riddle of *Arthur Gordon Pym,*" *Southern Literary Journal,* 10 (1978), 75-92, an essay not cited by Pollin, although it discusses what he regards as a significant influence on *Pym,* Jacob Bryant's *A New System; or An Analysis of Antient Mythology.*

Yeats's Politics

Richard J. Finneran

Grattan Freyer. *W. B. Yeats and the Anti-Democratic Tradition.* Totowa, N.J.: Barnes & Noble Books, 1981. x, 143 pp.

Bernard G. Krimm. *W. B. Yeats and the Emergence of the Irish Free State, 1918-1939: Living in the Explosion.* Troy, N.Y.: Whitson Publishing Company, 1981. xvii, 305 pp.

Elizabeth Cullingford. *Yeats, Ireland and Fascism.* New York: New York University Press, 1981. viii, 251 pp.

In May of 1938 Yeats came across an article by Archibald MacLeish entitled "Public Speech and Private Speech in Poetry," published in the *Yale Review* two months earlier.[1] The remarks on Yeats were mostly quite positive. MacLeish called him "the best of modern poets," particularly because "his poetry is no escape from time and place and life and death but, on the contrary, the acceptance of these things and their embodiment" (p. 544). But MacLeish also voiced what was by then the standard criticism of Yeats by the "Auden generation":

The later poetry of Yeats, because of Yeats's somewhat isolated situation in Ireland and because of Yeats's age, has not been called upon to employ the results of the poetic revolution at the point where those results may prove to be most useful. Yeats has moved only briefly and unwillingly at the point where the poetic revolution crosses the revolution in the social and political and economic structure of the post-war world, which so deeply concerns our generation in this country. But it is precisely at that point that the greatest victories of modern poetry may be won. [p. 545]

Writing to Dorothy Wellesley on 24 May 1938, Yeats seemingly overlooked the double slight on his Irishness and his age: "There has been an article upon my work . . . which is the only article on the subject which has not bored me for years. It commends me above other modern poets because my language is 'public.' That word, which I had not thought of myself, is a word I want."[2] But, Yeats was not about to allow MacLeish's criticism to go unanswered: his letter to Wellesley concludes with what is in effect his rejoinder, the poem "Politics." Taking as his epigraph a quotation from Thomas Mann included in the essay—"In our time the destiny of man presents its meanings in political terms"—Yeats offered the following defense of his work:

> Beside that window stands a girl;
> I cannot fix my mind
> On their analysis of things
> That benumb mankind.
> Yet one has travelled and may know
> What he talks about;
> And one's a politician
> That has read and thought.
> Maybe what they say is true
> Of war and war's alarms;
> But O that I were young again
> And held her in my arms.[3]

After some revision, the lyric was published in the *London Mercury* for January 1939. Moreover, when Yeats, a few weeks before his death, drafted a table of contents for a collection of poems and plays, he placed "Politics" as the final poem in the volume.[4]

That Yeats should feel compelled to reply to MacLeish, and that he should give a poem entitled "Politics" such a prominent position in his canon, should come as no surprise. Indeed, his career had hardly ever been free of "politics." In his early years he was often urged to put more propaganda and less obscurity in his poems and to spend more time on the lecture platform than in the study. When these entreaties came from Maud Gonne, they were difficult to ignore: Yeats later recalled that some of his proselytizing activities were motivated by "much patriotism and more desire for a fair woman" and that he "came to hate her politics, my one visible rival."[5] After the turn of the century, he was charged with allowing if not actually urging the Abbey Theatre to present plays which were an insult to the Irish nation—notably Synge's *The Playboy of the Western World* and O'Casey's *The Plough and the Stars*. He served in the Irish Senate from 1922 to 1928, but his diligent attendance at meetings and his positive contributions (e.g., selecting the designs for the Irish coinage) were overshadowed then and since by his speech on divorce: "We against whom you have done this thing are no petty people. We are one of the great stocks of Europe. We are the people of Burke; we are the people of Grattan" and so on — good oratory if ineffective politics.[6] Finally came Yeats's involvement in the summer of 1933 with "Fascism" — or, more precisely, with General Eoin O'Duffy and his "Blueshirts" movement.

Though Yeats's critics have not been silent on the question of his politics, especially the matter of Fascism, the three books under review are the first full-length studies of the topic. Of these, Grattan Freyer's *W. B. Yeats and the Anti-Democratic Tradition* is distinctly the slightest. It adds almost nothing to the extant criticism while introducing new errors of its own. It is not scholarly, offering no documentation beyond a two-page "Note on Sources," which mentions some of the standard accounts while overlooking numerous others, such as essays by Roger McHugh, George Mills Harper, Mary Carden, and David Fitzpatrick, and a recent book by G. J. Watson.[7] The concluding chapter traces some of the critical debate about Yeats's Fascism in a perfunctory way. Most of Freyer's study is little more than an elementary sketch of Yeats's life and works, with occasional emphasis on politics. The level of literary interpretation seldom advances beyond plot summary and paraphrase. New material is not a virtue of the study, Freyer admitting that "I have had only limited access to unpublished material" (p. ix) — even though microfilms of Michael B. Yeats's collection of manuscripts have been on deposit at the National Library of Ireland (and the State University of New York at Stony Brook) since 1976. Nor is the work strongly unified: whenever a name such as Davis or Ferguson is mentioned we are treated to a potted biography; the discussion of the Abbey Theatre bears little relation to the supposed topic; and we are not freed from numerous asides on the order of "Boucicault's reputation eventually came full circle, and three of his Irish plays with their simple message of romantic patriotism played to delighted Abbey audiences in the 1960s and 1970s" (p. 45) or "an ironic coda to the controversy over the *Playboy* was provided when the players of Ireland's national Abbey Theatre in a special audience with the Pope in 1968 presented him with a specially bound edition of this play" (p. 51).

It might be argued that there is a place and perhaps even a need for a brief, journalistic outline of Yeats's political activities; but if so, an account more accurate than *W. B. Yeats and the Anti-Democratic Tradition* will have to be provided. Take, for example, the following commentary on Yeats's marriage: "John MacBride fought in the Dublin

Rising of 1916 and was executed by the British. By this time Yeats, aged forty-eight, was again contemplating a permanent union with an English girl, several years younger than himself, Miss Hyde-Lees. He broke off the engagement to propose once more to Maud Gonne, and once more was refused. He married Miss Hyde-Lees on 21 October 1917" (p. 13). The first sentence is correct, though "Dublin Rising" is not a common term for the Easter Rebellion. In the next sentence Yeats's age is off by either two or four years, depending on what is meant by "this time," the time of the rebellion and executions (24 April–12 May 1916, when Yeats was 50) or the time of the proposals (summer-autumn 1917, when Yeats was 52). Further, "several years younger" does not quite describe a difference in ages of twenty-seven years. In the third sentence Yeats is depicted as the Don Juan of his time, becoming engaged and unengaged at the drop of a hat. But Freyer offers no evidence of any formal engagement between Yeats and Georgie Hyde-Lees before the autumn of 1917, *after* the proposals to both Maud and her daughter, Iseult (inexplicably omitted here but referred to on p. 68), had been refused. In a letter to Lady Gregory on 19 September (1917), Yeats noted that "I am going to Mrs. Tucker's in the country on Saturday or Monday at latest and I will ask her daughter to marry me. Perhaps she is tired of the idea. I shall however make it clear that I will still be friend and guardian to Iseult."[8] This hardly sounds like someone asking to be taken back after breaking a prior engagement. In *The Man and the Masks,* Richard Ellmann — doubtless drawing on conversations with the woman in question — notes that the marriage took place "after a short engagement."[9] Furthermore, in an unpublished letter from Mrs. Tucker to Lady Gregory of 30 September (1917), asking her to persuade Yeats not to marry her daughter, a prior broken engagement is not one of the charges brought against Yeats.[10] Finally, in the last sentence quoted above, Freyer repeats a common error and places the marriage on 21 October rather than 20 October.

This passage probably contains the largest concentration of errors in the book, but it is not altogether atypical. And sometimes the omissions are equally important. For instance, after a far too brief discussion of Yeats's involvement with the Blueshirts movement, Freyer suggests that although Yeats was probably never a formal member, "Frank O'Connor claimed to have been embarrassed to meet him for dinner at the Kildare Street Club and to find him wearing a blue shirt" (p. 107). But Freyer fails to offer an explanation, again provided by

Ellmann over thirty years ago: "Although Yeats was often seen in a blue shirt at this time, he had been wearing blue shirts since 1925 or 1926, and the reason was not political but esthetic. If he had learned the habit from anyone, it was from William Morris."[11] Indeed, even the epigraph to *W. B. Yeats and the Anti-Democratic Tradition* is not free from error: what Freyer describes as "T. S. Eliot in an Obituary Address in Dublin in 1939" is in fact Eliot's lecture "The Poetry of W. B. Yeats," the First Annual Yeats Lecture, delivered to the Friends of the Irish Academy at the Abbey Theatre in June 1940.[12]

Compared with Freyer's volume, Krimm's study is more restricted in scope, covering only the last two decades of Yeats's life, but more ambitious in attempting to extend our understanding of Yeats's politics. Krimm tries to demonstrate "the grounding Yeats's writing had in . . . the intense political situation in Ireland," stressing "his attempts to reach the public about practical political concerns" (p. xiii). The approach is roughly chronological, combining biographical information and speculation with interpretation of selected works. Though he is not especially thorough in surveying the previous scholarship, he has undertaken an impressive amount of research in both unpublished materials, such as Lady Gregory's journals in the Berg Collection of the New York Public Library, and newspaper archives.

The result of these labors is a study that is often interesting but finally flawed. To start with, the volume has been atrociously produced: there are few pages without misprints, and at one point almost two pages of material have simply been repeated (pp. 169.22–170.33). There is no index. The book contains some errors which could easily have been avoided, including "John Stewart Parnell" for Charles Stewart Parnell (p. 177), "G. R. Barrio" for George Barnes (pp. 235, 292), "Crazy Jane and the King" for "Crazy Jane on the Mountain" (pp. 239, 240), "DeValera" for de Valera (passim).

However, the major problem with *W. B. Yeats and the Emergence of the Irish Free State* is the allegorical approach Krimm takes to Yeats's works, especially the plays. To cite just one instance, Krimm argues that "in *The King of the Great Clock Tower* Yeats seems to be celebrating Ireland's final achievement of freedom through the 1931 Statute of Westminster" (p. 202). Indeed, in the title of the play "Yeats was thinking of Big Ben, perhaps the most famous clock tower of all for the English-speaking world, the clock tower that represented Britain and British rule" (p. 212). These are the kinds of suggestions that, once made, are perhaps impossible to refute (though Irishmen would be surprised to learn that the 1931 Statute was "their final achievement of freedom"). But the evidence offered in support of these and similar assertions is seldom convincing. Krimm's usual method is to seize upon certain elements in a work that might support his thesis while ignoring the remainder. With *The King of the Great Clock Tower,* he uncharacteristically admits, though only in a note, that he cannot "explain the political significance of all the details," especially the introductory songs, and lamely argues that "I do not try to reduce the play to a strict allegory" (p. 289, n. 35a). Yet the body of his discussion points toward just such an allegory. Are parts of the play allegorical and others not? If the play is essentially political and allegorical, and if, as Krimm suggests, Yeats "felt he *would* communicate with the Irish people with this play" (p. 219), what is the significance of the fact that no one in the audience at the Abbey on 30 July 1934 seems to have grasped its meaning? Finally, as Krimm conveniently neglects to mention, in revising the play to *A Full Moon in March* Yeats eliminated both the person and the symbol that supposedly represent England, explaining that "in 'The King of the Great Clock Tower' there are three characters, King, Queen and stroller, and that is a character too many; reduced to the essentials, Queen and Stroller, the fable should have greater intensity."[13] It is difficult to reconcile Yeats's attempt to present a political statement in 1934 with his removal of any such possibility from the play a year later.

Similar allegorical readings are found throughout *W.B. Yeats and the Emergence of the Irish Free State,* notably in the interpretation of *The Herne's Egg* as a satire on Eamon de Valera (in the person of King Congal). Yet, despite its shortcomings, the book does offer some new information on Yeats's political activities and adds resonance to our readings of some of his works. With substantial revision, it might well have been recommended to anyone with a serious interest in Yeats.

Such a recommendation can be given, with a few qualifications, to Cullingford's study. To dispose of the qualifications: first, the book is badly mistitled, as it offers an account of Yeats's politics throughout his career, with only two of its twelve chapters concentrating on the matter of Fascism. Secondly, it does not sufficiently acknowledge the previous scholarship: in addition to missing all but one (McHugh) of the works cited above in conjunction with Freyer's book, Cullingford overlooks monographs by Peter Faulkner, Brian Cleeve, and Fahmy Farag as well as essays by Donald Torchiana and Sandra Siegel; and Pearce's edition of *The Senate Speeches* is somehow omitted from the list of works by Yeats.[14] Thirdly, for some unpublished materials she relies on another scholar's transcriptions, a procedure never to be recommended: for "on public or local grounds" read "on public, or local, grounds" (p. 108), the single passage I was able to check. Finally, she does not always avoid allegorizing Yeats's works, as in her comment that "in Yeats's first considerable work, *The Wanderings of Oisin*, a chained maiden — Ireland — is held captive by a demon — England — against whom Oisin fights for a hundred years" (p. 32). This is indeed an arguable interpretation — Yeatsians will recall it from *The Man and the Masks* — but it is certainly not the only one.[15]

Nevertheless, *Yeats, Ireland and Fascism* offers a solid, sensible, well-written account of Yeats's politics. Cullingford begins with the influence of John O'Leary and William Morris and proceeds through the career, concluding with a commentary on *On the Boiler* and some of the late poems. She consistently maintains the proper balance between fault-finding and idolization, as in this: "*On the Boiler* can be explained, but probably it cannot be justified; its stridency is ultimately repellent. However it must not, despite its late date, be taken as the final word on Yeats's politics" (pp. 230-31). Assisted by an appendix on "Books of political interest in Yeats's library" (pp. 236-37), she is adept at sketching the contemporary environment in which Yeats's ideas developed. Her recognition that "Yeats's poetry escapes simple political labels because it is essentially dialectical" (p. viii) also serves her well. Cullingford concludes — rightly, to my mind — that "the nature of his convictions makes it wrong to place him in any school save that of a nationalist of the school of John O'Leary. His devotion to Ireland, which survived circumstances that drove most other Irish writers into despairing exile, also dictated his attitude to other political philosophies" (p. 234). Rejecting the labels "socialist," "democrat," "Tory," or "conservative," she suggests that "of all political stances he was probably closest to that of Burke's Old Whigs: an aristocratic liberalism that combined love of individual freedom with respect for the ties of the organic social group" (p. 235).

Cullingford's treatment of the question of Yeats's "fascism" is representative of the high standards of this study. First, she stresses the importance of distinguishing between fascism as a political philosophy of the 1930s and the results of that philosophy, especially in Germany, seen through a post-World War II perspective. Moreover, Yeats's conception of fascism was developed from the information then available to him, much of it supplied from propaganda machines. Given that "Yeats's curiosity about fascism centered upon Mussolini" (p. 144), Cullingford detects three incorrect assumptions by Yeats: (1) "that Mussolini governed through an hierarchy of intelligent assistants"; (2) "that Mussolini's opposition to democracy was comparable to his own"; and (3) that Mussolini fostered "the values of personality and of the soul's autonomy" (pp. 148-49). With these misconceptions, as well as with the influence of Ezra Pound during his several visits to Italy and the cyclical theories of *A Vision*, many of Yeats's pronouncements can be seen in a different light from that offered by some earlier critics—particularly, of course, Conor Cruise O'Brien in his controversial essay on Yeats's politics.[16] Cullingford also demonstrates that by October 1935 "Yeats's disillusionment with fascism was complete" (p. 144). Likewise, in her examination of the "Blueshirts" episode, she shows that "the period of Yeats's involvement with the Blueshirts, an involvement which was in any case never formal and existed largely in his own over-heated imagination, did not extend beyond the summer months of 1933" (p. 207). Rather than abandoning the movement only as it was being discredited, as O'Brien had suggested, "Yeats dissociated himself from the Blueshirts at the height of their success and popularity" (p. 212)

Near the end of *Yeats, Ireland and Fascism*, Cullingford offers a new piece of evidence on the question of Yeats's attitudes toward fascism, one that warrants further investigation. She quotes from the *Memoirs* of Pablo Neruda, describing his activities in helping to organize the Second International Writers' Congress in Madrid during the Spanish Civil War.[17] Neruda explains that in response to an invitation to attend the conference, "priceless replies poured in from all over. One was from Yeats, Ireland's national poet; another from Selma Lagerlöf, the notable Swedish writer. They were both too old to travel to a beleaguered city like Madrid, which was being steadily pounded by bombs, but they rallied to the defense of the Spanish Republic" (p. 223). Cullingford explains (unfortunately without documenting her source) that "at the first session in the capital letters from those unable to attend were read out, among them presumably the one from Yeats described by Neruda. He had stepped, briefly but decisively, out of the purely Irish context; he had made public his rejection of fascism" (p. 223). This is indeed possible, but one would like to recover the full text of Yeats's letter before sharing Cullingford's certainty. Perhaps it may be found among Neruda's papers; failing that, perhaps the

Madrid newspapers of the time (July 1937) will contain at least a quotation from the letter.

It is with such matters that Cullingford might well concern herself, should a new edition of *Yeats, Ireland and Fascism* be called for. She has already provided an impressive study, and as further materials become available—F. S. L. Lyons's authorized biography, the new *Complete Letters*—she will have the opportunity to refine and extend it. Yeatsians will be even further in her debt if she accomplishes that task.

Notes

1. MacLeish, "Public Speech and Private Speech in Poetry," *Yale Review*, 27 (March 1938), 536-47.

2. *The Letters of W. B. Yeats*, ed. Allan Wade (London: Rupert Hart-Davis, 1954), pp. 908-9.

3. Ibid., p. 909. The conclusion of "Politics" is also indebted to MacLeish's essay, which quotes "the anonymous poet of the Western Wind":

> O western wind when wilt thou blow
> That the small rain down can rain: —
> Christ, that my love were in my arms
> And I in my bed again. [p.540]

4. *Last Poems and Two Plays* (Dublin: Cuala Press, 1939). In *Yeats's "Last Poems" Again*, Dolmen Press Yeats Papers, No. 8 (Dublin: Dolmen Press, 1966), Curtis Bradford argued that there is no authority for the different order of poems in *Last Poems & Plays* (London: Macmillan, 1940). Bradford's assertion can be confirmed by a letter from Mrs. W. B. Yeats in the archives of Macmillan, London, and the 1939 order will be followed in my forthcoming *The Poems of W.B. Yeats, a New Edition* (London: Macmillan, 1983).

5. *Memoirs*, ed. Denis Donoghue (London: Macmillan, 1972), pp. 59, 63.

6. *The Senate Speeches of W. B. Yeats*, ed. Donald R. Pearce (Bloomington: Indiana Univ. Press, 1960), p. 99.

7. McHugh, "Yeats and Irish Politics," *University Review* (Dublin), 2 (1961?), 24-36; also *Texas Quarterly*, 5 (Autumn 1962), 90-100; Harper, "Yeats's Intellectual Nationalism," *Dublin Magazine*, 4 (Summer 1965), 8-26; and "'Intellectual hatred' and 'intellectual nationalism': The Paradox of Passionate Politics," in *Theatre and Nationalism in Twentieth-Century Ireland*, ed. Robert O'Driscoll (Toronto: Univ. of Toronto Press, 1971), pp. 40-65; Carden, "The Few and the Many: An Examination of Yeats's Politics," *Studies* (Dublin), 58 (Spring 1969), 51-62; Fitzpatrick, "W. B. Yeats in

Seanan Éireann," in *Yeats and the Theatre*, ed. Robert O'Driscoll and Lorna Reynolds (Toronto: Macmillan, 1975), pp. 159-75; Watson, *Irish Identity and the Literary Revival* (London: Croon Helm, 1979).

8. *Letters*, p. 633.

9. Ellmann, *The Man and the Masks*, new ed. (New York: W. W. Norton, 1979), p. 222.

10. I am grateful to Professor Mary M. FitzGerald for information about this letter.

11. Ellmann, p. 281. One is reminded of T. S. Eliot's comment about the relevance to scholarship of a writer's laundry lists.

12. First published in *Purpose*, 12 (July-December 1940), 115-27, and often reprinted.

13. *The Variorum Edition of the Plays of W. B. Yeats*, ed. Russell K. Alspach (New York: Macmillan, 1966), pp. 1311-12.

14. Faulkner, *William Morris and W. B. Yeats* (Dublin: Dolmen Press, 1962); Cleeve, *W. B. Yeats and the Designing of Ireland's Coinage*, New Yeats Papers, No. 3 (Dublin: Dolmen Press, 1972); Farag, *The Opposing Virtues: Two Essays*, New Yeats Papers, No. 14 (Dublin: Dolmen Press, 1978); Torchiana, "'Among School Children' and the Education of the Irish Spirit," in *In Excited Reverie: A Centenary Tribute to William Butler Yeats, 1865-1939*, ed. A. Norman Jeffares and K. G. W. Cross (London: Macmillan, 1965), pp. 123-50; Siegel, "Yeats's Quarrel with Himself: The Design and Argument of *On the Boiler*," *Bulletin of Research in the Humanities*, 81 (Autumn 1978), 349-68.

15. Ellmann, *The Man and the Masks*, p. 53.

16. O'Brien, "Passion and Cunning: An Essay on the Politics of Yeats," in *In Excited Reverie*, pp. 207-78. Cullingford might have cited some of the rebuttals of O'Brien, particularly Patrick Cosgrave's "Yeats, Fascism, and Conor O'Brien," *London Magazine*, 7 (July 1967), 22-41.

O'Brien, of course, was by no means the first critic to accuse Yeats of Fascism. George Orwell issued one of the earliest broadsides in "W. B. Yeats," *Horizon*, 7 (January 1943), 67-71, a review of V. K. Narayana Menon's *The Development of William Butler Yeats* (London: Oliver and Boyd, 1942).

17. Neruda, *Memoirs*, trans. Hardie St. Martin (New York: Farrar, Straus and Giroux, 1977).

Nick Adams in the Round

Scott Donaldson

Joseph M. Flora. *Hemingway's Nick Adams*. Baton Rouge: Louisiana State University Press, 1982. 285 pp.

Joseph M. Flora began with a fine idea for a book: to "focus on Nick Adams and his experience and the artistry of the work that reveals him" (p. 14). Hemingway's first and most autobiographical protagonist has often been considered critically, of course, but never with the comprehensiveness he deserves. Flora's valid assumption is that all of the Nick stories — or rather all the stories he so designates — should be examined as a whole, with sensitivity to their thematic and artistic interconnections. Thus when the warmly maternal Mrs. Garner asks Nick to fetch her son Carl home in "Ten Indians," one can and should be reminded of the neurasthenic and tyrannical Mrs. Adams sending her husband after Nick on a similar errand at the end of "The Doctor and the Doctor's Wife." Similarly, the supportive Mrs. Packard in "The Last Good Country" contrasts with Nick's emasculating mother not only in that fragment-of-a-novel, but also in "Fathers and Sons" and "The Doctor and the Doctor's Wife." Flora traces many such parallels. Moreover, he explicates individual stories with thoroughness, including those not much written about since appearing for the first time in the 1972 *Nick Adams Stories*.[1]

Often these explications are enlightening. Flora rightly refuses to be as harsh on Dr. Adams as most other critics. He calls attention to the journey motif running through the stories and observes how Hemingway gradually shifted from third person to first person narration as he moved from *In Our Time* to *Winner Take Nothing*. Best of all, Flora hears the tension in Ad's silence in "The Battler" and in the talk of "The Killers," a story he characterizes as basically a "one-act play." Not enough has been done on the subject of Hemingway's talent for drama, though James Hinkle has recently noted how reading his dialogue aloud brings out the flavor of the situation, adding humor or pathos. This skill is much more apparent in the fiction than in *The Fifth Column* and emerges as much in subtext (particularly in silences:

see for example the developing reticence of Jake Barnes as his emotional world deteriorates) as in the spoken words themselves.[2]

At times Flora's interpretations verge on the radical, and not always persuasively. Dr. Adams is cleaning his shotgun, he states without elaboration, "in case Dick Boulyon returns" (p. 38). "Big Two-Hearted River" is "Hemingway's account of Genesis" and is about marriage as well as war (pp. 157, 179). In addition, what is probably the most important point in the book—that Nick Adams is not simply a boy things happen to, but a boy, youth, and man who takes considerable initiative in making things happen as he grows older—is somewhat undermined by Flora's moralistic insistence that he develops into an optimistic and mature adult. Is he "confident that he will be a great writer" when he prays for that at the finish of "Summer People"? Does he really "welcome the fact of Helen's pregnancy" in "Cross-Country Snow"? (pp. 187, 212). Such issues of interpretation aside, however, there are three important reasons why *Hemingway's Nick Adams* fails to achieve its potential.

First and foremost, Flora has not consulted the papers in the Hemingway collection at the Kennedy Library. Not every study of Hemingway's work must be textually oriented, obviously, yet the professional scholar can ignore his manuscripts and typescripts only at peril. Had Flora read the aborted ending of "The Light of the World," for instance, he would have found some surprising support for the way Nick feels about Alice. Philip Young did not include this fragment in *The Nick Adams Stories* (though he did include "Three Shots," the beginning Hemingway chopped off "Indian Camp"), but it is available in Boston along with drafts of many Hemingway stories. Also on hand is the typescript of "Cross-Country Snow" in which the main character is called "Mike Adams" more than thirty times, and then, in all but two cases, a hand other than Hemingway's has crossed out "Mike" and written "Nick" instead. No one having seen that document would be likely to insist that Mike is a nickname for Nick and that it indicates the degree of comradeship between the two skiers. The point about Mike and Nick was made in the spring 1981 issue of *Hemingway Notes*. Appearing in the fall 1980 *College Literature* was Philip Young's acknowledgment that he had probably got the chronology of "The End of Something" and "The Three-Day Blow" wrong; Flora corrects Young on that point anyway.[3] Another unconsulted source is the Scribner archive at Princeton, where the correspondence between Hemingway and Maxwell Perkins (only a portion of which is reprinted

Nick Adams in the Round

in Carlos Baker's *Selected Letters*) might have provided solid documentation for the footnoted assertion that from "first to last, Hemingway used placement of his stories [within collections] to emphasize meanings" (p. 252).

Secondly, the book is not particularly well presented. The publishers have been responsible for a minor annoyance by using unjustified right-hand margins (inside an extremely handsome jacket). Still more troublesome are the typographical errors and misquotations: I ran across a dozen without searching for them. But the misquotations from Hemingway rankle most. Spot-checking turned up ten errors in eight separate passages, including the three italicized in the following quotation, from "Fathers and Sons": "His father had summed up the whole matter by stating that masturbation *produced* blindness, insanity, and death, while a man who went with prostitutes would contract hideous venereal diseases and *that* the thing to do was to keep your hands off *of* people." *Hemingway's Nick Adams*, on page 239, alters "produced" to "caused" and omits the relative pronoun "that" and the preposition "of."

In allowing such misquotations to pass, Flora and his editors are not at all unusual. Recently, while selecting and editing essays for a collection on *The Great Gatsby,* I was struck by how often—even in the most perceptive work by the most renowned scholars in the best journals—a word or phrase was transformed in its journey from novel to critical article. Few of these errors were substantive, just a few of Flora's are. Nonetheless, they matter. If those of us in the academy do not cite texts with exactitude, who will?

Finally, the book draws conclusions from unreliable biographical sources in two cases. Usually Flora does not attempt to make connections between Hemingway's life and his fiction, and when such connections are inevitable he almost always relies on the soundest available source, Carlos Baker's *Ernest Hemingway: A Life Story.* Thus it is odd to find him adducing evidence about Hemingway's careerism from Gertrude Stein, hardly an unprejudiced source, and making a good deal out of Gregory Hemingway's swipe at *The Old Man and the Sea* ("sentimental slop") without taking account of the then extremely bitter relations between father and son.

These important limitations prevent Flora's book from making as significant a contribution to Hemingway studies as it might have done. Yet *Hemingway's Nick Adams* retains considerable merit. Flora is a fine close reader, and it is doubtful if anyone could know these stories about "a sensitive boy's learning to accept his own and the world's limitations" (p. 18), and the interconnections between them, more comprehensively than he does.

Notes

1. Ernest Hemingway, *The Nick Adams Stories* (New York: Scribners, 1972). Phillip Young wrote a short preface for this volume but edited nothing in it. In " 'Big World Out There': *The Nick Adams Stories,"Novel*, 6 (1972), 5-19, reprinted in Jackson J. Benson ed., *The Short Stories of Ernest Hemingway: Critical Essays* (Durham: Duke Univ. Press, 1975), pp. 150-59, Young discussed the book and his part in its development at some length. He also refers to it in "The Hemingway Papers, Occasional Remarks," *College Literature*, 7 (1980), 310-18, reprinted in Bernard Oldsey, ed., *Ernest Hemingway: The Papers of a Writer* (New York: Garland, 1981), pp. 139-47.

2. This issue is explored in Nigel Cutting, "Hemingway's Sub-Text in *The Sun Also Rises,"* M.A. thesis, College of William and Mary, 1976.

3. Scott Donaldson, "The Case of the Vanishing American and Other Puzzlements in Hemingway's Fiction," *Hemingway Notes*, 6 (1981), 15-19; Young, "Papers" 316-18. I am aware of the difficulty of keeping up with current scholarship while meeting early book publishing deadlines.

The Continuing Relevance of William Morris

Gary L. Aho

Peter Faulkner. *Against the Age: An Introduction to William Morris.* London: Allen and Unwin, 1980. xi, 193 pp.

Peter Faulkner. *Wilfrid Scawen Blunt and the Morrises.* The First Annual Kelmscott Lecture of The William Morris Society, given at the Society of Antiquaries, 30 September 1980. London: William Morris Society, 1981. 45 pp.

Mary Lago, ed. *Burne-Jones Talking: His Conversations, 1895-1898, Preserved by His Studio Assistant, Thomas Rooke.* Columbia: University of Missouri Press, 1981. xi, 211 pp.

Margaret A. Lourie, ed. *William Morris: The Defence of Guenevere, and Other Poems.* Garland English Texts, Number 2. New York: Garland, 1981. xv, 262 pp.

Carole Silver, ed. *The Golden Chain: Essays on William Morris and Pre-Raphaelitism.* New York and London: William Morris Society, 1982. vii, 148 pp.

William Morris and Kelmscott. London: The Design Council, 1981. 191 pp.

Duncan Robinson and Stephen Wildman. *Morris and Company in Cambridge.* Catalogue of an Exhibition at the Fitzwilliam Museum, 30 September-16 November 1980. Cambridge: Cambridge University Press, 1980. xiv, 111 pp.

Oliver Fairclough and Emmeline Leary. *Textiles by William Morris and Company, 1861-1940.* London: Thames and Hudson, 1981. 120 pp.

A Book of Verse by William Morris. London: Scolar Press, 1980. vii, 49 pp.

John J. Walsdorf, ed. *Printers on Morris.* Beaverton, Oregon: Beaverdam Press, 1981. 37 pp.

Florence Boos, ed. *Socialist Diary by William Morris.* Iowa City: Windhover Press, 1981. ix, 38 pp.

Penelope Fitzgerald, ed. *The Novel on Blue Paper by William Morris.* London: Journeyman Press, 1982. xv, 79 pp.

Of the many scholars and critics who continue to explore the work of William Morris, insisting upon its relevance to our times, Florence Boos is one of the most active and incisive. Her comprehensive introduction to Morris's *Socialist Diary,* an introduction that I shall comment upon later in this review, opens with this statement: "Morris's achievements routinely exhaust the enumerative abilities of his biographers. When in 1883 William Morris joined the Social Democratic Federation, he had already been a writer of narrative poems and prose romances; pioneer in the decorative arts; translator of Icelandic sagas; designer of stained-glass windows, wallpapers, and tapestries; illuminator of manuscripts; vigorous man of business; founder of the Society for the Protection of Ancient Buildings (SPAB); and loyal personal friend and relation to an impressive range of people."[1] And Boos does not mention that Morris sketched and painted (his large oil, *La Belle Iseult* is one of the major attractions of the Pre-Raphaelite Collection at the Tate); composed lyric poetry as well as narrative (his twentieth-century reputation as a poet has rested mainly on a few of the *Defence of Guenevere* poems); wrote travel literature of the first order (all agree that his *Icelandic Journals* remain one of the best accounts of that ultimate island, twice visited by Morris); translated classical as well as Icelandic literature (his rendition of Virgil's *Aeneid,* Peter Faulkner suggests in his recent biography, has been unjustly ignored); and even attempted a sort of formal masque (*Love Is Enough,* "an interlude in the late medieval manner," also ignored, perhaps happily so).[2]

An astonishing array, and all before 1893! In the twelve years remaining to him he gave dozens of lectures to audiences ranging in size from a handful on a Hammersmith street corner to hundreds in halls in Glasgow.[3] He also wrote articles for *Justice* and *The Commonweal*, launching and keeping afloat the latter, the official organ of the Socialist League, from 1885 to 1890. He wrote for it not only editorials and articles, mundane notes and reviews, but also inspirational socialist narratives like *A Dream of John Ball, The Pilgrims of Hope,* and *News from Nowhere.* These first appeared serially, as did "Socialism from the Root Up," a series of articles written with Ernest Belfort Bax and later revised and published as *Socialism: Its Growth and Outcome.* Morris during these years also produced socialist poems and continued to translate Icelandic sagas, branching over into Old English to do *Beowulf* as well. He became a well-known collector of illuminated manuscripts and incunabula, and during his leisure moments, as a form of relaxation, he composed eight long prose romances, which (thanks to the popularity of Tolkien's *Lord of the Rings*) have recently gained a new audience and nourished new claims that Morris is the "father of heroic fantasy."[4] And few would dispute the claim that, as the founder of the Kelmscott Press in 1891, Morris initiated a revolution in book publishing. The care and intelligence lavished upon the fifty-three works (in sixty-six volumes) published between 1891-1898 make them unique, a continuing inspiration to booklovers and to the dozens of small presses that have attempted to emulate this final achievement of a remarkable Victorian polymath.

William Morris's energies and interests were almost boundless, leading him into activities and work that he almost invariably finished: hence the wide-ranging achivements enumerated above and also the continuing attention he receives from scholars and critics, many of them convinced not only of his relevance to their disciplines but to our urgent social problems as well. I shall comment on some of this recent attention, beginning with the only biography on the list, a study that does much more than enumerate the achievements of William Morris.

Samuel Johnson is reported to have said that the best biography should be "written by the subject himself; in other words the best biography is autobiography."[5] Morris never wrote an autobiography, but his *Icelandic Journals,* the *Socialist Diary,* and certain lectures and articles, especially "How I Became a Socialist," are autobiographical in content.[6] So too of course are some of the letters, especially a long one that Morris wrote to an esteemed socialist colleague, Andreas Scheu, in 1883.[7] Peter Faulkner has hit upon the neat device of opening the first five of the six chapters that make up his introductory biography, *Against the Age,* with long quotations from this letter, one in which Morris attempts to explain what influences and events led to the socialist attitudes he shared with Scheu. An autobiographical authority, a kind of backdrop, is therefore always available, and against it Faulkner places both his own commentary and analyses and also that of many of Morris's contemporaries. Such commentary is thereby highlighted, often receiving a sort of validity from the quotations. That backdrop, moreover, has the effect of suggesting that events became cumulative, leading Morris toward firmer and clearer realizations that as writer, decorator, and honest human being, he simply had to grow into someone who was "against the age." We can thus see Morris, as he confronts obstacles that the "Age of Shoddy" has laid across his path, moving inexorably to the left and into the role of socialist agitator and educator.

Faulkner repeats the phrase "against the age" several times, in appropriate contexts, thereby stressing the fact that Morris must be regarded as a rebel. Moreover, the social and political conditions that he rebelled against still abide: "As long as our industrial society continues to perplex us with such problems as pollution, delinquency, commercial acquisitiveness and violence, so long will we stand in need of Morris's vision of a society of equals in which every man and woman finds proper fulfillment" (p. ix). Faulkner threads such admonitions through the fabric of this short attempt to explain and reveal Morris to "new readers," urging them to take advantage of Morris's vision and to draw from it, and from Morris's own vigorous efforts to attain it, ways to respond to social forces that now do more than just blur Morris's vision.

It is today clear that the more virulent strains of corporate and nationalistic capitalism threaten all humanity; the men and institutions responsible must be confronted. We can be sure that Morris would have found ways to do so: "Morris was too involved with humanity, too passionate in his belief that a man's daily work should be a source of satisfaction to him, to retreat into an ivory tower. He wanted to share the satisfactions which the life of creative activity gave him, and this is what makes him relevant to us when we contemplate our own wasting world" (p. x). Faulkner, here and throughout, wants his "new readers" to perceive that Morris was never the "idle dreamer" celebrated by many of his early biographers. He was instead a rebel, someone who realized early on that the real gifts of life and nature might be won only by those who took up arms "against the age."

Obviously the battle must still be waged: hence the relevance of William Morris and of biographers like Faulkner. Perhaps long and patient work on Morris makes rebels out of the scholars and critics so engaged. This seems true of Faulkner, and it is certainly the case with E. P. Thompson, Morris's greatest modern biographer and at the present time one of the most articulate and energetic spokesmen for the antinuclear movement in Britain and Europe.[8] Recently, when an American journalist asked him about his politics, he replied "I am a Morrisist." He offered only a brief explanation: "a disciple of William Morris — with a certain affinity for Marxism."[9] Thompson is one of a handful of scholars who in the last decade have undertaken a systematic review and critique of modern Marxist theory and practice. Many modern Marxists, they suggest, continue to stress the economic and political aspects of social groups while ignoring the creative and artistic. Morris did not do so, and Marxism might be improved, might indeed even prove workable, if Morris's social ideas and theories were removed from categories like "Utopian Romance" and brought back into serious theoretical discussion. Faulkner is obviously sympathetic with Thompson's arguments, and his ability to draw political and social lessons from the material he sifts through is one of the strongest features of this introduction.

The book is not overtendentious, nor does Faulkner spend his time making political points or shouting relevant aphorisms. His general observations regarding rebelliousness or relevance always follow specific descriptions of the object at hand, whether poem, stained-glass window, or prose romance. For instance, he succinctly describes the several illuminated manuscripts Morris made between 1869 and 1875, during which time he produced some 1,500 pages in different styles of calligraphy. About the first of these, *A Book of Verse,* Faulkner says that "[the manuscript] shows a development from the early pages with powdered ornamentation to a more vital organic style later on, with growth from the base of the rectangle filling the right side and often mounting into the spaces between the stanzas. . . . We can see in this [arduous, loving hours of work with pen and brush] his consistent attachment to an idea of the potential richness and beauty of life which sets him at odds with his age's pride in its technological achievements" (p. 66). And after commenting on the imagery employed in *Love Is Enough,* Faulkner includes a reference to Morris's contemporary reality, noting that "Morris always responds, as both poet and designer, to the simple beauties of the countryside, which offered a haven to his imagination from the grimmer aspects of his age" (p. 69).

William Morris's love of nature was as deeply felt as Wordsworth's, but it was combined with a practical concern for what happened not just to individuals out of tune with nature's harmonies but to whole societies. Faulkner demonstrates how such practical concern grew out of Morris's work with various arts and crafts, how it was hammered into clear and prophetic messages in various lectures, and how it finally flourished in the vision of a future society where humans are in accord with each other because they are in tune with nature. Faulkner's short analysis of *News from Nowhere* is brilliant. He shows how Morris's ideas on art and work and nature — both human and otherwise — here culminate, and how and why the book "remains relevant and suggestive in our time" (p. 143).

Faulkner's discussions of the poetry, from *The Defence of Guenevere* (1856) through *Sigurd the Volsung* (1876) mix paraphrase and New Critical analyses of specific passages. Faulkner also offers a wealth of contemporary critical reactions, something we might expect from the editor of the *Critical Heritage* volume on Morris.[10] Always keeping an audience of beginners in mind, yet never talking down to them, he speaks of common themes in the poems in the *Defense* volume, of an awareness of the complicated and perverse ways that beauty mingles with crisis and violence in the lives of figures that Morris resurrected from Malory and Froissart.

Faulkner avoids (as many recent critics have not been able to) any temptation to read the poems as autobiography, to see in them Morris working his way through Oedipal problems or marital disjunctions. For instance, Faulkner concludes an explication of the structure and rhetoric of a difficult poem, "Concerning Sir Geffray Test Noire," in this quiet manner: "It may be appropriate to look for a psychological explanation of this in the young Morris's sexual feelings. In the poetry the result is powerful, strange, and disturbing" (p. 20). Indeed it may be "appropriate," but Faulkner obviously doesn't think so. Quiet common sense also informs his speculations about why Morris might have abandoned poetry for a number of years, attributing the lapse, in part at least, to the condescending reviews of *The Defense of Guenevere* and to the fact that only about 250 copies of the book were bought. Other critics have argued that various psychic disorders must have caused the temporal and stylistic gaps between Morris's first two volumes of poetry.

A strength of this book is the wealth of quotation from contemporary critics, and Faulkner uses other contemporary witnesses as well. To indicate the nature of the prevailing tastes in interior design that helped to bring Morris and Company into existence, Faulkner offers us the following, from the memoirs of a wealthy Victorian lady: "You remember our dear little house in Curzon Street; when we furnished it, nothing would please us but watered paper on the walls, garland of roses tied with blue bows! Glazed chintzes with bunches of roses, so natural they looked . . . gilt pelicans or swans on candlesticks, Minton's imitation of Sevres, and gilt bows everywhere."[11] A quotation from a mawkishly sentimental American novel of 1872, Annie Hall Thomas's *Maud Mohun,* lauds the Morris wallpapers with their "wonderful greyish-blue backgrounds on which limes, lemons and pomegranates with their respective foliages intertwine luxuriantly."[12] These quotations are neatly fitted into a concise discussion of Morris wallpaper and textile designs. They suggest how widespread, only a decade after its birth, had become the reputation of Morris's firm. Attitudes about his designs had spread into the popular consciousness across the Atlantic long before Oscar Wilde dropped Morris's name into his American lectures.

Given the brief scope of the book and the audience it is aimed at, Faulkner's discussions of particular poems are often surprisingly full, fresh, and rich. Though Faulkner ignores most of the narrative verse of *The Earthly Paradise* (1868-1870), he comments upon "The Lovers of Gudrun" (Morris's own favorite of the twenty-four tales) and demonstrates Morris's skill in dealing with the original saga narrative.[13] I do not share Faulkner's esteem for the poem, which sentimentalizes and distorts the Icelandic original, but Faulkner cogently presents Morris's argument. He conjectures about the reasons for some changes, draws on contemporary reactions, and suggests an analogy between Morris's description of Kjartan and "Yeats's tribute to Robert Gregory, 'soldier, scholar, horseman' " (p. 52). Such analogies support one of the major points of the book: Morris's modernity, his relevance to the twentieth century.

Faulkner treats works that other critics and biographers brush by or ignore. In his discussion of *The Life and Death of Jason* (1867), for example, he paraphrases the action across the seventeen books and quotes dozens of lines. A few pages are even devoted to the largely forgotten masque *Love Is Enough* (1872) which Morris wrote between the two Icelandic trips. Morris's reputation as a translator, whether good or bad, rests on his and Magnússon's renderings of the Icelandic sagas. The translations of the Mediterranean classics are seldom dealt with, a situation Faulkner would remedy. He compares selected lines from Morris's *The Aeneids of Virgil* (1875) with the same lines in Cecil Day Lewis's translation of 1952. He quotes a dozen lines from each and concludes: "The modern version is less obviously poetic; the intention is to give the reader a neutral version which will remind him of the original but not compete with it. Morris makes a far stronger impression, but not without strain. The long lines, indeed, hardly achieve the Virgilian sweetness, and sometimes appear clumsy. Yet at the end there is a sense of poetic energy which is likely to carry the reader onward, and this is a basic quality for a narrative poem. *The Aeneids* is not an unqualified success, but it is no disgrace to Morris as either poet or classicist" (pp. 77-78).

Faulkner has little to say of the famed Morris-Magnússon translations, and that little is rather misleading, for he quotes an atypical passage from an early translation of an Icelandic tale which, contrary to Faulkner's assertion, does not exemplify the archaic and clotted diction and syntax of the translations of the longer family sagas and of the *Heimskringla*.[14] Of the *Icelandic Journals,* only passing mention is made of that for 1871, the fullest and the one that Morris revised. Regarding the 1873 journal Faulkner makes this puzzling statement: "Morris's response to the stark simplicity of the country was even deeper than before. The image of the land and the lives of endurance of its people suggested an alternative to Victorian industrial England which appealed deeply to Morris's imagination. The people of the island, it seemed to him, had a dignity and self-respect which were rapidly being destroyed in his own country by the profound and uncontrolled changes which were part of the Industrial Revolution" (p. 75). Here Faulkner makes the same mistakes most commentators on Morris and Iceland have made, confusing his high regard for the saga heroes with his very muted reactions (especially in these journals) to the abject and poverty-stricken nineteenth-century Icelanders he met. They had escaped the ravages of industrialism but not the effects of modern capitalism, since they were subject to harsh Danish rule in the form of a trade monopoly that conspired with geography to create actual famine in certain districts. Critics have been too willing to expand upon a few generalizations about the absence of class in a few of Morris's letters, and they have ignored the journals, where Morris himself seems to question his assumptions about Iceland's pastoral virtues.[15]

There are only a few other problems with Faulkner's book, and they, like the generalizations regarding Iceland, also occur elsewhere in Morris criticism. Though some extravagant claims have been made for the literary worth of the late prose romances, many readers still find their archaic diction and lofty style problematic. Faulkner suggests that such critiques are unfair. Choosing a passage from *Wood beyond the World* (1894), he points to the high proportion of monosyllables, claiming that in "sample passages analyzed, Morris achieved something like 80% of monosyllabic words" (p.167). He also comments on the benign nature of the diction in the sample passage. A "whereas" or two, he suggests, and a "youngling" don't really merit the epithet "Wardour-Street English."[16] True enough, but what causes creased brows is not only polysyllabic or archaic diction. It is the apparent distaste Morris had for simple locutions. For instance, in this passage, instead of "He fell in love," Morris wrote, "He had fallen into the toils of love of a woman." Faulkner thinks it "unfair to Morris's achievement in the romances to note the elements of archaism in the diction as if these superseded other elements of style" (p. 168). But it is not a question of archaic diction superseding so much as coming together with other elements of style. The final effect *is* to clog narrative movement.

Faulkner concludes his discussion of the prose romances by suggesting that they never really caught on because they were so unlike the realistic novels of the nineteenth century. He reminds us, however, that in the twentieth century there have been "departures from realism of many kinds, the most popular being the development of science fiction. In view of such developments and the enormous success of Tolkien's *The Lord of the Rings,* it is now possible to see Morris's romances not as failed realistic novels, but as unusual and interesting creative fictions of their own kind" (p. 175). Of course they're "unusual" and "creative," but they do not have the narrative power of Tolkien's ring trilogy, or of much twentieth-century science fiction or fantasy literature. In fantasy novels by Ursula Leguin, for example, consistencies of plot and character combine with prose of a high quality to make powerful narratives much better than any of the final seven prose romances by Morris. Some modern critics, in their incessant search for influences, have turned up these gently meandering romances as explanations for Tolkien's Hobbit stories or C. S. Lewis's Narnia tales. Tolkien and Lewis had read Morris, but a more significant current of influence runs the other way. The popularity of the twentieth-century narratives has created new readers, and vaunted claims, for the yarns that Morris undertook mainly as a form of relaxation.

Faulkner believes that Morris has been influential during this century in two main areas: "as an exponent of crafts, and as a social thinker" (p. 181). Working within the first area were men like Arthur Mackmurdo, who founded the Century Guild, and Ebeneezer Howard and Raymond Unwin, promoters of Garden City schemes. Within the second, a partial list would include Bernard Shaw, G.D.H. Cole, Middleton Murry, Granville Hicks, and two writers still active in socialist causes and still warm in their praise of Morris: Raymond Williams and E. P. Thompson. Faulkner concludes that "Morris would probably have been pleased to know that his influence had been strongest in these two areas, but he would have argued strongly that they are in fact one. His belief in craftsmanship, like his belief in socialism, is based on the view that it alone can fulfill fundamental human needs" (p. 181). Morris would also likely have been pleased with Faulkner's graceful, sensible, committed introduction to his work and its continuing relevance.[17]

Peter Faulkner is responsible for another interesting though much less substantial recent Morris publication: *Wilfrid Scawen Blunt and the Morrises*. This is a reprinting, nicely done up by the London branch of the William Morris Society, of "The First Annual Kelmscott Lecture," delivered in September 1980. As Faulkner says, "Wilfrid Scawen Blunt has long been known to students of Morris for passages in his autobiographical *My Diaries* (first published in 1919) concerning their conversations at Kelmscott Manor in 1889, and his fine tribute on Morris's death in 1896" (p. 7). Those conversations touched on many subjects, from fishing to Home Rule, and Morris's breadth of knowledge and strong intellect continually astonished Blunt. He thought his own growing distaste for political involvement (Blunt was vociferously anticolonial, pro-Irish and pro-Egyptian, an elegant gadfly who had buzzed around parliamentary potentates for years) might have caused Morris to retreat from socialist politics. We now know that Morris eased his ties with the Socialist League and then with *The Commonweal* for other reasons, that in fact there was not so much of a retreat as Blunt and others had suggested.

Blunt's papers have recently been made public. He was more than a warm admirer of William Morris: he was also Janey Morris's lover. This is apparent in Blunt's unpublished notebooks and in the 145 letters that Janey sent him between 1884 and 1913. Selections from forty of these letters, as well as complementary passages from the notebooks (letters that Blunt sent to Janey, if they survive, have not surfaced) make up the substance of this lecture, or lecture-presentation, for Peter Faulkner's wife joined him at the podium, reading aloud the letters from Janey. He read selections from Blunt, as well as his own interepistolary commentary. In the notes Blunt reveals parts of himself not seen in *My Diaries*, and in these letters Janey Morris is not just the plaintive hypochondriac who emerged from her correspondence with her first lover, Dante Gabriel Rossetti.[18]

These letters demonstrate Janey's sense of humor; she complains, for instance, that another guest at Castle Howard "seems to spend his spare time tramping up and down and throwing his teeth about" (pp. 15-16). She warns Blunt that Swinburne is sure to produce "various manuscripts, which he will read till everybody goes to sleep" (p. 17).

Janey comments on the laughter she shared with her husband when they learnt that Edward Burne-Jones had accepted a baronetcy: "My husband refused to believe it at first, but afterwards when the plain fact was known, he said, 'Well a man can be an ass for the sake of his children.' — it seems that Phil was the chief culprit — I did hear that Sir George Lewis started the idea — in case his daughter wanted to marry Phil, so that he might be their *equal in rank*. It is all too funny, and makes one roar with laughing" (p. 34). This suggests a moment of real communion between the Morrises; such moments are not found in many of the hitherto available sources. Morris's scurrilous comment has an authentic ring, and students of Burne-Jones might also find such material useful since it supplements other descriptions of the conflict Gladstone's offer of the baronetcy caused in the Burne-Jones household.

The letters reveal more about Janey's sad relationships with her daughters than with her husband. References to May's marital problems begin when she learns of a friend's engagement: "May said pathetically that a good part of her life is passed in preparing wedding gifts for her friends — her own marriage appears to be as far off as ever" (p. 23). But May's marriage was destined to occur soon, and in a letter of June 1890, Janey laments that "it has all been like a bad dream, but it must end sometime like all dreams — the wedding will be tomorrow" (p. 25). As her parents had feared, May's marriage to Halliday Sparling was not happy, and a few years later Janey reveals to Blunt that "May's married life has come to an end, and although we always expected some catastrophe or other in that direction, the blow is no less heavy now it has come" (p. 35).

Such suggestions of self-pity are much stronger in the references to Jennie, the elder daughter, and her recurring illness: "I have been much more seriously ill than I thought when I left home, my doctor says I must never again live with Jennie while she is in her present condition, my brain was suffering from it. We hope however to get her cured by some new treatment we are about to try, but nothing is settled for her yet" (p. 19). Indeed, nothing was ever settled for Jennie, the apple of her father's eye, and perhaps one of the causes of her mother's emotional problems, her "melancholia." It is hard to decide, from passages like the following, who deserves our sympathy: "I came back to town Tuesday as Jennie was so very much worse, and I could not bear being quite alone with her" (p. 23). Later, Janey apparently finds it difficult to be pleased that her daughter has mended: "She has recovered with her usual rapidity, and is quite unconscious of having caused me anxiety" (p. 24). It is an altogether sad and imbalanced situation, one that Morris himself evidently tried to hold in some sort of equipoise. Sickness often brings families together; Jennie's epilepsy had the reverse effect, especially on Janey who seemingly couldn't bear to be near this afflicted daughter, or even to have other loved ones nearby. Janey's frequent trips abroad, to fashionable spas, or to the gracious estates belonging to folk like the Howards (she first met Blunt at their Naworth Castle) were sometimes attempts to avoid her own daughter.

The perceptions these letters provide of Janey are not as negative as my remarks might suggest. Her sense of humor is apparent in several of them, as is her sensitive intelligence when she comments on Blunt's poetry or upon his troubles with the authorities in Ireland, where his protests led to a short jail sentence. Her remarks on the Kelmscott Press indicate a lively interest in this new venture, one that we needn't attribute solely to the fact that Blunt's poetry would be published in an early volume. But those strains of anxiety caused by her children and by her own weaknesses, physical and emotional, recur often enough to become a theme in these letters. Morris evidently bore the effects of such neuroses with patience and obdurate good will. That he continued to work so productively through such sickness and melancholia within his own family seems remarkable.

Of less interest is the romantic aspect of the letters: the love or passion indicated by Janey's memories of Blunt in this room or that garden, the effect of the salutation "Caro mio," and the like. Pursuing implications along these tangents makes one feel like a voyeur; suffice it to say that Janey did not feel uncomfortable with the role of pining and yearning mistress, within the confines of a stereotype centuries old.

In Blunt's notebooks there are fresh revelations about the Morrises. His comments on Morris and his stricken daughter, more dispassionate and less subjective than Janey's, seem more reliable and more moving. Blunt has less to say about May, and much of it is unfriendly. He saw her at a Hyde Park demonstration "looking like a French revolutionist going to execution" (p. 17); later "she had made a senseless engagement . . . with a worthless young socialist" (p. 23). After William Morris's death, Janey and May visited Blunt in Egypt, and he confides to his notebooks that the "visit has been rather a disappointment. . . . May is an obstinately silent woman and Judith [Blunt's daughter] is bored by her . . . with May it is impossible to keep up any conversation" (pp. 39-40).

Blunt's notebook offers fresh evidence about Morris and his attitude toward Janey: "She was a loveable and noble woman, but he knew that he had never touched her heart. Yet he was observant. What had taken place between her and Rossetti he knew and had forgiven. But he had not forgotten it. I used to think too that he suspected me at times" (p. 24). Blunt is obviously flattered by thoughts that he has become Rossetti's successor, for he returns to this theme — poor Janey the fragile link! — several times.

Blunt's fancied connections and correspondences deserve further commentary, but Faulkner seems unwilling to pursue them, partly because of the nature of his presentation, perhaps also because of his sense of decorum. I suspect it might be the latter, since he makes key changes in this passage: "Mrs. Morris slept alone at the end of a short passage at the head of the stair-case to the right. The hall was uncarpeted with floors that creaked . . . to me such midnight perils have always been attractive."[19] In Faulkner's version, nothing is said about the location of Mrs. Morris's bedroom; the phrase "floors that creaked" follows upon a statement that Blunt had described "numerous passage rooms." Another change: preceding "midnight perils" Faulkner has added the phrase, "ghostly atmosphere" (p. 24), thereby suggesting that the latter, rather than the "creaking floors," constituted the "perils." Longford's official biography of Blunt (she was the first scholar allowed to use the notebooks) offers many details about his numerous affairs and about his adolescent pleasure in the dangers that illicit love could offer; the closer he came to the precipice of an outraged husband's wrath, the more delicious became the entire assignation. There's something silly about such attitudes, something that Faulkner, perhaps rightly, did not want to include in this presentation. Hence, probably, the omission and interpolation discussed above.

Longford quotes Blunt on the strange ethics of cuckolding a friend and in this way drawing closer to him. He brags: "These are the secrets of the heart which are not known even to the best novelists."[20] Blunt kept few secrets from his notebooks; we learn of his willingness to use married women not just for sexual satisfaction but also to titilate that delicious sense of existential peril, and, moreover, to identify with husbands, even while betraying their trust. Using Janey, Blunt had the unique opportunity to identify with *both* Morris and Rossetti.

These selections from his wife's letters and from Blunt's notebooks do nothing to undercut the traditional views of Morris as loving father and stoic husband. He must have seen what went on between Janey and Blunt, just as he had between Janey and Rossetti. His silence on such matters seems admirable, and the scenes of free and open sensuality in the prose romances, and especially in *News from Nowhere,* I shall read with more understanding the next time round. In those scenes Morris was reacting to the ways in which Victorian society encouraged deceit, hypocrisy, neurotic behavior—"midnight perils" of many types. These, he hoped, might disappear with the dawning of a new society.

A book about Edward Burne-Jones, even though he was his closest friend, might seem out of place in a review of recent books on William Morris, but it is pertinent, for the book has new material on Morris, his friends, and his social milieu. Mary Lago's edition, *Burne-Jones Talking: His Conversations, 1895–1898, Preserved by his Studio Assistant Thomas Rooke,* presents for the first time (in a fully annotated text) the talk, both small and large, that Rooke overheard in Burne-Jones's studio during that period. The years 1895 and 1896 were, respectively, the years of the Kelmscott Chaucer and of William Morris's sickness and death. These subjects preoccupied Burne-Jones, and he often worried aloud to Rooke, his young assistant, or to visitors to the studio.

The text amounts to about one-third of the 416 foolscap pages that make up Georgiana Burne-Jones's holograph transcript. Her sources, Rooke's "jottings" and notebooks, do not survive, but both Mary Lago (who has carefully examined hundreds of Burne-Jones's letters) and Georgiana herself (who would have known) assure us that the transcribed record brings us very close to the master's voice. Lago says, "Again and again in his letters, he echoes opinions, and describes persons and events with the vocabulary, the nuances of meaning, the syntax and cadences that appear throughout Rooke's record of the conversations. All confirm that if Burne-Jones's authentic voice is to be found in his letters — and their great spontaneity certainly suggests that this is the case — Rooke has captured it with great faithfulness" (p. ix). And Georgiana, who copied out the entire text and then used Rooke's notebooks for parts of her monumental biography, *The Memorials of Edward Burne-Jones,* says in that work that "these jottings, afterwards filled up and sacredly kept from every other eye, [Rooke] brought to me when the end came. In them I recognized the mind, and even the voice of the speaker, and could only remain astonished at the disciplined memory which thus made the past live again in Edward's unmistakable words. From this storehouse, I shall now draw freely for the expression of his thoughts."[21] These conversations, especially as supplemented by Lago's discriminating notes, contain new information about Morris. Since Rooke's "jottings" are, moreover, a source for Georgiana Burne-Jones's biography of her husband, and since, as Philip Henderson has reminded us, "it has long been recognized that Morris is virtually the hero of Lady Burne-Jones' *Memorials* of her husband," it follows that anyone interested in Morris should find this book worthwhile.[22]

But it would have been a more useful book if Lago had edited the entire holograph, instead of just one-third of the original. Her rationale for the excisions seems vague: "I include here approximately one-third of the entire holograph text. In the remaining two-thirds, historians and biographers will find a wealth of new and interesting information and comment. I have selected for this edition passages that illustrate vividly the personalities, interests, and activities of Burne-Jones and his circle in the 1890s" (pp. ix–x). It is unfortunate that those "historians and biographers" will have to go over the same ground that Lago has already covered and then compare their findings with her abbreviated text.

There is another problem. Lago's notes do not record when, and how, Lady Burne-Jones borrowed from Rooke's "storehouse." For instance, she drew upon Rooke's entries for 12 February 1896 and 24 October 1896, when the discussions overheard concerned Morris's socialism, and merged the excerpts together, placing them within a denunciation of Morris's socialism that Burne-Jones might have made (readers are invited to believe) as early as 1879. By 1896, when the statements were actually made, Burne-Jones was much more rancorous on the subject of socialism than he had been earlier on in 1879, and his wife's casual concern for dates could easily create false impressions about the attitudes Burne-Jones had when Morris first embarked on his socialist adventure, or about ways that Burne-Jones's political ideas might have developed.

Furthermore, since the *Memorials* have become an important source for Morris biographers, such false impressions can endure and even spread. This in fact has happened with this particular denunciation; in his biography Philip Henderson used part of this passage erroneously in a chapter concerning events in 1883 and 1884. We now know that Burne-Jones *said* this, or something very like it, in 1896, since it was then transcribed by Rooke. That transcription was changed slightly and used by Lady Burne-Jones in a section of her biography covering the late 1870s. Henderson set the denunciation in the 1880s, adding the fiction that Burne-Jones wrote it down. Careful annotations by Lago might have spared future biographers such mistakes.

The entry for 24 October 1896, a few weeks after Morris's funeral, includes the following exchange between Georgiana (Rooke refers to her as "Mistress") and her husband. Their son-in-law, Mackail, had already begun work on his biography of Morris, and she was sorting through letters for him.

Mistress: Then there are a great many interesting letters about his social views.
E B-J: I hope it won't be a key note in the book.
Mistress: Well, but it was an important part of his life.
E B-J: It was a parenthesis in it; he was before all things a poet and an artist.
Mistress: But he talked much more to me about it than he did to you. [p. 118]

This exchange implies a great deal about the constraints under which Mackail had to do his research. That Georgiana, in her biography, chose to use only the one line, "It was a parenthesis . . . " (putting it after the 12 February 1896 entry, as mentioned above), suggests something about similar constraints she recognized. She deferred to her husband's prejudices and kept her own political views, often close to Morris's, under wraps. It's unfortunate that Lago's annotations do not touch upon the implications of Lady Burne-Jones's handling of such passages.

As noted earlier, one of Janey Morris's letters to Blunt reports the shocked reaction of the Morrises to Burne-Jones and his baronetcy. Here is what Rooke's diary has on this topic: "The one person in the house who distinctly disliked it was the mistress." Burne-Jones did not covet a title, but Phil, his son, was urgently in favor, and Burne-Jones confided to Rooke, "I didn't feel that I ought to let my own notions stand in his way or affect his life one can't tell how."[23] This jibes nicely with the content of Janey's letter and contrasts directly with Georgiana's own flat description: "The honour was accepted."[24] Rooke's unvarnished testimony provides glimpses into the realities behind the decorous surfaces of Georgiana's *Memorials*. But Lago, for reasons one can only speculate upon, chose to omit all the diary entries concerning the baronetcy.

If such entries had not been omitted and if the notes had included discussions of the ways that Georgiana Burne-Jones had used Rooke's "jottings," this edition would have been vastly more useful. But there is still much in this book to recommend it.

Lago's introduction evokes the atmosphere of Burne-Jones's studio: "a true workplace, cluttered, congested, tidied up only for rare special occasions and then only over the loud protests of its owner" (p. 1). The introduction also offers brief portraits of Rooke, who emerges from these journals as an "appealing personality" (p. 4), and it discusses his special relationships both with Ruskin, his second hero, for whom he undertook special assignments to the Continent, and with Burne-Jones, his master, for whom "Rooke was a kind of mirror in which all of Burne-Jones's agitations and dissatisfactions were magically transmuted" (p. 8). Rooke was, in other words, someone Burne-Jones talked freely with, and therefore the reported comments on Morris have a special authority and pathos. In this introduction Lago also touches upon several of the political topics broached in the conversations, alerting us to the radical and prescient nature of many of Burne-Jones's pronouncements:

He viewed events of the 1890s in South Africa, and British reaction to them, with deepest pessimism, foreseeing death and destruction to come — as they did, and do. He deplored the pompous complacency of the Queen's Jubilee Celebration in 1897 and was convinced that in time the Empire would dwindle — as it has done. He had only scorn for the British attitude toward the United States during the Venezuelan crisis of 1895, and he predicted that the day would come — as it did — when Britain would need American aid. He was nearly as fierce as Morris in his denunciations of industrial plundering of the landscape. [p. 15]

These conversations offer sharply convincing proof that Burne-Jones was not a romantic recluse; while it's true that he didn't join Morris in active agitation for revolution, he shared with him convictions about what needed changing, and why.

In the conversations, Burne-Jones reveals views on politics that are surprisingly radical and witty: Rooke records Burne-Jones on England's "different way of behaving to little states and big ones. With big ones it's arbitration, but with little ones it's ultimatum. Ultimatum to Burmah, Ultimatum to the Afghans, Ultimatum to Chitral, Ultimatum to Ashantee, Ultimatum to Transvaal, Ultimatum to Venezuela — but with America, arbitration. . . . By this time people ought to be ashamed of these quarrels between civilized nations; they're in essence nothing more than mean little parish squabbles about boundary stones. I'd take their guns and gunpowder away from them, stupid infants" (pp. 73-74). Rooke should have been on hand at those famed Sunday breakfasts shared by Morris and Burne-Jones; one now suspects that the talk on those occasions was not so apolitical as some biographers have suggested.

He was witty and irreverent on a host of topics, and with his keen sense of the ridiculous, he was almost as skillful at creating verbal caricatures (see the cameo of the clergyman in hobnailed boots and nightshirt: p. 131) as he was at drawing the other kind (seven of the latter appear, at apt locations, throughout the text). His verbal portraits can also be straightforward and quite moving; here is Burne-Jones, the morning after Morris's death, talking out his grief to Rooke:

He got to be such a shadow that he was no more than a glorious head on a crumple of clothes. His poor body had dwindled into absolutely nothing. The strain of watching it was terrible to me sometimes, and I felt that I could hardly bear it and I must get away and fly from the pain of it. . . . One thing that I was always frightened of has been spared; I was so dreading that this disease might have got to his brain, and that would have been quite unbearable — but he was himself to the very end. There was for a short period a look of something like indignation in him, but that soon passed away and his face became quite placid again, and he died like a little child. [p. 115]

Avoiding what seemed too personal and too painful, and perhaps borrowing from that last simile, Georgiana in her *Memorials* wrote only, "On October 3rd Morris died—as gently, as quietly as a babe who is satisfied drops from its mother's breast."[25] She omitted the rest of the graphic passage; now that Lago has published it, we can better understand the tender relationship that existed between the two men, and more strongly feel the devastating effects that Morris's deterioration had on Burne-Jones.[26]

Lago's painstaking research into archives and collections is evident in the new material she uses to supplement or elucidate the Rooke "jottings." Taken from a letter written immediately after, here is Burne-Jones's description of Morris's funeral: "The burial was as sweet and touching as those others [of Leighton and Millais] were foolish—and the little waggon with its floor of moss and willow branches broke one's heart it was so beautiful—and of course there were no kings there—the king was being buried and there were no others left" (p. 114). Because friends like Burne-Jones are allowed to express in their own words what Morris's death meant, we achieve a strong sense of Morris's contemporary importance; in the letters and diaries Lago has unearthed, in the studio conversations she has skillfully edited, we come upon a Morris uncontaminated by the restrictions within which a biographer or critic necessarily operates. Her book provides a new sense of how serious became Morris's passion during his last years for purchasing rare books and manuscripts (Burne-Jones chuckled over this affliction, but at one point contemplated lending Morris money to acquire an especially esteemed manuscript); a new sense of Rossetti's importance for Burne-Jones, who recognized and disliked Rossetti's shoddy treatment of Morris, but often praised Rossetti's personal generosity; a new sense of how stalwart Burne-Jones was in his loyalties to his friends and to his work. Anyone doing research on nineteeth-century painters, writers, or public figures would do well to check the full index in this edition, for oftentimes what Burne-Jones said or remembered goes beyond the merely anecdotal. And anyone interested in relatively minor aspects of Morris's life or work (such as matters Icelandic) will find new material in this book.[27]

Margaret A. Lourie's preface to *William Morris: The Defence of Guenevere and Other Poems* is generally accurate and helpful, presenting the usual biographical details (from Dixon via Mackail) about the Oxford years and about Morris's discovery that he could write poetry. Then Lourie reveals her intentions for this new edition of the thirty poems of the *Guenevere* volume, poems that for her are "so saturated in the materials of the Middle Ages and the poetry of the nineteenth century," that the "explanatory notes appended to the present edition aim chiefly at restoring to the poems their medieval and nineteenth-century contexts" (p. xv).

Few will share in her assumptions that such a restoration of context would be possible, even with the fullest and most inspired of explanations, or in her belief that the original audience, whether Morris's Oxford cohorts or those few who bought the 1858 publication, "instantly apprehended" the poems. But one must applaud the attempt to place these poems before a "wide audience." Many students of English poetry think Morris wrote only "The Haystack in the Floods," a poem from the *Guenevere* volume invariably anthologized; the imagery and prosody of the other twenty-nine poems adumbrate Yeats and Pound (connections that Lourie stresses in her introduction), and they deserve more readers. Lourie evidently had a student audience in mind, the sorts of "new readers" at whom Faulkner directed his biography, for statements in both the introduction and in the explanatory notes are keyed to a level that assumes no prior knowledge in readers of either the middle ages or the nineteenth century. And often these statements do shed light, so this edition could fit into the syllabi of upper-division courses in Victorian poetry. But few instructors are likely to order it, since forty dollars, even at today's inflated prices, is too much to ask students to pay for a single text.

The critical introduction is divided into three sections: "Morris and Medievalism," "The Nineteenth-Century Poetic Heritage," and "The Legacy of *Guenevere*." These titles promise an orderly and logical presentation of material necessary to the beginning student, and the promise is fulfilled: Lourie offers discussions of, for instance, poets lamenting "the lost simplicity of pre-industrial society and a coherent system of beliefs" (p. 1), of the importance to Morris of Ruskin's "The Nature of Gothic," and of the "Pre-Raphaelites, who kept the Romantic spirit alive through the inhospitable years of the mid-nineteenth century" (p. 19). In the final section Lourie makes strong claims for Morris's influence, saying that the *Guenevere* volume "turned the poetic tide of the nineteenth century toward the twentieth" (p. 28). Such claims (however overenthusiastic) might provoke new readings of these thirty poems, and Lourie has provided many perceptive suggestions about how those readings should proceed.

But there are several problems. Lourie sometimes falls into a perfervid style that obfuscates meaning, as when she says that nineteenth century poets, "seeking comfort in this cataclysm. . . . combed through history for soil in which their thwarted imaginations could take root" (p. 1). She is rather too free-wheeling with critical terminology, suggesting among other things that the revival of a "Keats or Tennyson fairyland" is somehow a "poetic technique" (p. 2). And she is careless with categories; she claims that Scott, Carlyle, and Ruskin are "three famous champions of the Gothic revival" (p. 4), but under that rubric surely Walpole and Pugin, with Ruskin, would make a more acceptable triad. In commentary like the following, Lourie is not only careless but rather callous: "Like the medieval court poet, the speaker of this poem ['Praise of My Lady'] assumes a supplicating and reverential posture toward a quasi-divine mistress, persistently urges his own unworthiness, and seems to expect disappointment. Remarkably, this cluster of courtly attitudes precisely parallels Morris' lasting self-abasement in relation to his wife, who apparently preferred the company of Rossetti both before and after her wedding" (p. 8). Anyone who has read recent biographies must be impressed with what the Rossetti-Janey Morris correspondence revealed of William Morris's saintly tolerance in the face of his wife's drawn-out and neurotic involvement with Rossetti.[28] Morris exhibited the same quiet tolerance when Janey took up with Wilfrid Scawen Blunt. "Self-abasement," if that term must be used, would seem more apt for other figures.

Perhaps Lourie is not being "callous" so much as naive. At any rate, naiveté is certainly apparent later in the introduction when she asserts that "the typical Victorian urgently needed to know how to live humanely in an increasingly ugly and impersonal world. For an answer he looked to poetry" (p. 20). A "typical Victorian" looked to poetry for answers just about as often as a typical Edwardian, or a typical American; the man on the street (especially on nineteenth- and twentieth-century urban streets) is blissfully unaware of poetry. Lourie shifts her ground slightly, moving from a "typical Victorian" to a "literary world pleading for answers to the great welter of Victorian questions and confusions" (p. 21), suggesting that Morris responded to such pleas with the *Guenevere* poems, which were, alas, ignored because they lacked social relevance. Lourie is correct that the volume quickly fell into oblivion, but she is misleading about the reasons why, misleading about the pressures that encouraged Morris to write the poems, and misleading about the influence the poems have had. Her enthusiasm, which one hates to criticize since she is trying to encourage new readers to perceive the significance of these poems, seems to lead her into rhetorical flourishes and naive overstatement.

Following the critical introduction is a shorter, more restrained editorial introduction that has a "description of the six significant *Guenevere* texts and a summary of the major differences among them" (p. 32). The six are manuscripts (for only two and one half poems); *Oxford and Cambridge Magazine* (for five poems); the first edition of 1858; the 1875 reprint; the Kelmscott Press edition of 1892; and the May Morris edition of 1910. Each poem has its own introductory note that includes information on dating and composition, a reading guide, and brief comments on sources, influences, and critical studies. Finally, there are notes to specific lines that "complement and further specify the introductory notes." This editorial introduction ends with a bibliography that "includes only published books and articles which deal with one or more of the poems in Morris' first volume and which take a literary rather than a biographical stance" (p. 37). Her decision to include only published works is unfortunate, since an extremely important dissertation is thereby ignored. Karl C. Chen's "The Sources of William Morris's *Defence of Guenevere and Other Poems*" (Yale, 1934) catalogues and discusses all potential influences, medieval and contemporary, on each of the poems. Another dissertation might have been listed: Thomas Drescher's "A Critical Companion to William Morris's *Defence of Guenevere*" (York University, Ontario, 1979). One is puzzled also by the omission of titles like Margaret Grennan's *William Morris: Medievalist and Revolutionary* (1945: rpt. Russell and Russell, 1970); with its brilliant discussions of the ways Morris applied his medieval readings, this book should be on any list of recommended studies.

The texts of the thirty poems are clearly and carefully printed, with wide margins. (But would anyone who paid forty dollars for the book actually write in those margins?) Textual variants are listed at the bottoms of pages, with the explanatory notes following the texts and concluding the edition. There are over 400 such notes to individual lines, and since the majority of them do offer clear explanations (a necessity, given the opaque and indirect nature of many of these poems), they testify to Lourie's diligent scholarship.

I did find the following mistakes, however: a note to "King Arthur's Tomb" records that Tristram "often defeats Dinaden in Malory" (p. 193); Dinaden is Tristram's companion, and he assiduously avoids battles of any kind. In a note to "The Chapel in Lyonness" one learns that "Lyoness is a name first used by Malory" (p. 200); but "Leonois" occurs in his French sources. In a note to "Praise of My Lady" Lourie says that Morris's only extant painting is called *Queen Guenevere,* (p. 253); it is really *La Belle Iseult.* A few apparent oversights: Lourie says that in a ballad, Morris used "intensifying" rather than "incremental" repetition (p. 247), and in a note for "Summer Dawn" she says, "If the chief criteria for a sonnet are fourteen lines and a final couplet" (p. 255), when she undoubtedly meant to write "twelve lines." These mistakes and oversights are less troubling than the misconceptions apparent in the following breezy certitudes: in a note to "Rapunzel," one that glosses "Norse torches" in line 87, Lourie writes, "Morris would have discovered from his reading of *Heimskringla* that for northern kings one popular way of dispatching enemies was to roast them in their castles" (p. 213). The flippant tone is gratuitous, and the note is wrong on a number of counts: Morris was not translating the *Heimskringla* in the 1850s, the practice of "burning-in" was never "popular" among the Norse (it was usually the last resort for villains or cowards), and Norwegian kings did not live in castles. These might seem to be quibbles, but there are other occasions when Lourie's assertions are simply too confident, e.g., the brunette in "Praise of My Lady" is "unquestionably Jane Burden" (p. 244), when Lourie's trendy rhetoric is simply inappropriate, as it is in the second sentence of the following note: "In 1871 Morris took Kelmscott Manor in joint tenancy with Rossetti and Janey. Gallant certainly to a fault, he split his time between his factory in London and visits to Iceland, leaving Rossetti and Jane to loaf in the suburbs" (p. 254).

I found the following typos: two pairs of quotation marks are missing at 187.4; at 234.24 "Heraldson" should be "Haraldson"; at 235.28 "Striklestad" should be "Stiklestad"; and at 244.26 "in" should be "is." Given the large number of foreign names and the esoteric content of many of the poems, the introductions, texts, and notes are remarkably free of typographical errors. Margaret Lourie and the editors at Garland Publishing should be commended for their careful work, for their endeavors to make these early poems of William Morris more easily available to modern readers. Perhaps they could bind subsequent editions in paper covers, reducing thereby costs and increasing the likelihood that these poems do reach a "wide audience."

Ironically, since it is obviously not aimed at a student audience, the next book under review is available in an economical paperback edition. Published by the American branch of the William Morris Society, *The Golden Chain: Essays on William Morris and Pre-Raphaelitism,* is the third volume in a series of studies intended to deepen appreciation of Morris's literary works.[29] Like the first two, this volume in both its appearance and content betrays the careful editorial work and stalwart cooperation of Joseph Dunlap and Carole Silver.

To the present volume, which takes its title from William Morris's "The Beauty of Life" (in which he celebrates the Pre-Raphaelite painters who "caught up the *Golden Chain* dropped two hundred years ago"), Carole Silver contributes an introduction and a substantial essay. In the former she reminds us that William Morris was an extremely popular Victorian poet, admired and read on both sides of the Atlantic. His *Earthly Paradise* volumes earned him this wide reputation and sustained it across his lifetime. He received accolades from the likes of Shaw and Yeats, Shaw placing *Sigurd the Volsung* on almost the same level as the Homeric epics. The earlier lyric poems (those now regarded as "Pre-Raphaelite") were, however, less well known, and by 1934 all of Morris's poetry had fallen into disregard. At centenary celebrations then, according to Silver, "speakers and writers lauded Morris's contributions to modernism and design, to architecture and the book arts, to socialism and the labor movement, but could only faintly praise his literary art" (p. 1). It wasn't until the late 1950s, when the New Critics were to find, especially in the *Guenevere* volume, the sorts of indirect and ironic density that best tested their analytical skills, that Morris's short poems began to receive considerable critical attention. And with growing interest in Pre-Raphaelitism generally, the prose romances Morris wrote at Oxford have likewise received new scrutiny. Silver comments that "with the ironic twist typical of literary history, Morris is again popular. But the works least valued in his lifetime—the short romances written for the *Oxford and Cambridge Magazine* of 1856 and the poems of *The Defence of Guenevere* of 1858—are now considered his most significant achievements. This volume, the first to be devoted entirely to his works of the 1850s, is a sign of that change in literary taste" (p. 2).

The volume includes the following essays: "Dreamers of Dreams: Toward a Definition of Literary Pre-Raphaelitism," by Carole Silver; "Acts of Completion: The Search for Vocation in Morris' Early Prose Romances," by Kenneth Deal; "Heroic Disintegration: Morris' Medievalism and the Disappearance of the Self," by Frederick Kirchhoff; "The Poetics of Repetition and *The Defence of Guenevere,*" by Diane

Sadoff; and "Rossetti and Morris: 'This Ever-Diverse Pair'," by Robert Keane.

Kenneth Deal says that the *Oxford and Cambridge Magazine* tales "deserve more than the usual cursory treatment given them as biographical documents or convenient expressions of the critic's pet motif" (p. 53). He proceeds to remedy the former, and by tendering them full treatment, he offers inadvertently a demonstration of the latter point, hanging all manner of biographical assertion and speculation onto various incidents in the tales. He calls them "initiation fables," not so much for their heroes as for Morris, "who attempts to discover himself vicariously in relation to work, women, his capacity for commitment, and an emerging awareness of personal values" (p. 53). Pursuing his "pet motif," Deal finds correspondences between, say, a narrator's pride and "Morris' decision not to give himself to the altruistic but nonetheless bourgeois life of the clergy" (p. 58). This sort of linkage seems simplistic, but since every author puts himself into his work somehow, such speculations can be interesting, can perhaps provoke new insights into Morris's situation in his early manhood. But other comments will probably provoke more puzzlement than perception. Here, for example, Deal is alluding to the notorious structural problems in the tales: "Inadvertent slips in the artistry of these works lead one to suspect their primary purpose involves a cathartic expression of psychical biography rather than an objective solution to Morris' intellectual dilemma" (p. 66). One is not persuaded, at least not by jargon of this nature, that the tales or their "slips" have any such "primary purpose." Such "slips" might also "involve" bad craftsmanship, revealing the haste and carelessness with which they were written rather than chapters in any "psychical biography."

Though her essay breaks new ground in discussing the importance of dreams both to Victorians generally and to specific Pre-Raphaelite poets, Carole Silver also at times rides a "pet motif" toward explanations that are neither convincing nor terribly helpful. When she says, for instance, that some of the extremely confusing poems in the *Guenevere* volume "are marked by a disjointed structure which is that of dream logic" (p. 33), going on then to remind us of the kaleidoscopic shifts in event and imagery in some of these poems, one is still confused. The oxymoronic "dream logic" explains nothing but perhaps isn't meant to, for she continues with this statement: "Characters behave and events occur as they do in dreams: they are bizarre, memorable, and in the final analysis, inexplicable." Fair enough: the poems, finally, defy explanation. But in the next line Silver says that "this pervasive effect is not due to Morris's carelessness or lack of interest in an audience beyond his group of intimates, but to his observation and imitation of dream phenomena" (p. 34). Just as Deal could find a "purpose" — albeit a psychical one — in the narrative disjunctures in the tales, Silver posits an intention behind the numerous disjunctures in the poems, turning apparent faults into craftsmanlike virtues, celebrating Morris's ability to imitate "dream phenomena" or to use dream "techniques," which by definition must remain vague, insubstantial, and "dream-like."

When she is talking of content rather than structure, what Silver has to say about dreams is enlightening. Her long essay goes most of the way toward proving its thesis: "Rossetti was the progenitor and Morris and Swinburne the shapers and transmitters of a literary tradition which, though never fully defined, has been called 'literary Pre-Raphaelitism.' It is a movement to which dream is central, a movement which utilizes accounts of actual dream, dream language, dream symbol, and most significantly, a movement with the characteristics of dream itself" (p. 5).

Frederick Kirchhoff's essay also speculates upon disjunctures in these tales and poems; he also links their medieval settings to Morris's psychology. Kirchhoff says, "I take it for granted that Morris used the medieval setting and characters of his early work to project an identity forbidden him by his own time and place in history — specifically to give freer reign to the promptings of his libido than more 'realistic' fiction would have permitted him" (pp. 75-76). And in similar fashion: "Medievalism overcame his inhibitions both psychosexual and poetic. But this is precisely the problem: the poems and romances are insufficiently repressed. Their shifting imagery and structure suggest the unrestrained function of Freud's primary process" (p. 77). Kirchhoff's essay includes provocative discussions of several of the prose tales, notably of "The Story of the Unknown Church," and a few of the *Guenevere* poems. These discussions attempt to demonstrate the validity of his speculations regarding medievalism: "the medium of Morris' libidinal projection" (p. 93).

Diane Sadoff, in the next essay, also makes sophisticated use of Freudian notions. She opens with figurative statements about past and present drawn from Kierkegaard: "On wild trees the flowers are fragrant; on cultivated trees, the fruits." And there is another from Pater: "Like some strange second flowering after date, [Morris's 'medieval' poetry] renews on a more delicate type the poetry of a past age, but must not be confounded with it." Sadoff then suggests that Morris's early poems "question the temporal tie between past and present" and thus create an "erotics of repetition" (p. 98). This phrase was suggested to Sadoff by Kierkegaard's speculations on our apparent need to seek repetition. After a brief discourse on these speculations and on Morris's repetition of medieval texts, she argues that since "eroticism and death pervade and embody the textures and structures of Malory's tales" (p. 104), a major source for Morris, it is not surprising to find these concerns emerging in the *Guenevere* poems. It is furthermore possible to "recognize the pattern of eroticism and death as the outcome of primal Oedipal repression" (p. 107). To her credit, Sadoff does not probe "the sources of his interest in the disguised Oedipal situation; we simply do not know enough about Morris's childhood to argue a causal link" (p. 108). But she reminds us of how often "triangular relationships" recur in Morris's work and concludes with comments about "repetition compulsion" (drawn from Freud) as part of Morris's aesthetic. The comments are provocative but murky.

One is uneasy with the formulations and conclusions in this essay for other reasons. Categories borrowed from Kierkegaard and Freud, as well as their rhetorical functions in their original contexts, need to be more patiently elucidated than they are here. So too do several of the conclusions about Morris's medieval sources; the assertion, quoted above, that "eroticism and death pervade" and somehow "embody the textures and structures of Malory's tales" is vague and misleading. Roger Ascham, for different reasons, made a similar remark about the *Morte*, condemning its "open manslaughter and bold bawdry."[30] But over the past five centuries the majority of Malory's readers, including Morris himself, have been attracted by other qualities of the *Morte Darthur,* by what Caxton saw as its "many joyous and pleasant histories, and noble and renowned acts of humanity, gentleness, and chivalries."[31] Those histories and acts are woven into Malory's cycle of prose romances; moreover, when he "unravelled" his French sources, he pruned scenes with violence and lust so that he could put into the foreground those that centered on personal honor and chivalric brotherhood. These themes do reappear in Morris's *Guenevere* poems; he did not ignore them, and when Sadoff disregards such themes to stress only those that support her "pet motif," she becomes unconvincing.

Literary texts, even when patiently and fully explicated, usually cast only a flickering light into biographical and psychic corners. In too many instances in the first four essays in this volume, but especially in those by Deal and Sadoff, partial and misleading explications reveal little either about Morris's postadolescent tribulations or about his controlling aesthetic. The essays might, however, cause readers to look again at the literary works Morris published in the 1850s.

The last essay in this volume touches upon these works, but its author's primary concern is to discuss a fruitful reciprocal relationship, one that began in the 1850s, between Morris and Dante Gabriel Rossetti. Robert Keane rehearses the usual biographical details regarding Rossetti's large reputation which attracted Burne-Jones, and then Morris, to London to live and work with the master. From these details Keane often draws fresh implications, ignoring, for instance, the hoary anecdotes about the Red Lion Square studio—the maid, the massive furniture—to comment upon how "the easy life of conversation, city walks, plays, and artistic production . . . fostered fresh ideas and shared literary and artistic influence" (p. 125). He stresses that the influence was shared, saying that "Morris carried Rossetti strongly into the world of Malory for awhile" (p. 127). Keane's discussions of Rossetti's watercolors on Arthurian themes and upon the ways Morris attempted to capture visual iconography in corresponding poems are refreshingly concrete. Similarities between Rossetti's watercolor *Arthur's Tomb* and Morris's poem "King Arthur's Tomb" exemplify how "Morris gives tongue to passion while Rossetti paints it in a moment's image" (p. 130). Keane's extended discussions of Morris's poetic response to two medieval watercolors he'd purchased from Rossetti (*The Blue Closet* and *The Tune of Seven Towers*) are fascinating, and so detailed that I found myself wishing these two paintings had been reproduced and included here, along with the copy of *Arthur's Tomb* that appears as frontispiece, so that readers could refer to them.

Keane devotes nearly one half of his essay to a demonstration of how the *Guenevere* poems "are in many ways closely connected to Rossetti's watercolors of this period. Rossetti influenced these poems in four ways: through a continued presence of Rossettian motifs and symbols, through a shared interest in themes from Malory, through Morris' direct use of certain Rossetti watercolors as subjects for poems, and through a mutual interest in the ballad form" (p. 128). The subsequent discussion of Rossetti's varied influence recalls points made about, say, dream in other essays in this volume; but since Keane talks of dreams as themes rather than techniques, and since he avoids speculation about Morris's psyche, his discussion is more satisfying and enlightening.

Stylization of the sort that has come to be called Pre-Raphaelite is easier to comprehend in paintings than in poetry; we can see the bright, flat colors and the overtly displayed symbols and thus ponder their effects more readily than when language must carry forward both basic meanings and stylistic variations. It is easier to categorize paintings as Pre-Raphaelite than to place poems and tales under that rubric. In some literary anthologies, consequently, the only feature that all the poems in a section headed Pre-Raphaelite have in common is their appearance in that section. It is a slippery category. We are therefore indebted to the authors of these essays in *The Golden Chain,* since their discussions of Morris's literary works of the 1850s — those regarded as essentially Pre-Raphaelite — can help us come to grips with the term. Their discussions should also deepen our appreciation of those works and help us to understand Morris's development as a writer and how it was influenced by a climate of opinion and by certain people in Oxford and London in the 1850s.

Because Keane charts only the mutually fruitful influences Morris and Rossetti had upon one another's work, he does not discuss their joint ventures into real estate. In 1871 they leased together an old house near the head waters of the Thames, and here with Janey Morris and the two daughters Rossetti enjoyed a few seasons of fitful happiness and artistic productivity. Morris loved the place, but it wasn't until Rossetti gave up his share of the lease in 1874 that he felt easy going there. From 1874 until his death in 1896, he went often. It was his favorite retreat, his one sure place of solace; and it is his tenancy that has made Kelmscott Manor world famous. Visitors have been attracted to the place both by Morris's reputation and by his descriptions of the manor ("a many-gabled old house built by the simple country folk of the long-past times") in the closing paragraphs of *News from Nowhere.* Since Janey and her daughters lived there permanently after Morris's death, bringing upriver with them their London possessions, visitors today can enjoy not just the lovely house and gardens, but also a treasure trove of artifacts: furnishings, books, paintings, embroideries either made by Morris or associated somehow with Kelmscott Manor. (Paintings and drawings done by Rossetti while he was a tenant hang on the walls.) To make these treasures known to a wider audience, the faculty of West Surrey College Art and

Design, in collaboration with the Society of Antiquaries, staged in November 1981 an exhibition entitled "William Morris and Kelmscott."

A book with the same title was published to accompany the exhibition. It contains a detailed catalogue of the many artifacts exhibited, from paintings and textiles to furniture and books (pp. 125–83), as well as sixteen essays: (1) "William Morris, Kelmscott and Farnham," by Leonard Stoppani, (2) "Kelmscott," by A. R. Dufty, (3) "The Appeal of William Morris," by Asa Briggs, (4) " 'An Artist of Reputation': Dante Gabriel Rossetti and Kelmscott Manor," by Joseph Acheson, (5) "Dear William," by Martin Shuttleworth, (6) "No Drawing Room Sort of Man," by Gillian Naylor, (7) "William Morris and Victorian Decorative Art," by Stuart Durant, (8) "William Morris and His Interest in the Orient," by Patricia L. Baker, (9) " 'Good Citizens' Furniture': William Morris and the Firm," by Helen Snowden, (10) "Traditional Furniture and Personal Items from Kelmscott Manor," by Dorothy D. Bosomworth, (11) "The Importance of Philip Webb," by John Brandon-Jones, (12) "The Socialism of William Morris," by Larry Baker, (13) "The Kelmscott Press: A Cornerstone of Modern Typography," by Ray Watkinson, (14) "Textiles at Kelmscott, an Introduction," by Jacqueline Herald, (15) " 'Red and Blue,' " by Deryn O'Connor, and (16) "On Designing Textiles with Birds," by Jacqueline Herald.

This list should indicate both the depth (implied in the names of well-known scholars like Dufty, Briggs, and Watkinson) and the diversity of these essays. Dufty offers a concise history of the manor and its various owners, Briggs a general overview that demonstrates why Morris appealed to his contemporaries and why that appeal (or relevance) has continued into the late twentieth century; he cites Morris's "concern for human relationships and for natural and built environment" (p. 22). Watkinson's essay is packed with detail about Morris's early and continuing love for the book arts, a love that culminated in the Kelmscott Press, where Morris was able to combine new ideas about typography with older ones about book decoration. Gillian Naylor has gathered excerpts from lectures and letters in which Morris assesses what his Firm had contributed to the Gothic Revival, and where he registers a self-doubt that at times rises to a "conviction that his life's work might add up to nothing more than 'make-believe' " (p. 57). Stuart Durant is convincing in his demonstration that "Morris's decorative design does not differ quite as radically as is sometimes claimed from the work of the more accomplished designers of his generation" (p. 66). Similar points are presented by Helen Snowden on the furniture made by Morris and Company, which was evidently not so innovative nor so sturdily simple as some contemporary manifestos and memoirs have suggested. John Brandon-Jones reviews Morris's friendship with the architect Philip Webb, stressing how important Webb was for the Firm and also for the Society for the Protection of Ancient Buildings. It was Webb who designed the unusual tombstone—like the roof of a Germanic hall—under which all the Morrises are buried, only a few hundred yards from the manor that inspired this exhibition and these diverse essays.

The two essays on Morris's textiles break new ground. Jacqueline Herald writes, "The process of selecting textiles for the Farnham exhibition was quite rigorous. For, rather than attempt to present a comprehensive survey of Morris's work in this field, as was done in Birmingham in April 1981 [the catalogue for that exhibition is reviewed below], two specific aspects were chosen—namely his use of red and blue and his impressions of birds in their design context" (p. 104). Deryn O'Conner remarks that red and blue "seem to represent richness, generosity and honesty for Morris" (p. 197), and she goes on to outline the arduous processes Morris mastered to produce his multicolored textiles. Jacqueline Herald points out that Morris "was never at a loss for words to describe birds in their natural surroundings, yet the portrayal of them in designs did not come easily" (p. 117). How Morris, with his typical industry, confronted problems of designs and dyes, studying real birds and experimenting with ancient dyes, is then set forth in some detail. Using notebooks that Morris kept when he was an examiner for the South Kensington Museum, comparing his patterns to those of the ancient textiles at the museum (now the Victoria and Albert), Herald in this detailed essay presents a great amount of new information on Morris and textile design.

The other essays, on Morris's socialism, Rossetti's tenure at Kelmscott Manor, and on certain "personal items" there, on Morris's interests in the Orient, all have information that would interest any viewer of the exhibition. They help to round out the introductory presentation of Morris which the exhibition, in part, intended. So too does the most puzzling and uneven of the essays in this book-catalogue. This is Martin Shuttleworth's strange epistle, "Dear William," a nearly interminable sixteen pages of reminiscing addressed directly to Morris: "Kelmscott Manor was a very private place. You rented it in 1871 when you were 37. . . . by the time that you were 37, you were already a fashionable prophet. It was not entirely your own fault. You began by writing extremely well, harsh poems out of Malory and Froissart. As a child I loved them" (41). I really don't know what to make of this second-person-familiar rehash of Morris's life and times; it reminds me of an awful television show popular years ago, "This Is Your Life," where an unctuous emcee would parade details and personages by an embarrassed celebrity who had to stand and take it while the audience cheered and chuckled. It is hard to imagine what audience Shuttleworth might have had in mind for lines like these: "It may seem ridiculous to write a letter to a man who would be 148 next March, but the majority of the problems that faced you and your age face us still and, besides, there are people still alive in Georgia and Kashmir who were toddlers when you were a toddler. If you had been born in some upland Asian valley and lived on yoghurt you might well be alive still" (p. 43).

Beautifically edited and produced, this book has dozens of black and white photographs and twelve stunning full-page color photographs of Kelmscott Manor interiors and Morris textiles. The catalogue section of the book describes fifty-two items exhibited under the category "Paintings, Prints, and Drawings" (thirty of these are by Rossetti), twenty-five items under "Textiles," nineteen under "Ceramics," eleven under "Firm's Furniture," nineteen under "Traditional Furniture and Personal Items," and forty under "Books at Kelmscott Manor." The descriptions are full and reliable, with the exception of two errors in the last category: instead of "Great Rift," "Thingvellir" should have been used; these "meeting-plains" are what Morris called the "most storied place of Iceland" (p. 169), and the comment on *Three Northern Love Stories* should not occur under *Volsunga Saga* (p. 177).

Another recent study arose from an exhibition; like *William Morris and Kelmscott,* it is more than a catalogue of items in an exhibition. Since it attempts to be comprehensive in its coverage, *Textiles by William Morris and Company, 1861-1940*, is an important contribution to Morris scholarship. Other articles and books contain useful information on Morris's textiles, but their discussions usually stop at around 1890 when the Kelmscott Press and problems with book design diverted Morris's attention away from textiles.[32] This book extends detailed commentary and descriptions for another fifty years, right up to the closing of Morris and Company in 1940. We thus can attain a much clearer sense of William Morris's influence on textile design both inside the Firm and out. Perceptive comments about Morris's relevance to twentieth-century design occur throughout the study, especially in its opening chapters.

There are six chapters: "Morris and Company," "Embroideries," "Printed Fabrics," "Woven Fabrics," "Carpets," and "Tapestries." Oliver Fairclough wrote the first, fifth, and sixth chapters, Emmeline Leary the remaining three. These six chapters, though fairly short, are detailed and comprehensive, adequate as introductions for those unfamiliar with Morris and with the fact that "textiles were, with stained glass, the most important part of Morris and Co.'s business, and were peculiarly Morris's own" (p. 13). The chapters can also serve as complementary readings for specialists to use along with the exemplary final section, "The Catalogue of Textiles," prepared by Emmeline Leary. That catalogue (pp. 77–116) is divided into five sections that correspond, respectively, to chapters two through five. In each instance an impressive array of information is presented, both under individual entries in the exhibit and then in tables and lists of known embroideries, printed fabrics and woven fabrics. The embroideries number 165, the printed fabrics 49, the woven 58. A list of tapestries had been published previously, and a comprehensive list is not attempted for the carpets.[33]

This attractive, impeccably edited book-catalogue has dozens of illustrations and a graceful introduction by Barbara Morris, an authority on Victorian embroidery.[34] She reminds us of Morris's status "as one of the greatest textile designers of all time" and, more importantly, of "the profound and beneficial influence that Morris's patterns were to have on designers of the succeeding generation" (p. 11).

The last catalogue examined here focuses not upon one achievement but again on a particular place. Just as Kelmscott Manor contains artifacts whose beauty and importance justified a major exhibition, so too does Cambridge. Though Morris attended the *other* university and though there are countless associations between him and Oxford, countless anecdotes about him and Burne-Jones at the Bodleian, or about painting the Oxford Union murals, and the like, there are also many associations with Cambridge, ones that have not received so much critical and scholarly attention. Because of a major exhibition mounted at the Fitzwilliam in 1980 and the handsome and informative catalogue that accompanied it, entitled *Morris and Company in Cambridge,* perhaps this situation will soon be remedied.

In a brief foreword to the catalogue, Michael Jaffe sketches in the importance of Sydney Cockerell as intermediary between Morris artifacts and the Fitzwilliam; as director of the museum, the one time secretary to the Kelmscott Press and long time friend of the Morris family brought dozens of rare items to Cambridge. In a short introduction Stephen Wildman, commenting on the appropriateness of this exhibition of nineteenth-century art and architecture, quotes Morris to excellent effect: "In these times of plenteous knowledge and meagre performance, if we do not study the ancient work directly and learn to understand it, we shall find ourselves influenced by the feeble work all around us."[35]

This catalogue should certainly aid such study. It is divided into four sections: "Section I makes use of a carefully chosen group of Pre-Raphaelite drawings to describe the artistic and personal debts of William Morris and Edward Burne-Jones before the formation of Morris, Marshall, Faulkner and Co. in 1861. In Section II, the activity of the firm is set into the architectural context of Cambridge in the second half of the nineteenth century. Section III includes all works connected with the firm in The Fitzwilliam Museum. Section IV is an account of Morris's life-long interest in the art of the book" (p. 3).

Section I has detailed commentary on twenty-two items, ranging from portraits of Rossetti to Burne-Jones; included are the necessary biographical details as well as references to previous exhibitions and pertinent bibliography. The second section stresses the effects of the Gothic Revival on Cambridge architecture, and it also discusses the ways that Morris's Firm, especially through contracts awarded by the architect G. F. Bodley, was able to contribute to that revival, or to its later manifestations. Some of the catalogue descriptions here — of the windows for Jesus College Chapel, for example — are actually essays on the designs, on the cartoons, or on matters like the negotiations that preceded the execution of the work. This is therefore the section with the most substantial commentary; its photographs and blueprints might, however, have made up the least interesting part of the exhibition itself. A variety of items is discussed in the third section: furniture, sketches for various design schemes, textiles, tiles, wallpapers. Section IV though devoted primarily to the Kelmscott Press, begins with discussions of Morris's early work with calligraphy and manuscript illumination. In 1873 he copied out, in delicate italic script and with splendid display capitals, three of the shorter Icelandic sagas which he and Magnússon had recently translated.[36] This manuscript of 244 pages he gave to Georgiana Burne-Jones; her initials, interlaced with flowering vines, appear at the bottom of the first page. She later gave this treasure, bound in citron morocco by De Coverly, to the Fitzwilliam; it was part of the exhibit. So was an almost complete set of Kelmscott Press books, the magnificent Chaucer among them, that May Morris (thanks to Cockerell) left to the Fitzwilliam in 1935. Details regarding these many books are clearly set forth in this final section.

Duncan Robinson assisted Stephen Wildman in the preparation of the exhibit and in the writing of this handsome catalogue; its many black and white plates are keyed to the descriptions of individual items, and it is thus a fine guide to the many ways that William Morris left his mark on Cambridge, where his influence continues to be felt.

During the late 1860s and early 1870s, when their marriages were undergoing heavy weather, William Morris and Georgiana Burne-Jones turned from the specters of Rossetti and Maria Zambaco to each other's company, and there they evidently found solace, if not refuge. Morris's regard for Georgie is apparent in poems he wrote for her and then copied out in a fine cursive hand for *A Book of Verse*. This illuminated manuscript, the most personal and beautiful of the four he made for her, Morris gave to Georgie on her birthday in 1870.[37]

It has just been published for the first time. In cooperation with the Victoria and Albert, which acquired the manuscript in 1952, Scolar Press has produced a facsimile edition of *A Book of Verse*. Careful and exacting work with process camera and printing plates is everywhere evident in the edition. The sharpness of painted pictures by Charles Fairfax Murray is remarkable, and the delicate colors of early summer that Morris himself worked into the decorations are particularly striking. The vines and tendrils that swirl and wind up the margins push their buds and blossoms, their pale green leaves, into the lines and stanzas of the poems themselves. And when these lyrics refer to nature's beauties, as they often do, the juxtaposition of verbal and painted images is striking indeed.

This facsimile edition was limited to a run of 325 with 300 numbered copies (sixty-two in vellum) for sale, at fancy prices. With such editions, Scolar Press is obviously aiming at a fairly limited audience: curators of rare book rooms in large libraries, wealthy aficionados of fine books, speculating collectors. It is therefore pleasant to report that a trade edition came out last year (just in time for Christmas).

The format is smaller, so is the price, and anyone interested in Morris or any aspect of the book arts can now purchase *A Book of Verse*.

Morris was an avid collector of manuscripts and early printed books. His deep understanding of their craftsmanship, his delight in their art, above all his determination and ability to use them as models for his own books made him an unusual and perhaps unique collector.[38] So beautiful are his own achievements in the book arts that they have in turn inspired collectors, but the majority of them are of the usual sort: merely acquisitive. John J. Walsdorf, an editor of another recent book on Morris, seems to be of this stripe, judging from the opening lines of his introduction to *Printers on Morris:* "The genesis of this book springs from fourteen years of collecting William Morris, which has *netted* [my emphasis] just one miniature on Morris, and that in Czechoslovakian! I felt a need, as a collector, for a Morris miniature. If I couldn't find such a book, then I would just do one myself" (p. 1). That's just what he has done, and those with enough money (the only thing not small about this book is its price) may herewith be treated to twenty-five blurbs from twenty-five personages, most of them printers, from Kegan Paul in 1883 to John Johnson in 1933. All of these abbreviated appreciations are available elsewhere (a few of them, especially Elbert Hubbard's with its silly mistake, should probably not have been resurrected at all).[39] Walsdorf's miniature does not advance Morris studies an iota.

It does, however, demonstrate one aspect of Morris's continuing popularity. Someone who owns a Kelmscott Press book has a hedge against inflation, since its monetary value has appreciated geometrically with each passing decade. In turning out this limited-edition miniature, gussied up with "Brother Rabbit" paper, a Barry Moser engraving of Morris, and a foreword by Basil Blackwell, Walsdorf was apparently trying to create a "collectible," a curious little artifact that others presumably will want to "net."[40]

A more positive manifestation of Morris's continuing influence on printing and the book arts is Florence Boos's edition of his *Socialist Diary*. In publishing this fascicle, the Windhover Press at Iowa City continues a tradition that goes back to the Kelmscott Press. Morris's insistence on craftsmanship, his loving attention to every detail of a book's publication from the design of its type to the manufacture of its paper, created a revolution in book design and publishing in America.[41] Though only a handful of the dozens of presses inspired by Morris's example survived for any length of time, and though fewer yet flourished, the tradition is still alive. It is reflected on every page of this Windhover Press limited edition, "set by hand in Dante types, with Bembo titling for display, and printed on Barcham Green's Windhover paper" (p. 38). The care and skill that went into the production of this volume are justified by the signficance of its content: a diary by William Morris never before published in its entirety, and a thoroughly competent preface by Florence Boos.

She also wrote the longer introduction and notes to this same diary when it appeared a year later for a different audience in *History Workshop Journal*. This edition is a scholarly tour de force and an impressively thorough job of editing and research. The diary is bracketed by eighteen pages of introduction and nineteen of biographical notes. The thirty-three pages of text would be far fewer without the dense mat of footnotes (195 of them, several amounting to short essays) upon which the entries rest. Throughout there are wide-ranging references to Morris's letters, lectures, and journalism, and to pertinent previous scholarship.

Morris kept this diary from 25 January to 27 April 1887. Justifying its publication nearly a century later, Boos says, "Its brevity and bluntness render it a more accessible introduction to his political activities and beliefs than the editorial notes of *Commonweal*, his more expansive essays, or his massive socialist correspondence to friends and comrades during this period. Morris's tactical analyses give a shrewd but admirably disinterested view of many of the political groups of his time: Gladstonian liberalism and the Liberal Unionists, Bradlaughian radicalism, Fabianism, Hyndman's Social Democratic Federation, several varieties of anarchism, and the antiparliamentarian and parliamentarian wings of the Socialist League. The *Diary* also records grim economic conditions, hostility of the newspapers and police, shifting responses of his audiences, and practical obstacles to his efforts at propaganda. Finally, it documents some of the movement's many achievements—its genuine intellectual variety and cooperation under stress, and a sense of excitement and anticipation, which deepened as well as intensified its doctrinal and tactical disputes" (pp. 2-3). Many scholars have recognized the importance of such material in the *Diary* and have tapped the original in the British Library or used excerpts May Morris placed in the introductions to the *Collected Works* and in *William Morris: Artist, Writer Socialist*. Long extracts were also previously published in Mackail's *Life* and in E. P. Thompson's massive political biography.[42]

Boos seems unfair about these earlier appearances of passages from the diary. About Mackail she says that "his virulent anti-socialist bias probably led him to omit passages describing Morris's more productive campaigns in the North, and to highlight accounts of the movement's internal debates and failures" (p. 4). But Morris himself highlights such problems, often lamenting his own failures as a mediator and as a lecturer. And there's nothing in Mackail about the April trips to the North because his extracts conclude with an entry for 24 March: "fifty-three years old today — no use grumbling at that." So he did not cut passages from those entries, and those trimmed from the earlier entries are inconsequential. While Mackail, a professor of classics, did not sympathize with all of Morris's political activities or acquaintances, he surely harbored no "virulent anti-socialist bias." Only a few years after completing his monumental and generally reliable biography, he lectured on the necessity for socialist reform.[43] About Thompson, Boos says that his "own electoral marxism may cause him to de-emphasize Morris's antiparliamentarian associations during this period and to deprecate his commitment to labour issues" (p. 4). But Thompson had written, "Ever since that day of bright sunshine in April, 1887, when Morris had addressed the striking Northumbrian miners he had been particularly responsive to events in the coal fields. Here he gained a sense of the tremendous power of the organized workers in action."[44] So Boos's puzzling speculation deserves documentation.

But Boos is rarely puzzling. Her comments on the numerous opportunities Morris had to become a mere liberal are provocative: "A 'political' temperament, which might have made Morris a good parliamentarian, Fabian, or trade-unionist at 53, might also have frozen him in any number of earlier, more 'reasonable' bourgeois roles; for example: (i) as a Christian socialist at 20 (his mother had wanted him to become a bishop, and as a young man he was fond of ecclesiastical lore); or (ii) as a restorationist architect at 25 (he apprenticed in the firm of G. B. Street, the most enlightened practioner of exactly the sort of restoration Morris later bitterly opposed); or, (iii) as a Gladstonian Liberal MP at 40 (his friends' expectation)" (p.11). Boos's ability to combine such intelligent speculation with the necessary presentation of biographical fact is also apparent in the following: "Periods in which more concrete or pragmatic aspects were dominant (creation of the Firm, Icelandic trips; formation of the Society for the Protection of Ancient Buildings; the political activity of the '80s) complemented and alternated with other periods of abstraction or introspection, in which he created highly intense and allegorical poetry, and the abstractions of his designs. Had this pattern continued, and Morris's health not deteriorated, he would have undertaken another cycle of social or political effort in the late 1890s. Who can guess what form this might have taken?" (pp. 16-17). Though objections immediately come to mind (Morris wrote *Sigurd the Volsung* the same year he founded the SPAB and joined the Eastern Question Association; he was creating wallpapers for Balmoral Castle in 1887 during the period of intense political activity recorded in the *Diary*), one must still admire the attempt to understand Morris through such patterns.

The footnotes are pertinent and specific; one even includes philological lore; in a note to "proclaimed the procession," Boos writes, "the use of 'proclaim' in this context seems to have been fairly recent," and she cites *OED* entries. It seems surprising that she does not comment on Morris's use of an archaic verb in this description of a Council meeting: "it was in the end quarrelsome: Donald captious and obviously attacking Lane . . . then I must needs flyte them, which I did with a good will, pitching into both parties" (p. 41). Morris must have recalled the numerous "flytings" in medieval poetry when he wedged this verb into a modern context. "Wardour-Street English" in his political writings is rare, and the use of "flyte" here demands attention.

Only a few of the biographical notes refer to well-known people; the majority, from James Allman through Charlotte Wilson, never found their way into the DNB. These notes often clarify the record (see the note on George Wardle whom Morris biographers have frequently confused with either Thomas or Thomas E. Wardle), and they rarely contain errors (John Carruthers did not go with "Morris on his last visit to Iceland in the summer of 1896." He went with Morris to Norway that summer). These notes provide insights into the practical concerns and modest achievements of politicans whom Morris knew well. Our sense of Morris the working socialist and his continuing signficance to the British Left (more than half of these people lived well into the twentieth century) is enriched. James Frederick Henderson (1868-1947), active with the Socialist League, was imprisoned for labor agitation in Norwich, was a journalist in London in the 1880s and stayed then at Kelmscott House. He held various political offices as a socialist, and served "eventually as Lord Mayor in 1939-40 of the city where as a youth he had been imprisoned" (p.

64). Charlotte Martin Wilson (1854–1944) was the "only upper-middle class woman to propagate revolutionary anarchism in Britain during the 1880s." Many of her ideas resemble Morris's, and "since they frequently spoke at the same meetings during the period, influence or cross-influence is conceivable" (p. 75). With such comments, Boos invited other scholars to turn their attention to these lesser-known figures.

Even in her discussions of the luminaries, Boos provokes fresh insights. Shaw's well-known memoir *William Morris as I Knew Him* praises Morris, but at the expense of his colleagues in the Socialist League. Shaw says of them, "They were romantic anarchists to a man, strong on the negative side, but regarding the State as an enemy, very much as the child regards the policeman. . . . Morris, who had been holding the League up by the scruff of its neck, opened his hand, whereupon it dropped like a stone into the sea, leaving only a little wreckage to come to the surface occasionally and demand bail at the police court or a small loan." Boos quotes this and then claims that the metaphors of stray dog and flotsam "establish Shaw's real antipathy to Morris's basic egalitarian ideals. Morris was capable of rage and contempt for the strong but not the weak, and not only children are properly wary of police and the massed power of a state in which they have no means of representation" (p. 71). She then turns to the oft-quoted conclusion of Shaw's memoir: "And with such wisdom as my years have left me, I note that as [Morris] has drawn further away from the hurly burly of our personal contacts into the impersonal perspective of history he towers greater and greater above the horizon beneath which his best advertised contemporaries have disappeared." Instead of applauding this graceful peroration, Boos asks, "Would Morris have wanted such a subtly apolitical canonization? The tribute is in good part a comment on Shaw, perhaps, and an act of nostalgic love for a long-dead spiritual parent. But a more measured and concrete respect for the intelligence and consistency of Morris's ideas and acts would serve his memory at least as well as such an apotheosis of him as a heroically misguided eccentric" (p. 71). Such invitations to reinterpret hallowed texts and to examine Morris's associations with lesser-known figures make these notes another resource for the continuing revaluation of Morris's political significance generally, to his times and our own.

Of Glasier's *William Morris and the Early Days of the Socialist Movement* (London, 1921), Boos says, "Its effort to present Morris as uninterested in Marxism have drawn upon it highly charged and heavily documented attacks by E. P. Thompson and Paul Meier, but Glasier's book seems to me insufficiently pointed to merit such artillery. Its Morris is a rather vaguely hearty well-wisher to Glasier, not a serious theoretician of any kind" (p. 63). This is true, but the heavy artillery was brought to bear because many scholars were eager to disassociate Morris from Marxism, and Glasier's accounts of Morris's inability to comprehend Marx became an important prop in an edifice R. Page Arnot called "The Morris Myth."[45] Using this myth, Morris's significance can be regarded as literary rather than political. He becomes a romantic or utopian socialist, never a serious one. This edifice has recently been undermined, thanks to the work of Arnot and Meier, of Raymond Williams and Perry Anderson, and especially of Thompson.[46] In the postscript to his revised edition of *William Morris: Romantic to Revolutionary,* he says, "It may be that Morris was a major intellectual figure. As such he may be seen as our greatest diagnostician of alienation. . . . And if he was that then he remains a contemporary figure. And it then must be important to establish the relation in which he stands to contemporary thought."[47] Florence Boos's exemplary work on Morris's *Socialist Diary* will become a part of a new edifice, one from which Morris is likely to be regarded as one of the nineteenth century's foremost socialist thinkers.[48]

Another recent edition of previously unpublished Morris material is of less far-reaching significance. This is *The Novel on Blue Paper,* edited by Penelope Fitzgerald, the biographer of Edward Burne-Jones. In her introduction to this fragment, she explains: "The novel which William Morris began to write early in 1872 is unfinished and unpublished and untitled. I have called it *The Novel on Blue Paper* because it was written on blue-lined foolscap, and Morris preferred to call things as they were" (p. v).

One wonders therefore what Morris himself might have called this book. May Morris once said that "no one felt more keenly than my father the wrong done to dead authors by gathering together every fragment of their writing regardless of quality, and in his lifetime he always refused to reprint his early prose."[49] In a letter advising Ellis to take great pains in choosing poems for the Kelmscott edition of Coleridge, Morris wrote, "It is these poems only that must be selected, or we burden the world with another useless book."[50]

But even fragments can reveal something signficant about an author's development, assuming that an editor has dealt carefully with the original manuscripts. Here is Fitzgerald on her methods in this edition: "I have corrected spelling, punctuation, omissions and repetitions, and regularized the names, ages, and place-names. I have also paragraphed the story which has meant cutting out one or two of the medievalising 'and so's,' divided it into short chapters and given them chapter headings" (p. xvi). She has in other words "Caxtonized" the original; one therefore cannot use her edition as the basis for sound comments about Morris's prose style or narrative technique. Fortunately a transcription of the manuscript (rather than a "version") is scheduled to appear in the 1982 *Dickens Studies Annual*.[51]

Literary fragments can also reveal something about an author's personality; perhaps fragments are even more significant than finished texts, for what has been suppressed or discontinued sometimes implies deep psychic truths, or fear of discovery, or the like. Fitzgerald assumes that this is the case with these few dozen pages of confusing narrative, for she quotes Mackail's famous comment on the Prologues to *The Earthly Paradise* — that they contain "an autobiography so delicate and so outspoken that it must needs be left to speak for itself." Fitzgerald adds, "That, we have to conclude, was the trouble with the novel on blue paper; it did speak for itself, but much too plainly" (p. vi). Because it was so revealing, Georgiana Burne-Jones evidently told Morris to lay it aside (Fitzgerald even suggests that Mary Zambaco was the model for one of the characters in the fragment). The two brothers in love with the same woman parallel, of course, the situation with Morris, Rossetti, and Janey; but Fitzgerald sees in them still deeper meanings: "in the two boys, John and Arthur, he represents the opposing sides, as he understood them, of his own character" (p. xiii).

For those who appreciate psychoanalytical approaches, this book should represent a significant contribution to Morris studies. Others might be interested in the elegant architectural descriptions, which prefigure those in the lectures, or in the landscape descriptions, which, in their hints of ways that landscape affects emotion, are similar to those in the *Icelandic Journals* and the late prose romances. These elegant descriptions offer marked contrasts to the confusing and contradictory exposition, the weak dialogue and characterization, the general heavy-handedness everywhere evident in Morris's only attempt to write realistic prose fiction. Those interested in theories and structures of narrative might find this book useful.

The Relevance of William Morris 115

The edition is further evidence of Morris's continuing appeal, of the relevance that diverse scholars and critics can apprehend in Morris's achievements — even in his failures. One must therefore be pleased, though Morris would not have been, that *The Novel on Blue Paper* is finally in circulation. But the publication of his *Socialist Diary* is more significant, for we are in real need of what Morris can teach us about ways to achieve a decent society. Since his political writings are so clear and compelling, one hopes that the future will see new editions of the socialist lectures, of *A Dream of John Ball*, of selections from his contributions to *The Commonweal*, and the like. High quality work on all of Morris's achievements, work of the kind that I have discussed in this review, is likely to continue. Morris brings out the best in his admirers. But more attention needs to be paid to the ways that all his diverse achievements intersect in his visions of a better society.

Notes

1. Boos, ed. "William Morris's Socialist Diary," *History Workshop Journal*, 13 (1982), 1.

2. Philip Henderson, *William Morris: His Life, Work and Friends* (1967; rpt. Harmondsworth: Pelican, 1973), p. 160. The authorized biography is J. W. Mackail, *The Life of William Morris* (London: Longmans, Green, 1899).

3. Eugene D. LeMire, ed., *The Unpublished Lectures of William Morris* (Detroit: Wayne State, 1969).

4. Lin Carter, "Introduction," *The Wood beyond the World* (New York: Ballantine, 1969), p. xv. See also Richard Mathews, *Worlds beyond the World: The Fantastic Vision of William Morris* (San Bernadino, Calif.: Borgo Press, 1978).

5. Quoted in Mark Schorer, "The Burdens of Biography," *The World We Imagine: Selected Essays* (New York: Farrar, Straus and Giroux, 1969), p. 228.

6. *The Icelandic Journals* have been reissued as a volume in the "Travellers' Classics" series with an introduction by James Morris (Fontwell, Sussex: Centaur Press, 1969). "How I Became a Socialist" originally appeared in *Justice*, 16 June 1894; it is reprinted in *Political Writings of William Morris*, ed. A. L. Morton (London: Lawrence and Wishart, 1973).

7. This letter was published in the *Socialist Review* (March 1929) and in *The Letters of William Morris to His Family and Friends*, ed. Philip Henderson (London: Longmans, Green, 1950).

8. Thompson, *William Morris: Romantic to Revolutionary*, rev. ed. (London: Merlin Press, 1977).

9. *New York Times,* 13 November 1981, p. 2.

10. Faulkner, *William Morris: The Critical Heritage* (London: Routledge and Kegan Paul, 1973).

11. Quoted in Faulkner, *Against the Age,* pp. 33-34.

12. Ibid., p. 73.

13. The original tale of doomed love, in one of the greatest of the family sagas, is available in a fine translation: *Laxdoela Saga,* trans. M. Magnússon and H. Palsson (Harmondsworth: Penguin, 1969).

14. *The Saga Library*, trans. Eiríkur Magnússon and William Morris, 6 vols. (London: Quaritch, 1891-1905).

15. Gary L. Aho, "William Morris and Iceland," *Kairos,* 1 (1982), pp. 102-33.

16. London's Wardour Street was known for shops that sold fake antiques.

17. I found one printing error: the second line has evidently been omitted on p. 170.

18. John Bryson, ed., *Dante Gabriel Rossetti and Jane Morris: Their Correspondence* (Oxford: Clarendon, 1976).

19. Quoted in Elizabeth Longford, *A Pilgrimage of Passion: The Life of Wilfrid Scawen Blunt* (London: Weidenfeld and Nicholson, 1979), p. 279.

20. Ibid., p. 156.

21. *Memorials* (New York: Macmillan, 1904),II, 174.

22. Henderson, *William Morris: His Life,* p. 176.

23. Quoted in Penelope Fitzgerald, *Edward Burne-Jones* (London: Michael Joseph, 1975), p. 251.

24. *Memorials,* II, 241.

25. Ibid., p. 288.

26. Fitzgerald observes that the figure of Arthur in Burne-Jones's canvas *Avalon* is actually William Morris: "a glorious head on a crumple of clothes" *(Edward Burne-Jones,* p. 276).

27. There's an anecdote about Charles Faulkner trying to buy tinder from a stubborn Scotsman ("Ye'll be having it in foot lengths") and nearly missing the boat for Reykjavik, another about Burne-Jones asking Morris if there really is a Greenland Saga; Morris's reply is typically abrasive. I found three typos: on 41.13 "prese,ted" should be "presented," on 107.5 "mighw" should have been "might," and on 184.37 "promiees" should be "promises."

28. See, e.g., Jack Lindsay, *William Morris: His Life and Work* (London: Constable, 1975).

29. The earlier two are *Studies in the Late Romances of William Morris,* ed. Carole Silver and Joseph Dunlap (New York: William Morris Society, 1976) and *The After-*

Summer Seed: Reconsiderations of William Morris's "Sigurd the Volsung," ed. John Hollow (New York and London: William Morris Society, 1978). I found a few typos in the present volume: on 5.16 "Fair" should be "Pair," on 64.12 "and" should be "and a," on 76.15 a verb (perhaps "point"?) is needed, on 123.4 "retures" should be "returns," and on 135.2, "enchanged" should be "enchanted."

30. *The Scolemaster,* ed., R. J. Schoeck (Don Mills, Ontario: J. M. Dent, 1966), p. 67.

31. "Caxton's Preface," *The Works of Sir Thomas Malory,* ed. Eugene Vinaver (Oxford: Clarendon Press, 1967) p. cxlvi.

32. See Paul Thompson, *The Work of William Morris* (New York: Viking, 1967), and Ray Watkinson, *William Morris as Designer* (London: Studio Vista, 1967).

33. Such a list appears in H. C. Marillier, *History of the Merton Abbey Tapestry Works* (London: Constable, 1927).

34. Barbara Morris, *Victorian Embroidery* (London: Herbert Jenkins, 1962).

35. This is from Morris's lecture "The Decorative Arts," given on 12 April 1877. Reprinted as "The Lesser Arts," it is available in the A. L. Morton edition cited in note 6.

36. These are "The Story of Hen Thorir," "The Story of the Banded Men," and "The Story of Howard the Halt." They reappeared later in vol. 1 of *The Saga Library.*

37. Joseph Dunlap writes that the title "takes on special meaning when one realizes that in the earlier version of FitzGerald's translation of the *Rubaiyat* (which Morris wrote out later for Georgy) the familiar stanza reads: 'Here with a Loaf of Bread beneath the Bough/A Flask of Wine, a Book of Verse and Thou' " ("William Morris: Calligrapher," *William Morris and the Art of the Book* [New York: Oxford, 1976], p. 57).

38. Paul Needham, "William Morris: Book Collector," ibid., pp. 21-47.

39. Elbert Hubbard, an American original, founded the Roycroft Press and supposedly visited Morris twice during the 1890s. He says, however, that Morris was a famed blacksmith. See *William Morris Book* (East Aurora, N.Y.: Roycrofters Press, 1904, p. 36)

40. What Walsdorf has netted in his fifteen years of collecting appeared in two recent exhibitions: *A Collector's Choice: The John J. Walsdorf Collection of William Morris in Private Press and Limited Edition,* a catalogue of an exhibition at George Washington University, 26 November 1979-15 February 1980 (Washington, D.C.: George Washington University, 1980) and *William Morris in Private Press and Limited Edition,* a catalogue of an exhibition at the University of Missouri, 14 September 1980-9 October 1980 (Kansas City: University of Missouri, 1980).

41. See Susan Otis Thompson's *American Book Design and William Morris* (New York: Bowker, 1977).

42. In Mackail the extracts are in vol. 2, pp. 170-80; in Thompson, pp. 430-34, 440-42, 445-46, 752-53, 757. The extracts are in complementary distribution.

43. Mackail, *Socialism and Politics: An Address and a Programme* (London: Hammersmith, 1903).

44. Thompson, *William Morris: Romantic to Revolutionary,* p. 587.

45. This is the title of the opening chapter in Arnot's *William Morris: The Man and the Myth* (London: Lawrence and Wishart, 1964).

46. Paul Meier, *William Morris: The Marxist Dreamer* (Sussex: Harvester Press, 1978); Raymond Williams, *Politics and Letters* (London: New Left Books, 1979); Perry Anderson, *Arguments within English Marxism* (London: New Left Books, 1980).

47. Thompson, p. 801.

48. Soon to appear, published by the William Morris Society, is an edition by Boos of Morris's juvenilia.

49. May Morris, "Introduction" *Collected Works*, I (London: Longmans Green, 1910), xv.

50. Quoted in Henderson, *William Morris: His Life,* p. 412.

51. See J. Kocmanova, " 'Landscape and Sentiment': Morris's First Attempt in Longer Prose Fiction," *Victorian Poetry,* 13 (1975), 103–17.

After Strange Gods

Christian K. Messenger

Robert J. Higgs. *Laurel and Thorn: The Athlete in American Literature.* Lexington: University Press of Kentucky, 1981. xi, 196 pp.

There was a man in my class at Princeton who never went to football games. He spent his Saturday afternoons delving for minutiae about Greek athletics and the somewhat fixed battles between Christians and the wild beasts under the Antonines. Lately — several years out of college — he has discovered football players and is making etchings of them in the manner of the late George Bellows. But he was once unresponsive to the very spectacle at his door, and I suspect the originality of his judgments on what is beautiful, what is remarkable and what is fun.

F. Scott Fitzgerald

Fitzgerald's story is about a Yale football player learning to love his sport.[1] The story by extension is a treatise on coming to understand what is "beautiful," "remarkable," and "fun" in our lives and learning to care about it for itself as something intrinsically valuable for the spirit. A half century later Americans are squarely in Fitzgerald's corner, almost slavishly attentive "to the very spectacle at [their] door." America has indeed "discovered" football players, not only as popular heroes, but also as objects to be transformed into art. The same holds true for many other sports and their players. "Sportsworld" *is* the American environment: we need look no further for the pattern of our lives — their rhythms, victories, and frustrations.[2] We know now that the spectacle is not just at our door but in our daily round, expressive of life beyond that spectacle, that how we conceive of sport as a nation is a record of our cultural preferences and the contradictions of our social arrangements.

The shift that Fitzgerald describes is one that led from the historical study of sport to its popular cultural appreciation, with the result that American authors could create art out of what was close at hand. The legacy of sport in American fiction is that of authors such as Ring Lardner, Fitzgerald, and Ernest Hemingway, who proved that modern American society may be imaginatively conceived and explained through its games and players. Contemporary American authors write in their wake both in subject matter and mode of narration.

In *Laurel and Thorn* Robert J. Higgs attempts to study this modern and contemporary literary phenomenon, but he is actually an example of Fitzgerald's Princeton man, delving into Greek models and Christian parables while turning away from his nominal subject matter. Higgs's book searches for a value-laden wholeness among honorable men and sorts out a variety of deficient athletic heroes in quest of that wholeness. However, Higgs boxes himself in very early with disclaimers about his own method and goals. He doesn't want to write a "traditional literary study" (p. viii); his book "does not undertake to assess the authors aesthetically, to examine form and content; rather the approach is cultural. The concern here is not primarily with how well the author has done his job, how artistic a product he has created in his athletic hero but with the view he takes of his figure and his milieu" (pp. viii–ix). As a result, this book creates an unsophisticated art-versus-life dichotomy, opposing the aesthetic to the cultural, in contrast with virtually all recent criticism that confirms the union of the two in any relevant critical discourse. Furthermore, sport and play have intrinsically aesthetic properties that cannot be ignored by critics of sport in literature.

In a murky first chapter, "Game Plan," only five pages are given to a search for the roots of Western mind-body dualism. Higgs asks, "What is the mind?" and in the next sentence concludes, "As far as I know, no one has the slightest idea" (p. 3). This statement probably will not drive students of Kant, Berkeley, and Hume down into trade, but it is an accurate portrayal of Higgs's dogmatism. He wants to think everything through from an original stance and thereby contorts himself into abstractions beyond his scope. The same problem appears in his tripartite grouping of sports heroes into three classes: those of Apollo, Dionysus, and Adonis. Basically, the Apollonian heroes are described as conformists while Dionysians and Adonics are rebels. The Apollonians are contrived and artificial; the Dionysians are indulgent and "natural"; and the Adonics are a mediating group who seek a union between body and self on the side of nature. Adonics don't conform but are not hedonists. They seek a mixture of *Arête* (excellence) and *Aidos* (respect). It is not that research into the associations of such mythological figures cannot have a general currency in discussing modern heroic types or be made extraordinarily vivid as in the work of Nietzsche in *The Birth of Tragedy* and, recently, of René Girard in *Violence and the Sacred*. But Higgs wants to torment the modern athletic hero into one of his three categories without the requisite American cultural and social context that the subject demands.

In *Laurel and Thorn* the Apollonians and Dionysians are the bad heroes, hypocrites and sensualists, while the Adonics comprise a brotherhood of the Golden Mean and include almost every modern hero validated by New Criticism and Existentialism: "The folk hero, the fisher king, the scapegoat, the absurd athlete, and the 'secret' Christian" (p. 11). Higgs is most comfortable when invoking a predetermined set of categories, as when he quotes Northrop Frye, Joseph Campbell, and Lord Raglan. How well does this structure of mythological referants elucidate modern American athletes in literature? Much depends on how the structure is programmed, which authors and heroes are examined, which are favored, which cast out, and, most significantly, which ignored. The literature that Higgs cites and examines in his study is far more eclectic than that treated in any other book about sport in American fiction.[3] Higgs indeed has found athletes in authors and texts where no one else has even looked, and occasionally this search has paid off. For example, we are reminded of Elmer Gantry's college football days and his muscular Christianity, and while most critics would cite Irwin Shaw's short story "The Eighty Yard Run" in any discussion of sport in fiction, we find an original analysis of *The Troubled Air*, Shaw's novel of the McCarthyite era. *Laurel and Thorn* is most thorough on the role of the athlete in American drama (Sherwood, O'Neill, Inge, Miller, Albee) and also refers extensively to sports narrative by Anderson, Runyon, and Farrell, although the value of the latter material is often minimal.

What is troubling, however, in the "Apollo" section is a cursory and often trivializing reading of Lardner and Fitzgerald. This section confuses the very differing geneses of the "busher," or "rube," and the college sporting hero and draws almost entirely on secondary sources for a limited understanding of the Frank Merriwell phenomenon. It is simply wrong to concur in Gilbert Seldes's view that before Lardner all baseball players had been thought of as college gentlemen (p. 23). Lardner's Jack Keefe is seen as supplanting Merriwell, a judgment that ignores almost a century of the development of American humorous fiction and reveals a failure to know the narrative history of the subject. Higgs concludes that Lardner's portrayal of baseball heroes in an ironic mode was so deft that contemporary baseball novelists cannot continue in this vein. Modern baseball is said to be "devoid of humor and absurdity" (p. 27) as reflected in its fiction, an observation difficult to accept in light of Robert Coover's *The Universal Baseball Association*, Philip Roth's *The Great American Novel*, and Jerome Charyn's *The Seventh Babe*. If Higgs is not interested in authors "aesthetically," why does he devote more space to labeling Lardner's inheritors of subject than he does to describing Lardner's Jack Keefe on and off the field?

A similar problem occurs in a discussion of Fitzgerald's Tom Buchanan, the All-American end from Yale in *The Great Gatsby*, one of the most potent symbolic athletes in American fiction. Higgs appears to dislike Fitzgerald intensely and Buchanan as well. While it is not difficult to dislike Buchanan, Higgs fails to support his negative judgment with sufficient examples, and this despite Fitzgerald's intricate characterization of Buchanan's physical power and menace. Instead Higgs provides the conventional sentimental picture of a Fitzgerald so taken with football heroes that his worship destroyed his judgment. By stating that "there is not in Fitzgerald anywhere a good example of strength and beauty" (p. 37), Higgs ignores such complex, strong, and beautiful characters as Jay Gatsby, Dick Diver, and Monroe Stahr, all of whom suggest Fitzgerald's intense romantic identification with youthful heroism, of which his valorization of the athlete was a significant part.

Although the subtitle of Higgs's study, "The Athlete in Literature," indicates no specific time period, Higgs early on specifies that he is investigating the period from Jack London's *The Game* (1905) to Walker Percy's *Lancelot* (1976). In fact, the book addresses little fiction written after 1960, and thus there are many troubling omissions. Only bare mention is made of Coover, Norman Mailer, Dan Jenkins, and Frederick Exley; and there is nothing about Ken Kesey, Don DeLillo, Peter Gent, or Leonard Gardner.[4] These authors have written the text of contemporary sports fiction. One suspects they are distasteful to Higgs because of their pessimism and their self-reflexive playfulness as well as their confrontation with professional sport. Higgs shies from discussing professionalism which, along with its opposite, free play, forms the marrow of any current study of sport in fiction. Indeed, in the one pro football novel that Higgs takes on, James Whitehead's *Joiner*, he purports to see Dallas Cowboy tackle Joiner as the "secret Christian," an ideal hero of excellence and concern, but a figure more at home with Arthur at the round table than with Tom Landry at the Cowboys' training camp.

Higgs is angry about the shallowness of modern sport. His ideal is an archaic Christian *gentillesse,* and he appears much happier in discussing Sir Philip Sidney and Rupert Brooke than Jack Keefe and Tom Buchanan. This ideal hero would temper strength with the knowledge of real value. Higgs fails to create an American historical or literary context for his study, however. Instead he favors a mythological schema to yield variants of the Christian gentleman, a grid now far removed from American cultural realities. Higgs combines one part myth, one part hectoring religiosity to set up his heroes of value: the above-mentioned Joiner, Louis Auchincloss's headmaster Frank Prescott in *The Rector of Justin,* Percy's Lancelot Lamar, and most of the "cripples" and "naturals" in American sports literature. What Higgs writes of Frank Prescott may stand for Higgs as well: "He uncompromisingly evaluates the character-shaping institutions he attends against the severe standard that the Hellenic-Christian synthesis suggests" (p. 52).[5]

Such austerity sends Higgs after strange gods, a quest not aided by his inelegant, overwrought discourse. Donatello in Hawthorne's *The Marble Faun* is "too faunish" to be a real hero (p. 16); the ideal of the "superman of strength and beauty died with Nietzsche" (p. 18), a rueful judgment at the end of this catastrophic century. Higgs reminds us that "to look good, however, is not to be either whole or holy" (p. 82), a phrase worthy of the Reverend Mr. Gantry himself. "For the most chilling words in American Literature" (p. 102), Higgs nominates a Willie Stark pragmatism in *All the King's Men;* a remark in *Rabbit, Run* "hits the unsuspecting reader like a thunderbolt" (p. 163); and in a Melvillean burst, he concludes about *Rabbit Redux,* "Ah Skeeter, Ah Humanity" (p. 166). In a single paragraph the reader learns that "it is not just a myth that blacks and Indians like to dance," that Jack London perpetuated "the myth of the young white God raised in the boonies," and that London "sought the Holy Grail all his life and had no more success than Monty Python" (p. 124).

Higgs's narrow views show at a number of junctures. He appears to take Robert Cohn's "hard, Jewish stubborn streak" (in Hemingway's words in *The Sun Also Rises*) at face value without explanation (p. 43). He seconds conventionalities in his own terminology. Thus the Apollonian Indo-Europeans are committed to doing and thinking while those dancing Dionysian-Adonics, "the black and the North American Indian" (p. 124) are characterized by being and feeling. Higgs dislikes spectators, professionals, alumni, "pretty boys," "naked beasts"; the list goes on.

Higgs gives the clearest statement of his own credo relatively early in the book:

> Over the years I have become more and more suspicious of strength, even when that strength is moderated by the professed spirit of sacrifice. I believe in the combination of strength and beauty or strength and wisdom—the ideal of God as revealed throughout the Old and New Testaments—but I do not believe that this ideal can ever be fully articulated or captured in art, though it can be suggested and approximated. The danger, though, is always mistaking the shadow for the substance, the symbol for the thing symbolized, creeds and codes for the Unknown and the Unknowable. [p. 68]

Higgs does not really trust athletics or the symbolic representation of them, a fact which suggests that he does not trust modern literature itself. Neither sport nor sports literature can approximate the ideals he professes, at the heart of which is a basic denial of art in a polarized relation with religion. Higgs is an apologist for a cluster of pieties well back beyond American athletes and their fictional representations. His book does not bridge the gap between his conservative sentiments and the achievements of sport in modern American literature.

Notes

1. F. Scott Fitzgerald, "The Bowl," *Saturday Evening Post*, 21 January 1928, p. 6.

2. "Sportsworld" as a total environment is defined by Robert Lipsyte, *Sportsworld* (New York: Quadrangle, 1975), pp. ix-xv.

3. See Wiley Lee Umphlett, *The Sporting Myth and the American Experience* (Lewisburg: Bucknell Univ. Press, 1975); Leverett T. Smith, Jr., *The American Dream and the National Game* (Bowling Green: Bowling Green Univ. Popular Press, 1975); Christian K. Messenger, *Sport and the Spirit of Play in American Fiction: Hawthorne to Faulkner* (New York: Columbia Univ. Press, 1981); Neil David Berman, *Playful Fictions and Fictional Players* (Port Washington, N.Y.: Kennikat Press, 1981); Michael Oriard, *Dreaming of Heroes: American Sports Fiction, 1868-1980* (Chicago: Nelson Hall, 1982).

4. In contrast, Berman in *Playful Fictions* deals solely with five novels, none of which are discussed by Higgs. They are Gardner, *Fat City*; Gent, *North Dallas Forty*; DeLillo, *End Zone*; Lawrence Shainberg, *One on One*; and Coover, *The Universal Baseball Association*.

5. Higgs appears to be seconding Matthew Arnold's concepts of Hellenism (spontaneity of consciousness) and Hebraism (strictness of conscience) formulated in *Culture and Anarchy* (1869).

Those Blessed Structures

Maurice English

John Hollander. *Rhyme's Reason: A Guide to English Verse.* New Haven: Yale University Press, 1981. 54 pp.

> Those blessed structures, plot and rhyme—
> Why are they no help to me now
> I want to make
> Something imagined, not recalled?
>
> "Day by Day," Robert Lowell

How to go beyond the praise that John Hollander's little book has already received for its joyful craftmanship, its sparkling display, like jewels spread out on a velvet cusion, of the riches of English prosody, and of the author's own bright inventiveness? Perhaps by stressing the fact that beyond delighting all readers, *Rhyme's Reason* can also serve to remind his fellow poets that these neglected resources are still ready for the taking.

But if they are indeed there for the taking, why are they not taken? Why is the very idea of poems written not (of course) in sestinas or in rime royal but in forms derived from practice in the writing of those and their companion structures an idea to which there is, here and now, no answer, or a derisive one?

Ours is an unlikely decade in which even to raise the question. In an appreciative review of a recent volume by Czeslaw Milocz, translated from the Polish but full of responses to his years in America, Leon Edel quoted the Nobel prize winner reminding us of the central question of American poetry: "Who am I?" Perhaps it would be truer to say, sampling the books of poetry which win prizes today, that the question, in the last decade and so far into this one, can no longer be asked.

The poetry being offered us, at least by poets in their twenties and thirties, is no longer the poetry of anxiety (the poetry of "Dream Songs," for example) or of alienation; it is, as other poets and critics have pointed out, a poetry of anomie, of a succession of disheartened Rimbauds, in a world grimmer than his with no escape by excess or perversion or violence—no Ethiopia where the concentration camps are not already receiving their local bards. The poetry of anxiety can still, as in Lowell's "Life Studies," seek an answer to the question "Who am I?" But the characteristic poets of these years seem to be asking, instead, like Lowell in his last book: "yet why not say what happened" — in a tone which does not imply that it truly matters.

I am not being presumptuous; I do not suggest that there are no contemporary poets to carry on the traditional American search for a personal poetic identity. The feminist poets do, the black poets do, other minority poets do; isolated, awkward, not-to-be labeled loners do; Ashbery, Kinnell, and their peers do. To the extent that they are substituting polemics for passion, those I have put in groups are keeping alive the poetry of anxiety or alienation; to the extent that they are embarked on voyages of self-discovery, any or all of these poets may be helping to revive what seems an increasingly dispirited art.

But, in the meantime, more and more poems are being published without rhythm, without even off-rhymes or internal rhymes; without any of the subtler resources deployed in *Rhyme's Reason* and others with which John Hollander is not concerned.

Two characteristics of contemporary poetry have seen sensibility and wit. But disillusion increasingly damps down the first and surrealism (substituting, wrote Wallace Stevens, invention for discovery) the second. The poems we are now being offered are not only without a strong beat, they are often written in stanzas that can readily be reduced to prose: "I went to parties to persuade myself it was useless preparing for emergencies, but people kept talking about the season's emptiness, the weather's delay. So I returned to my apartment, sold everything, and listened." This is a stanza from a recent prize-winning book of poetry, which I have copied out as prose. It is nicely phrased, and contains a note of ambiguity. It is the kind of passage that — all the more because of the absence of imagery — might just as well be found in a contemporary novel or short story. It lacks passion, or even feeling.

It lacks passion largely because it lacks rhythm. And, of course, the reverse of that statement is equally true.

Are there, then, no poems written without a marked rhythm, which yet succeed on their own terms? All of us have read such poems, occasionally it is even possible to recall them, or parts of them; there are moments of love, or rage, or anguish that force their way into the poet's voice, onto his page, in defiance of any regularity of meter. But it is true, I think, that they are rarely memorable, least of all at any length. And perhaps that is why so much contemporary poetry has sunk to a level of description, of (again) sensibility and wit which so seldom offer us the sound of transcendence. Or, if that is too much to ask for, then, simply, *relatedness*. (But that raises the specter of imagery again: so often a ghost on the page of the poets of the day.)

Perhaps this is a good point to step back for a larger view of the scene in which we are situated, and have been since early in our century. The dilemma of American poetry, and of modern poetry generally, began with a quest made inevitable, perhaps, by the collapse of traditional society and finely put by Milocz — the quest for an answer to "Who am I?" first undertaken by Whitman and Dickinson, with both of them deliberately renouncing the conventional prosody of their time, bringing the gains for which, in their cases, the losses are a price worth paying.

The gains and losses they imposed on the future of our poetry must concern us more today. Whitman, if not Dickinson, succeeded to a degree in the ambition of modern poets, to write a personal epic or myth. Dickinson if not Whitman, succeeded in creating an idiom in which the broken patterns of the past could be contained; and made the basis for recurring struggles between belief and disbelief — those struggles which, though with a flagging energy, continue in the work of some poets today, and are in a sense the theme of these remarks.

Explicitly in the one case, covertly in the other, Whitman and Dickinson gave body to views of their world whose intensity — even in its contradictions — compel our assent or our attention. Whitman did this in his greatest poems by curbing his compulsion to offer us catalogs and exhortations, even the biblical rhythms which animate much of his work. These typically give way at moments of exaltation to meters more central to English, the simplest, most eloquent and most memorable our language bestows on us:

> and from time to time
> Looked up in perfect silence at the stars
> * * * * *
> I was the man, I suffered, I was there.

As for Emily Dickinson, we all know how much her explorations have benefited the poets who came after her — but also how much those explorations were based on a recurrent going-from, and returning-to, the established beats and measures of the traditional lyric in

English. How readily her finest poems take their place in, and enrich, a great tradition, while releasing her successor poets to test their own freedom within it. No fault of hers, if that freedom is so often renounced for free verse — the stanzas so readily accommodated as prose paragraphs.

But what has happened, beyond our loss of faith in our own society, and its survival — assuming doubtfully that we can or should seek to go beyond these — to cause our poets (who testify for the rest of us) to renounce that element in poetry which so clearly makes it memorable — in both senses: easy to recall, and bearing a weight of meaning and emotion that separates it out from an also memorable jingle?

Poetry is memorable when it is passionate; and when it is passionate, typically through the course of its history in Europe, it expresses that passion in rhythm and often in rhyme. This means that it is written, as many older poets of this century came to believe, with the whole body. Not only the senses, but also the internal organs, whose rhythms play a role (in some sense a speaking role) in the creation of poems (and not, of course, of poems only, but all that, as the truly human, comes to consciousness).

"The body is the soul" — never more so than when the poet draws, however unconsciously, on all his inner being. The senses may be the least of all the parts of the-body-that-creates, except in being, with the brain, the link between the rhythms of the external world and the repetitions and responses of the world within us, to which the heartbeat gives witness for all the others that silently regulate our lives. Silently, except when they orchestrate the inner rhythms that emerge in the pulse and beat of all the arts, poetry among them, that make us human. Yet, but during these last decades, how faintly heard, if at all. The measures to which we move as social beings, in the ceremonies of custom, tradition, and the natural order, have been drowned out by the depersonalizing effects of technology and the prospect of annihilation — and these have reduced the poet to the sequence of anxiety, alienation, anomie.

Which brings us to a conclusion it was no part of Hollander's purpose to make, or even to imagine emerging from his text — but which may have a clarifying force for the reader of his little book who turns to contemplate the majority of the "lyric" poems written today, devoid of all or most of the devices he so skillfully deploys. But much worse, devoid of the spirit which animates even the slightest of his verses.

These devices, of course, are not needed for the contemporary poet. What is needed is the passion that evokes pattern — the patterns that fix our passions on the page. That passion, and those patterns, if they are rendered inaccessible by the disjunction between our world and our innermost selves, will not emerge from the examples in *Rhyme's Reason*, or any others of the sort. Who knows from what sources, if any, they may spring, what ultimate resistance or ultimate survival may lead many or few back ultimately to that commonality of meaning that makes a poem, and can make of a poem a myth? — that is, in this context, a statement that is somehow true for everyone who can hear it, wherever its rhythms are heard.

Two on the Aisle—
More or Less

John A. Williams

Tony Buttitta and Barry Witham. *Uncle Sam Presents: A Memoir of the Federal Theatre, 1935-1939*. Philadelphia: University of Pennsylvania Press, 1982. 249 pp.

E. Quita Craig. *Black Drama of the Federal Theatre Era: Beyond the Formal Horizons*. Amherst: University of Massachusetts Press, 1980. 239 pp.

It is sometimes a great satisfaction to discover that a few ideas in one book may well be elaborated and more fully explored in another, enlarging booking on the same topic. This is one of those times. The topic under discussion by E. Quita Craig and by Barry Witham and Tony Buttitta (who seems to be the person who wrote the book, since it is told in the Buttitta first person singular) is the Federal Theatre of the depression days. Buttitta outlines its successes and failures, its politics, some of its major figures and, above all, the advent, for the most part, of good inexpensive theater in the United States that sought both to enlighten and entertain some of the twenty-five million people who saw the Federal Theatre productions. Craig's perspective, by contrast, might loosely be called one of the black aesthetic. She examines the interior meanings of the black dramas that were produced and of those, although scheduled for production, that never were. Few of the names and plays she mentions will be recognized; not so with Buttitta's litany of stars and plays.

Reading the two books, one reflects on Wordsworth looking at royal England from "Calais Beach" in republican France and thinks of Arnold later looking from "Dover Beach" over the channel toward France, separated by time, personal experiences and, naturally, ideas. Buttitta writes about the Federal Theatre from an insider's perch. He was a functionary who, in his capacity as *Federal Magazine* and publicity writer, had contact with the director of the program, Hallie Flanagan, and with countless producers, directors, and actors. *Uncle Sam Presents* is memoir without much depth, but it does have value. The key point of departure that separates—and necessarily complements—the Buttitta and Craig books is stated by Craig: "The theatre of the thirties that was inhereited by the federal project was a product of white racism. It was a segregated affair that varied considerably in degree from city to city, and even from theatre to theatre" (p. 9).

Of course. The society of the thirties was redolent of what was to become known as racism. The history is immutable, persisting today, and will almost certainly be with us in the future, as contemporary theater reveals. But Craig is of West Indian heritage and also considerably younger than Buttitta. She looks down the tunnel of the past with much aggression and some digression as well. The former is well-placed, and the latter finally wends its way home in telling fashion.

This is not to say that both authors avoid political commentary. They do not. Buttitta's commentary is spiced with the tarnished mellowness of a soldier, dumped unceremoniously upon an invasion beach, who has somehow managed to survive. Craig missed the action but has captured analysis. She give credit where it is due, and this includes to Mrs. Flanagan who, battling the egos of showfolk on the one hand and the nervousness of politicians on the other, made the Federal Theatre work mightily for the four short years it existed. Both books in different ways represent a tribute to her. That there was pettiness among the minor officials goes without saying. There were baby witch hunts for Communist sympathizers, as Buttitta notes, and there was from the beginning congressional suspicion of the political nature and political power of the Federal Theatre and its fewer than 11,000 workers.

There was one-act experimental theatre; and there were classical, repertory, children's Negro youth, poetic, popular price, Negro, Anglo-Jewish, Yiddish and other ethnic components of the Federal Theatre; but it was the experimental "Living Newspaper," headed by Morris Watson and composed mainly of out-of-work newspeople, that first drew congressional wrath and censorship. Both books discuss *Ethiopia*—a production, with a minimum of props, about the Italian invasion of Ethiopia. Washington was afraid to antagonize Mussolini, and so the production was shelved. The playwright, Elmer Rice, head of the New York City project, resigned saying: "I don't think the decision to ban *Ethiopia* was made until Morris Watson and I outlined some of The Living Newspaper's future productions to Washington officials. Plays dealing with the Scottsboro case, sharecroppers, unemployment and relief problems" (p. 37).

Rice, according to Buttitta, supported the concept of a Federal Theatre, but the playwright complained that "it was constantly attacked in Congress as wasteful, immoral and Communistic. . . . Had funds been provided for continuance, upon an artistic basis divorced from unemployment relief, the foundation would have been laid for a nationwide theatrical structure that would have brought enlightenment and enjoyment to millions" (p. 37). The blame for banning *Ethiopia*, and later Marc Blitzstein's *The Cradle Will Rock*, is laid on the desk of David Niles, the WPA information officer. Blitzstein told Buttitta: "Some say [*The Cradle Will Rock*] is proletarian, but I say it's middle-class. Ordinary workers and average Americans being swallowed up by big business and industry. My 'stormbirds' sound like they're bringing a warning of the threat posed by home-grown dictators, political or industrial, and such fascist front groups as the Liberty League of America" (p. 133).

Cradle was influenced by the works of Brecht and Weill and was to have been directed by Orson Welles and produced by John Houseman, whose names are almost like stepping stones through *Uncle Sam Presents*. They presented *Macbeth* with an all-black cast, in the Lafayette Theatre in Harlem, which is, by the way, the only black production to receive much notice in Buttitta's book. It was the judgment of the veteran black actress Rose McClendon that blacks interested in theatre could learn most from Houseman and Welles, and she requested them for the Lafayette. *Conjur Man*, Buttitta tells us, was directed for the Lafayette by Joseph Losey. Craig does not mention the play in her book, nor the production of *Androcles and the Lion*, which was never presented. Buttitta was stationed in New York and therefore productions outside the city are not well covered in his book. In fairness, though, the centerpiece of the Federal Theatre was the New York project.

One of the hilarious sections of *Uncle Sam Presents* deals with Sinclair Lewis readying *It Can't Happen Here* for production. Although Lewis was unsure of himself and Dorothy Thompson told him that one draft of the play smelled, it played a combined total of 260 weeks, the equivalent of a five-year run on Broadway. The play was also given credit for reelecting Roosevelt. Broadway, by the way, was not all that pleased with the success of the Federal Theatre; it needed every paying customer it could get at Broadway prices and could not compete with Federal Theatre prices for plays like Eliot's *Murder in the Cathedral*.

Uncle Sam Presents is a good reference work, and it is valuable for no other reason than the author demonstrates that, when theatre is removed from its middle-class pedestal and returned to the people, it works as it has always done from the ancients to the nineteenth century. Theatre, exclusive of vaudeville, became an entertainment and perhaps an education for some of the people; but certainly not all. While the National Endowment for the Humanities and for the Arts, together with the respective state councils of the Arts, are invaluable, they cannot do what the Federal Theatre did. And it is obvious that they consider the Federal Theatre a fossil. Nevertheless, the arts have forever been underestimated as a political force in some U.S. circles, and overestimated in others. But they are a force.

E. Quita Craig understands this. She is a product of a generation for which the disguises no longer work. If Buttitta is willing to discuss political censorship, Craig is more than eager to square off with a more insidious censorship, based on racism no one admits to. In *Black Drama of the Federal Theatre Era*, Craig has no more to say about Rose McClendon than does Buttitta, so we are left to ponder what her actual role was in Lafayette Theatre. Of one thing we are sure—*Macbeth* seems to have been the major production by a black New York unit. It is the one that drew the most critical acclaim, but critics, as Craig points out, based their opinions on factors outside the black experience with predictably negative results.

During her digressions—intended to provide a compound education for those who may not know anything of black history and life, even at this late date—Craig provides a background for the Federal Theatre productions she does discuss. In New York perhaps the most successful was *The Trial of Dr. Beck*, which opened in Newark in 1937 before moving to Manhattan. Craig calls it a success; Buttitta does not mention it. We have to agree with Craig's assessment, for Hughes Allison was then commissioned to write a trilogy, the first of which was *Panyared* (kidnapped), which anticipated Haley's *Roots* (or Courlander's *The African*) by more than a quarter of a century. If we recall the impact of the book and especially the television production of *Roots*, we may begin to suspect how powerful Allison's play was. *Panyared* framed the eternal African myths and aspirations, but it was not produced, and there is no record as to whether Allison wrote the other two plays. Theodore Browne's *Natural Man* was produced in Seattle in 1937 and was revived in 1941 by the Negro Theatre, a surviving offshoot of the Federal Theatre. Built on the framework of John Henry, *Natural Man* was a departure from the white myth and an arrival at the concept of revolutionary hero.

Lest we miss the essential difference of a play about black people, written by whites, and a play about black people, written by blacks, Craig takes us on a tour, citing O'Neill's *Emperor Jones* and Paul Green's *Hymn to the Rising Sun* as examples of white stereotypical portrayals of "the brute Negro," while Browne's *Natural Man* portrays the black folk hero in whose soul the best of the racial characteristics are combined. "The brute Negro" stereotype was satirized by Langston Hughes' Suitcase Theatre production *Em-Fuehrer*. Craig draws additional comparisons between the work of Theodore Ward and his *Big White Fog*, not produced by the Federal Theatre, though Flanagan fought for it (the play advocated a merging of black and white to fend off bigotry), and *Return to Death*, which *was* produced by the Federal Theatre, and was written by Washington Porter and John Wexley, both of whom were white. *Black Empire* by Christine Ames and Clarke Painter, who were white, was produced in 1936. *Troubled Island*, dealing with the same island, Haiti, and about the same time period, the Haitian Rebellion against the French, was not produced by the Federal Theatre. Its author was Langston Hughes.

Many plays written by black writers were not produced, but it was not until 1974 that both their works and Federal Theatre records concerning them were uncovered in an old airplane hangar near Baltimore. Although listed as having been produced, none of Georgia Douglas Johnson's one-act plays ever were; Theodore Browne's *Go Down Moses* and *Liberty Defended*, by Abram Hill and John Silvera, are among many others that simply never made it to the boards. Craig insists that it was because they spoke too forcefully of black freedom.

It is not likely that all of these plays were superb or matched Craig's enthusiasm for the Hall Johnson *Run Little Chillun*, which was produced in Los Angeles in 1936. The lack of production represents a not unusual pattern of discrimination, aided and abetted then and now by producers and critics alike. Some of the unproduced plays, says Craig, were innovative in concept and structure above the norm for most Federal Theatre productions.[1] No wonder, then, that Black theatre people protested: "A brief, prepared in 1939 by the Negro Arts Committee of the Federal Theatre Council, specified a number of alleged acts of discrimination in employment practices, in producing adequate facilities for bringing black theatre to the black population, and in the selection of plays by black dramatists for production" (p. 61).

Combined, *Uncle Sam Presents* and *Black Drama of the Federal Theatre Era* provide a vision of the artistic struggles of the time. The vision, even in Buttitta's less aggressive book, is disturbing . Two levels of censorship are detailed—political and racial—and they are markers of the distance we have traveled, not only in theatre, but as a nation. That we have not traveled very far is the message. But these books are good records to have around, just in case one day we do decide to kick old, murderous habits.

Note

1. Craig's opinion here is echoed by James Vernon Hatch in *Black Image on the American Stage: A Bibliography of Plays and Musicals, 1770-1970* (New York: DBS Publications, 1970).

"To Make Yee All Blithe":
Recent Studies in John Skelton

Ian Lancashire

Robert S. Kinsman. *John Skelton, Early Tudor Laureate: An Annotated Bibliography c. 1488-1977*. Boston: G. K. Hall, 1979. liii, 179 pp.

John Skelton. *Magnificence*. Ed. Paula Neuss. The Revels Plays. Manchester: Manchester University Press; Baltimore: Johns Hopkins University Press, 1980. xvi, 229 pp.

Skelton: The Critical Heritage. Ed. Anthony S. G. Edwards. London: Routledge & Kegan Paul, 1981. ix, 224 pp.

> Therefore I pray yee,
> Contentedly stay yee,
> And take no offending,
> But sit to the ending.
> Likewise I desire,
> Yea would not admire
> My rime so I shift.
> For this is my drift,
> So mought I well thriue,
> To make yee all blithe:
> But if ye once frowne,
> Poore Skelton goes downe,
> His labour and cost,
> He thinketh all lost,
> In tumbling of bookes
> Of Mary goe lookes.
> The Sheriffe with staues,
> With catchpoles and knaues,
> Are comming, I see,
> High time tis for mee
> To leaue off my babble
> And fond ribble rabble.

This, Anthony Munday's sketch of Skelton as leader, prologue, and Friar Tuck of a troupe of Robin Hood players in *The Downfall of Robert,*

Earl of Huntington (1601) is an anachronistic offshoot of the jesting-Skelton tradition of *Merie Tales*. Yet Munday's Skelton is perceptively close to life: professional entertainer, master of metrical shape-shifting, impolitic mocker of unjust authority, his own first critic, and somewhat embarrassed don. He does misbehave out of school. To some scholars his lapses have been regrettable, even unforgivable: grammarian William Lily, whom Skelton attacked, thought him "neither learned, nor a poet"; C. S. Lewis, who read Skelton for pleasure and came away cheered, terms him artless, amateur, "always in undress." Erasmus called the tutor of young Prince Henry "that incomparable light and ornament of British letters," rather too formal to ring true. The only scholars who saw nothing in Skelton for which to apologize were scholar-poets like himself: Spenser, Jonson, Wordsworth, Graves, Auden. These put scholarship in the context of professional entertainment, teaching in delighting, and came away cheered by a don who, as Munday perceived, worried about raising a frown in his audience where one was not intended.

Two books have just appeared to document the history of these two reputations, surviving concurrently through the four centuries since Skelton's death in 1529. Robert S. Kinsman draws on several decades of research during which he has dominated scholarship on the poet to produce the "formal bibliography" that C. S. Lewis regretted did not exist in 1954. Anthony S. G. Edwards, in the Critical Heritage series, contributes an edition of texts and excerpts from texts that form a companion volume to Kinsman's comprehensive guide and illustrate in detail the history of taste for Skelton's poetry.

Kinsman accurately describes his book as a "bibliographical guide and literary index." It is far more than a list of publications. In about 680 entries dating from 1488 to 1977, he exhaustively surveys, in chronological order, not only primary materials such as life records and editions but also critical commentaries in four languages, important anthology selections, geneaological notes, catalogue entries, and unpublished masters theses and doctoral dissertations. Kinsman describes his method of selection modestly as "calculated arbitrariness," but in fact he omits only minor remarks in general histories and anthologies having relatively brief and uninfluential excerpts of Skelton's works. Each entry is a titled bibliographic item with a commentary that summarizes the document or work and points out sources or errors. Kinsman brings wide knowledge to these compact entries; they frequently give new information as well as save hours of labor. The largest entry, for Skelton's *Workes* (1568), itemizes its contents and gives a succinct account of their probable compiler, John Stowe. A typical small entry, for Gordon Woodwin's "Commissary Court of Westminster," *N&Q*, 10th ser., 3 (1905), 125, draws attention, for the first time, to the discovery of the document recording William Mott's administration of Skelton's estate in 1529. The only important omission known to me is Henry R. Plomer's "An Inventory of Wynkyn de Worde's House 'The Sun in Fleet Street' in 1553," in *The Library*, 3d ser., 6 (1915), 233, where twelve copies of "thenterlude of magnifycence" are listed. Kinsman also omits two life records, a court payment of 1497 to the king's mother's poet, and a similar payment in 1502 to the duke of York's schoolmaster, but these do not name Skelton.[1]

A guide of this sort, if without convenient finding lists, would be frustrating to use, but Kinsman has well anticipated his readers' needs. His introduction defines the scope of his book and gives a critical overview of the periods of Skelton's reputation and of scholarship on him and his works. There are three indexes, one each for authors, subjects, and titles. The subject index, unusually, is organized under twenty-two headings, each one of which is a miniature bibliography. For example, the thirty-two items under "Biography: Life Records & Contemporary References," listed by record date, provide a brief life of the poet. "Criticism" has six subheadings: General; Influences on Skelton's Works; Linguistic and Philological; Prosodic; Techniques of Composition; and Specific Works and Passages. Other headings concern the dating of editions and poems, emendations, and even musical settings and recordings.

Anthony Edwards' careful edition of fifty-five critical documents, from Caxton's prologue to *Eneydos* (ca. 1490) up to C. S. Lewis' discussion in his Oxford History of English Literature volume (1954), can be used profitably with Kinsman's guide. Edwards' introduction also traces the development of Skelton's reputation as a touchstone for "fluctuations in literary taste from the sixteenth century through to our own age" (p. 1). Only two of Edwards' selections are without entries in Kinsman's guide: Hippolyte Taine's rude comments in his English literary history (1863; cf. Kinsman, p. xxv), and James Russell Lowell's brief mention of Skelton in his 1899 address to the Modern Language Association. Although Kinsman and Edwards acknowledge each other's assistance in their prefaces, Edwards has independently searched for materials. He mentions some additional references that are not in the guide: Alexander Barclay's "Contra Skeltonum," allusions to "Philip Sparrow" by George Gascoigne and Shakespeare, two versions of it by John Bartlet and Robert Herrick, and several more published notes by Graves (pp. 12, 40 nn. 66, 70). The combined breadth of coverage by Kinsman and Edwards is impressive. Edwards' volume also has three useful indexes: General; Comparisons with Skelton; and References to Specific Works.

Kinsman classifies the "basic shifts" in Skelton's reputation into nine periods, his own career (1488-1529) and eight succeeding blocks of time: (2) 1530-86, "Goodly Recognition yet Fading Laurels"; (3) 1589-1662, "Critical Division, Poetic and Dramatic Imitation, Installation as a Worthy"; (4) 1675-1737, "Notoriety Prevails"; (5) 1739-1831, "Antiquarian Recovery and Poetic Recrudescence"; (6) 1832-82, "Editorial Restoration"; (7) 1883-1915, "Skelton Considered as Dramatist and Satirist"; (8) 1916-33, "Skelton and the Modern Poets"; and (9) 1935-79, "Skelton and the Academic Critics." Edwards stresses opinion on Skelton as a poet, whereas Kinsman's approach touches, as well, Skelton as "literary object . . . about whom facts are to be collected" (p. xxvii). For these reasons I turn to a comparison of their findings.

Kinsman and Edwards agree that the key elements of Skelton's reputation are fully realized in 1529: at first his learned poetics (asserted by Erasmus in 1499, and later by Henry Bradshaw and Robert Whittinton), and from about 1509 his satiric power, his unruliness, and his eroticism (an attack initiated and sustained by Alexander Barclay). Edwards suggests that these two contrasting perceptions of Skelton may have been developed by the changing ways in which his texts were disseminated and by a resulting shift in their audience: at first in manuscript copies for an elite, close-knit courtly audience; and then, from about 1512, with Skelton's appointment as "orator regis," in printed editions of poems "which stress courtly attitudes or 'establishment' positions" for a broad audience. Possibly Skelton's own retirement from court from about 1504 to 1512, or an officially condoned sanction against him, may also explain aspects of his unfavorable reputation, publicized by Barclay in 1509 and 1514. In any event, Skelton's former pupil, Henry VIII, restored him to a position of favor that lasted until the anti-Wolsey poems, unpublished until after the deaths of Skelton and Wolsey, were written about 1521-1522.

Kinsman's next two periods are ones of action and reaction. In the sixty years after his death Skelton's achievement was honored by the publication of *Collyn Clout* and *Magnificence* in 1530-1531, and of *Workes* in 1568, and by sincere imitations by Spenser and others, but a growing movement to describe Skelton in a popular mythic fashion as the "pleasant, conceyted fellowe" whom William Webbe mentioned in 1586 and whom the *Merie Tales* of 1567 showed as a jester compromised the former laureate. George Puttenham's frank attack in 1589 led to widespread denigration; and even the poet's characterization as "witty curmudgeon" in the short fiction and popular plays of the Renaissance did not make for much respect. Kinsman, however, finds enough "high esteem" in imitations by Drayton and Jonson to describe the consensus at that time as a "Critical Division." Kinsman argues that Jonson "completely understands Skelton as poet, personality, satirist, and as collector's object" (p. xxx), that enough of *Magnificence* is in Jonson's *Cynthia's Revels* to represent serious emulation, and that Jonson's own Skeltonics and use of Skelton as persona in the masque *Fortunate Isles* (1624) are "popular *and* fitting." In contrast, Edwards' darker interpretation is that Jonson represents Skelton as a comic burlesque and dismisses the poet's verse form as lacking value. Edwards also explains Bale's sympathetic account of the poet as biased by their similar satiric bent, calls Churchyard's prefatory praise in *Workes* "disappointingly feeble," "a blurb, a puff," and sees Drayton's praise as "qualified" and "defensive" (pp. 10, 12, 15). For Kinsman, Skelton is a poet whom the seventeenth century inclines to neglect as time goes by, whereas Edwards sees a more calculated dismissing of Skelton as mere jester, like Scoggin, speaking a tedious and clumsy verse (pp. 13, 15).

In their comments on the next period, "Notoriety Prevails" (1675-1737), Kinsman and Edwards agree that Skelton is generally neglected or faintly damned by literary historians, but whereas Kinsman stresses the undoubted bad influence of Pope's "beastly Skelton," a reaction to a reprint of *Workes* in 1736, Edwards finds in the anonymous preface to a reprint of "Elynor Rumming" in 1718 some reason to see a new attitude. This preface praises Skelton for "just and natural Descriptions" and his admirers for their "extensive Fancy and just Relish," both signs of movement away from the "trivialized view" of Skelton's art in the Renaissance and from the neutral biographical criticism of the Restoration.

Kinsman breaks down the next 175 years into three periods. In 1739 Francis Blomefield's first two volumes of his Norfolk local history, which documented Skelton as rector of Diss, ushered in antiquarian research and book collecting by men like Thomas Tanner, William Herbert, and T. F. Dibdin, who sleuthed out new Skelton texts and biographical facts. This scholarly attention led in turn to critical attention. Thomas Warton's *History of English Poetry* fully, if also negatively, reviewed Skelton's satire and social commentary for an era that should have been receptive to it (but was not). The realization of what Wordsworth called Skelton's "demon in point of genius" was left to the Romantics, in particular Robert Southey. He enthusiastically called for a new edition of the complete works and this initiative begins the next period, of editorial restoration, marked by the still standard two-volume 1843 edition by Alexander Dyce, supplemented in 1882 by John Ashton's annotated facsimile of its only omission, "Ballade of the Scottyshe Kynge." Early Victorians like Isaac Disraeli and Elizabeth Barrett, though isolated in this respect, were caught up with this delight in Skelton, but the late nineteenth century and the next period, from 1883 to 1916 (when Robert Graves rediscovered him for modern poets), is characterized by scholarly activity: editing selections for anthologies, reediting *Magnificence* for the EETS, explicating some of the longer poems (notably John Berdan's work), and resurveying in a biobibliographical way the Skelton tradition (the work of the German scholars Friedrich Brie and Elise Bischoffberger).

Edwards' account of this era parallels Kinsman's but of course centers on the critical reception of Skelton's art. Warton's *History* marks the "beginning of modern Skelton criticism" because it attempts to control "instinctive prejudice" and to serve analysis and illustration (pp. 19-20). Edwards agrees that Southey's enthusiasm for Skelton's extraordinary value in representing the English language and British history at a crucial period has been "an important but largely unremarked feature" in the poet's critical rehabilitation, but instead of mining the romantics for all their (not always well-informed) comments, Edwards chooses to print Disraeli's essay of 1840 (pp. 93-98), the unsigned review of Dyce's edition in the *Quarterly Review* of 1844 (pp. 101-21), and the unsigned article on Skelton in the 1866 *Dublin University Magazine* (pp. 123-46). All three are important: Disraeli presents a rational basis for Skelton's satire, the *Quarterly* reviewer systematically answers the attacks of Pope and others, and the *Dublin* essayist describes the poet's excellences in a historical perspective. These works appear to exhaust critical reassessment of Skelton until the 1920s.

Kinsman marks 1935 as this century's breakpoint in Skelton

criticism. Until that date modern poets, including Graves, Richard Hughes, and Auden, embraced Skelton (as Eliot and others did Donne) "as a living writer in a vital metrical and satirical tradition" (p. xl). Afterwards, academic critics and scholars, notably William Nelson, H. L. R. Edwards, Ian Gordon, Maurice Pollet, Arthur Heiserman, and Stanley Fish, analyzed Skelton's poetry as an outgrowth of Henrician political, religious, and social life, searched for the roots of Skelton's biography and humanism, or undertook systematic generic and psychoaesthetic studies. Kinsman's synopses of academic articles and books up to 1977 are especially excellent. They show how resolutely university researchers have failed, as a group, to respond to the perceived "critical division" on the question of Skelton's merits, an issue that is central, Edwards shows, for the poets on the one hand and for C. S. Lewis on the other. To Graves, Skelton is "the dedicated poet"; to Edmund Blunden and Auden, a consummate metrist; and to both Auden and E. M. Forster, a professional entertainer and comic. Lewis sees Skelton as an amateur reveling in fortuitous art. Kinsman seems less aware than Edwards of this critical disagreement, but in turn Edwards neglects a critic looming large in Kinsman's mind, Robin Skelton, another poet-scholar who has made a sustained, orderly defense of his namesake as "The Master Poet . . . Conscious Craftsman" (1973), "omnicompetent, multi-lingual, and self-assertive." Read together, Kinsman and Edwards imply that a new critical synthesis of old divisions may be in hand.

Paula Neuss's welcome edition of *Magnificence* in the Revels Plays series will strengthen the case of Graves, Auden, and Robin Skelton against those persuaded by Lewis. The Revels *Magnificence* shows Skelton to be a totally professional writer, no "gifted amateur." Far from being an eccentric *jeu d'esprit*, by an artless personal genius, this play falls into three traditional dramatic subgenres; it is at once a moral interlude like *Mankind*, a debate proceeding to proof of a thesis, and a near tragic exemplum, skillfully woven together into what is probably the best-made play in English until Udall's *Ralph Roister Doister*. Inside an old dramatic moral competition between virtue (Measure) and vice (Liberty, unleashed by Fancy and others) for control of a type of mankind (Magnificence), Skelton develops a neoclassical argument on the theme "Measure is treasure," and then humanizes both the moral and prudential by superimposing on them the life of a medieval prince in the tradition of Lydgate's *Fall of Princes*. Neuss shows how well these three levels, allegorical, philosophical, and narrative, fall together into one under Skelton's hand. In doing so, she nicely bears out Glynne Wickham's view that almost all early English drama can be characterized as tragicomedy.

"John Skelton's reputation," Neuss beings, "is not that of a person we would expect to have written *Magnificence*." That is quite true, as Kinsman and Edwards well document, but we should not conclude as a result that Skelton did not write the play, but rather that those who formed his reputation never bothered to read the play. The unavailability of *Magnificence* from the mid-sixteenth century until 1843 must have contributed to early bias against Skelton. This is a point that neither Kinsman nor Edwards makes. Neuss admits "inconsistencies" in Skelton's combined learning and ribaldry, and in the alternation of his "formless Skeltonics" and more closely patterned poems, but she also stresses that these are part of his truly "Protean" energy in exploring and expanding the most fundamental resource of our literature, the English language itself. In reading Neuss's introduction, one's impression is precisely of a *Protean* Skelton disciplining himself to some very exacting demands, a doubling scheme requiring only five actors to play eighteen parts, a theme of "magnificence"—in its varied senses, from generosity to honor and impressive display—revealed on a bare hall floor with a "minimum of props" and "simple" costumes, and a timeless high seriousness nicely complemented by the desire to entertain people with "various games and bits of comic business" that justify themselves by paralleling, underlining, or parodying that very seriousness (as vices will do, to their own undoing). Skelton manages this wonderfully varied unity by a mastery of language, the common tool of most great authors. Skelton's English, for the understanding of which we have to thank not only Dyce but also F. M. Salter, moves from aureate, long-line verse for the virtues to slangy Skeltonics for the vices. With seeming ease, Skelton shifts tones, speech styles, and rhyme patterns, so that, for example, rime royal is at one point a vehicle for stately Measure, at another a borrowed trick of the vices' hypocrisy.

The special care taken in preserving and annotating Skelton's language is a special value of Neuss's edition. Although hers is the first critical edition to appear with modern spelling, she has sensibly modified usual Revels practice so as to retain the text's obsolete words, old rhymes, meter, and the semantically rich antiquated spellings—in short, to protect early Tudor English. The very pressure to consider modernization for each word must have sharpened her sensitivity to nuance. The edition has at least a thousand glosses for 2,568 lines, frequently with new illustrative parallels from contemporary works, and at least forty instances that supplement existing lexical or proverbial information in the *OED*, Tilley, and Whiting. To this care over Skelton's poetics the edition brings a delight in stage business and theatrical commentary: these are well represented in the commentary and by the staging section of the introduction.

My own preference in editing is for more conventional Revels editorial apparatus than is found in Neuss's edition. Less than a page, for example, is spent on textual criticism, the interpretation of the collation, the history of early printed copies, and the play's editorial tradition. There is, unhappily, no separate section on Skelton's sources (but see pp. 19-20). Kinsman's guide, which was published too late to be available to Neuss, leads one to Maurice Pollet's suggestion that *The Castell of Labour*, translated by Skelton's enemy Alexander Barclay and printed several times *ca.* 1503-1510, was an influence here, and to Gordon Kipling's argument that Skelton's idea of magnificence is less Aristotelian than Burgundian in origin. No one would have been better qualified than Neuss to comment on these things. Finally, Neuss makes no great use of the period's rich historical materials calendared in *Letters and Papers of the Reign of Henry VIII* (a single reference only at line 328n.) or listed in Conyers Read's bibliography of the Tudor period.

Possibly she has combed these materials thoroughly, with little to show, but what seem to me to be problems in the sections on dating and the satire of Wolsey suggest otherwise. Neuss dates *Magnificence* between 1515, when Wolsey had a mistress named Lark to whom Skelton seems to allude here, and 1523, when the play is mentioned in a printed edition of the *Garland of Laurel*. These are sensible limits, and indeed the first is Neuss's own discovery (although Wolsey and Lark were together by at least 1511). In narrowing the dates to about 1520-1522, on the basis of a proposed satire of Wolsey, instead of the traditionally accepted date of 1518 (proposed by Ramsay in the context of the disgrace of the king's "minions" then), Neuss uses an argument I do not follow. She clearly wishes to associate the play with Skelton's anti-Wolsey poems, *Parrot, Cloute,* and *Why Come*, written about 1521-1522 (although not printed until later). Three pieces of evidence are cited. In *Why Come* (1522) Skelton satirized Wolsey as one "To whose magnificence / Is all the Conflewence" and as a noble man who would fall from felicity by an overgreat will. Yet is this any reason to redate the play? If it were written in 1518 about Henry and his "minions" and not about Wolsey, Skelton would undoubtedly have applied the terms of his play anyway to his satirical subject in 1521-1522, Wolsey. Second, Neuss well argues that "when Abusion offers Magnificence a 'lusty lass' 'to acquaint you with carnal delectation' (1548) [and when] Magnificence cries 'I would hawk whilst my head did wark, / So I might hobby for such a lusty lark' (1564-1565)," Skelton is punning on the name of Wolsey's mistress Lark; and Neuss cites, in proof, Skelton's attack on Wolsey in *Cloute*, "Some say ye . . . hauke on hobby larkes, / And other wanton warkes, / Whan the nyght darkes." This is a very likely "local hit." Yet does one such allusion make Magnificence, and the vices, figures for Wolsey? Finally, Neuss cites some nonliterary attacks on Wolsey that stress his pride, extravagance, and political double-dealing, all of them features touched on in the play. Yet the fact remains that no vice in the play is plainly represented as a churchman (rather insistently Skelton depicts them as fools and fops) and that Magnificence is described repeatedly as a prince (once "prince royal") and noble man. Further, Magnificence compares himself to kings and terms himself best of barons and dukes (1499-1500). One piece of evidence actually points to a date several years before 1520, when Wolsey still had the trust of his king, the reputation of being a pillar of justice, and the love of his people. This is Fancy's reference to Folly's dog as "Grimbaldus greedy" (line 1156), a clear "hit" at John Baptist de Grimaldi, one of Henri VII's "promoters" who was disgraced in 1510 and was probably an object of caricature in a play of 1514, *Hick Scorner*.[2] It seems unlikely that Skelton would have been attacking Grimaldi in the early 1520s, for he was by that time restored to a position of trust. The allusion to Mistress Lark that Neuss has herself discovered, dating from 1511, points, like the Grimaldi reference, to a date in that decade.

 I will close with a comment on a final important contribution that this edition makes toward our understanding of *Magnificence*. Neuss draws on two allusions, the first a remark that "Measure is meet for a merchant's hall" (line 382), and the second a comic reference to eating sauce at the Taylors' Hall (line 1405), to suggest that the play was first performed in a London guild hall, probably that of the Merchant Taylors. The more one reads the play, the more persuasive this suggestion becomes. "Master Measure" (line 84), the play's virtue, is exactly what one would expect to find glorified in the company of *tailors*, and a variety of other allusions to clothes and fashions can be read as audience-pleasers in this way. Alone of all the companies, too, the Merchant Taylors enjoyed a king as presiding master; Henry VII was reputed to have sat as head of the guild at various hall feasts. "Magnificence" would be no stranger there. If Neuss is right, and *Magnificence* is not a play designed (like Medwall's *Nature* or anonymous household plays like *Youth*) for the court or a noble or royal sponsor, but for a professional playing troupe to act before a third party, Skelton's is our first surviving "commercial" play-text from the London area.

Notes

1. See H. L. R. Edwards' *Skelton* (London: Jonathan Cape, 1949), pp. 288–89.

2. See my *Two Tudor Interludes, Revels Plays* (Manchester: Manchester Univ. Press; Baltimore: Johns Hopkins Univ. Press, 1980), App. I. B.

Flannery O'Connor's *Via Extrema et Negativa*

Melvin J. Friedman

Frederick Asals. *Flannery O'Connor: The Imagination of Extremity*. Athens: University of Georgia Press, 1982. xi, 268 pp.

Writing about Flannery O'Connor continues to be an ongoing and healthy activity. More than a half-dozen books have appeared since 1980, bringing the total close to twenty-five. There have been disturbed rumblings of late about this proliferation of commentary on a writer who managed just two novels and thirty-one stories during her lifetime. Jerome Klinkowitz, assessing the situation for O'Connor and Walker Percy in the latest *American Literary Scholarship*, made these unencouraging remarks: "Criticism on O'Connor and Percy may be having a Greshman's [sic] Law effect on literary scholarship of the American South: the most useful work on each of them having been done several years ago, mediocre and repetitious criticism is smothering their reputations in banality and allowing precious little room for either genuinely new interpretations or for much consideration at all of other Southern writers"[1] Robert Coles's *Flannery O'Connor's South* receives the brunt of his attack. Coles did not fare well either in Joel Conarroe's review in *American Literature* which dismissed his effort as "a compendium of mistakes, misreadings, and missed opportunities."[2] Coles himself, who is genuinely appreciative of much of the commentary written about O'Connor, even questions at one point: "How much more critical attention can a couple of dozen stories and two quite slim novels, however brilliantly and originally crafted, manage to sustain—without some recognition from all of us that the time has come for a bit of a pause?"[3]

Frederick Asals enters the arena, then, at an unpropitious time for a new book on Flannery O'Connor. His arrival on the scene should cause no particular surprise as he has been writing about O'Connor since 1968; those essays of his that I have read, two of which are listed in his bibliography, are useful contributions to our understanding of the Georgia writer. Indeed his credentials were firmly established by the time *Flannery O'Connor: The Imagination of Extremity* arrived.

Even those who feel most keenly that a moratorium should be

declared will probably welcome Asals's book to the critical canon. Klinkowitz is not likely to view it as "mediocre and repetitious"; Conarroe is not likely to despair at the discomforting sight of errors and misreadings. Asals offers a knowing glance at all phases of O'Connor's oeuvre, and he studies in depth a handful of the stories and the two novels. His readings are invariably original and perceptive.

He sees in the fiction what Henry James once called a "rich passion . . . for extremes." Words like "polarities," "dualism," "dualistic imagination," "ironic duality," "tension of opposites" are part of Asals's special vocabulary; he views O'Connor's work as systematically avoiding a comfortable via media.

After an introductory chapter of definitions and presentations of critical strategies, Asals looks at the pre-*Wise Blood* stories and offers a full-scale analysis of *Wise Blood* itself. His discussion of her first novel parts company with the usual notions of its sacramental nature and its apprenticeship status in the O'Connor canon. He sees it as "an odd, angular book" (p. 24), much in debt to Poe, Nathanael West, and the existentialists, which goes its own disruptive "Manichean" way—almost in defiance of its author's widely advertised Catholicism. He insists on the special qualities of this first novel: "This sense of release, this aesthetic exuberance, exercised as that exuberance is on the frightening and the repellent, is not to be found elsewhere in O'Connor's fiction. It is one of the marks of the uniqueness of *Wise Blood*" (p. 62).

The extremities, grotesqueries, and naturalistic tensions of *Wise Blood* capture Asals's fancy. For him, it reads like "a naturalistic novel gone berserk" (p. 50). He reluctantly leaves it at the end of his first chapter, only to return to it intermittently through the remainder of his book. The novel becomes his yardstick for measuring "the gradual extension of her resources" (p. 67) in the later work.

Asals's next three chapters concentrate on a variety of the short stories. His chapter titles, "The Duality of Images," "The Double," and "The Aesthetics of Incongruity," point once again to O'Connor's consuming passion for polarities and tensions. Asals's strategy is to offer a close reading of a single story or a group of stories under each of these headings. Thus when treating the duality of images in her work, he concentrates on "The Artificial Nigger," which he sees as completely realizing "her mature sacramentalism, that double vision which seeks to use imagery both literally and symbolically" (p. 79). Asals ends by stressing the singular position this story occupies: "The result is the uniqueness of 'The Artificial Nigger' among O'Connor's works: a story that ends not in violent death or estrangement or in an apocalyptic vision but in human reconciliation and the promise of a genuine future in this world for the protagonists" (p. 90). Interestingly, another recent critic of O'Connor, Carol Shloss, also sees "The Artificial Nigger" as different from the rest of the fiction — but for somewhat different reasons. Shloss, who finds "heavy ambiguities" virtually everywhere in O'Connor's scenes of revelation, exempts the encounter that Mr. Head and Nelson have with the statue of the artificial Negro from this charge.[4]

In his chapter on the double, Asals suggests the vast literature on the subject created by Poe, Dostoevski, Conrad, and James and then proceeds to find their legacy in stories like "A View of the Woods," "Good Country People," and "The Comforts of Home." The first two are seen as using "the double motif in almost directly contrary ways" (p. 107). "The Comforts of Home," analyzed at considerable length, is a classic instance of the type, with Sarah Ham acting as Thomas's "instinctual double" (p. 113).

"A Good Man Is Hard to Find" receives most of the attention in the chapter on the aesthetics of incongruity. Asals explains at great length how the two halves of the story work so well together "despite the rather disparate action contained in each" (p. 149). We are reminded again and again in this chapter of "the distinctive tension of her work" (p. 159).

The fifth chapter is entirely devoted to *The Violent Bear It Away*. For Asals, this novel derives from the "lyric" tradition ("short, intense, symbolic works" [p. 161]) which carried from Poe's *Narrative of Arthur Gordon Pym* through West's *Miss Lonelyhearts*. Next he brilliantly juxtaposes *The Violent Bear It Away* with *Wise Blood*, concentrating on their differences. The following sentence puts the matter in sharp focus: "If *Wise Blood* takes the astringent comic perception, the episodic action, and the nonmimetic techniques of *Miss Lonelyhearts* and pushes them beyond West's boundaries, *The Violent Bear It Away*, with its dense concentration, exquisite sense of form and structure, and movement between the examination of inner struggle and dramatic scenes of confrontation, is reminiscent of the methods of Hawthorne's *The Scarlet Letter*" (p. 163). Asals finds the doublings and polarities in *The Violent Bear It Away* that he uncovered elsewhere in the fiction, but he also falls back heavily on triadic movements and motifs, with a helping hand from "Jung's psychic 'Trinity' " (p. 179). Before the chapter is finished, Northrop Frye and Joseph Campbell have joined Jung to put something of a strain on O'Connor's text. The mythic contours of the novel are more restrained, it seems to me, than Asals makes them out to be. This suggestive if not always convincing treatment of *The Violent Bear It Away* concludes with another glance at *Wise Blood* and the proposed mating of Hazel Motes and young Tarwater, "these dreadful mutilated heroes" (p. 196), to show how different the novels are from the stories.

The final chapter concentrates on the religious and prophetic dimensions of the work. This section has a different rhythm from the earlier parts; it overviews a variety of texts and does not offer close readings of any of them. Asals locates O'Connor in the ascetic tradition with the accompanying "dualities of an Augustinian cast of mind" (p. 206). He also sees the "deep strain of asceticism" as increasingly offering "a complement to her sacramentalism" (pp. 231-32).

This chapter-by-chapter glance at *Flannery O'Connor: The Imagination of Extremity* does not do justice to the subtleties of the book. It merely suggests the range of Asals's preoccupations and the formidable critical tools he brings to bear on O'Connor's work. Few other critics have gotten this close to the nerve center of her fiction. His readings of *Wise Blood* and a handful of the stories, like "The Comforts of Home" and "A Good Man Is Hard to Find," are as sensible as any I have seen.

Asals writes well and often manages elegant turns of phrase. He also displays a sense of humor, appropriate when dealing with a writer who possesses an "incorrigible sense of comedy" (p. 233). Foreign expressions, often in Latin, thread their way through his text. Once he comes up with *"imitatio Rayberi"* (p. 181), Latinizing the name of the schoolteacher in *The Violent Bear It Away* which nicely calls attention to the ludicrousness of Rayber's rigidly ordered world view. It is also perhaps Asals's nod to Flannery O'Connor's "aesthetics of incongruity."[5]

As a critic of O'Connor, Asals avoids the extremes he finds in her work and invariably walks a controlled via media. He eschews those "religious interpretations" of O'Connor's apologists which Josephine Hendin found so unpalatable in her study *The World of Flannery O'Connor*.[6] He also stays clear of the nay-sayers' positions of Hendin herself (for whom O'Connor was "the pure poet of the Misfit") and of Martha Stephens and Carol Shloss (who agonized respectively over tonal problems and ambiguities). His elaborate notes and extensive bibliography attest to his knowledge of the significant criticism; he seems to have read with care and discrimination virtually all of it, and occasionally he offers useful correctives.

Oddly enough, his bibliography does not list a single item published after 1979 and fails to mention Dorothy Tuck McFarland's tidy 1976 study *Flannery O'Connor*, which also addresses the Georgia writer's "fascination with incongruities."[7] Much of the post-1979 criticism, like James A. Grimshaw's *The Flannery O'Connor Companion* or Lorine M. Getz's *Flannery O'Connor: Her Life, Library and Book Reviews*, is scarcely worthy of Asals's attention, but he should certainly be aware of Coles's and Shloss's books and the major study by Marion Montgomery, *Why Flannery O'Connor Stayed Home*. Despite Klinkowitz's and Conarroe's negative reactions to Coles's *Flannery O'Connor's South*, I find it an indispensable work. Coles's pages on the Manichean and Gnostic heresies should certainly be of interest to a critic who labels *Wise Blood* "a 'Manichean' book" (p. 58) and who feels that its author "seems to have been an inveterate 'Manichean' " (p. 120). Besides, it is always a pleasure to read the wide-ranging discourse of Robert Coles—for the quality of his mind as well as the sharpness of his insights. Asals should no longer delay approaching this gifted social scientist, trained in psychiatry, who occasionally directs his talents toward literary criticism. Coles on O'Connor (or on Walker Percy, who is the subject of his *Walker Percy: An American Search*) offers something of the same sort of experience as Jung on Joyce's *Ulysses* or on Goethe's *Faust*. The books by Shloss and Montgomery have perhaps less to do with Asals's preoccupations, but they should certainly be noted in any bibliography concerned with Flannery O'Connor.

To end on the positive note which *Flannery O'Connor: The Imagination of Extremity* deserves: it is a careful, discriminating, original study. It does so many things—and does them so well—that maybe, in fact, little is left for future O'Connor critics.

Notes

1. Klinkowitz, "Fiction: The 1950s to the Present," in *American Literary Scholarship: An Annual/1980*, ed. J. Albert Robbins (Durham: Duke Univ. Press, 1982), p. 317.

2. *American Literature*, 53 (March 1981), 139. For a more positive view of *Flannery O'Connor's South*, see my "Robert Coles' South and Other Approaches to Flannery O'Connor" in the Fall 1982 *Southern Literary Journal*.

3. Coles, *Flannery O'Connor's South* (Baton Rouge: Louisiana State Univ. Press, 1980), p. xxiii.

4. Shloss, *Flannery O'Connor's Dark Comedies: The Limits of Inference* (Baton Rouge: Louisiana State Univ. Press, 1980), p. 123.

5. Latinizing Rayber's name made me think of a similar gesture on Samuel Beckett's part when he substituted Murphy for God in the following distorted quotation from Spinoza's *Ethics*: *"Amor intellectualis quo Murphy se ipsum amat"* (epigraph used before the sixth chapter of Beckett's *Murphy*). This fractured Latin, in which a stock Irish name appears in the midst of a solemn philosophical statement, produces rather a fine sense of incongruity.

6. A large number of her endnotes disparagingly begin "For a religious interpretation see" (Hendin, *The World of Flannery O'Connor* [Bloomington: Indiana Univ. Press, 1970], esp. pp. 167–72).

7. McFarland, *Flannery O'Connor*, Modern Literature Monographs (New York: Frederick Ungar, 1976), p. 6.

The Regensburg *Morte Arthure*

Mary Hamel

Karl Heinz Göller, ed. *The Alliterative* Morte Arthure: *A Reassessment of the Poem.* Arthurian Studies, II. Cambridge: D. S. Brewer, 1981. 186 pp.

I am told that, when participants in the Twelfth International Arthurian Congress arrived in Regensburg in the summer of 1979, they were greeted by schoolchildren bearing banners in praise of the Middle English alliterative poem *Morte Arthure.* Professor Karl Heinz Göller of the English faculty at the University of Regensburg, it seems, had taken up the cause of "this unique and previously neglected poem" (preface, facing p. 1). That advocacy was seen also in the fact that there were no fewer than four papers on the poem presented in the course of the Congress, all by members of the Regensburg English Department.[1] Those four papers, much revised, form the nucleus of the present collection: the contributions of Göller and Gleissner, Haas, and Ritzke-Rutherford. All but one of the other contributors to this volume were also present, and one infers that the collection was planned and contributions solicited there.[2] Hence the title of this review.

According to the editor's preface, the contributions "form an integrated whole"—a description that may put off the unwary reader if he begins at the beginning and lets first impressions guide him. The quality of scholarship, criticism, and writing in this group of essays varies from excellent to poor, and the editor's own contributions are not at the higher end of the scale, nor does his central thesis promise much illumination about the poem as a work of art. Fortunately there is a certain amount of inconsistency in what follows the opening essays, and it would be misleading to attempt to evaluate the book as an "integrated whole," an approach that might lead to the undervaluing of several important contributions. Thus in what follows here I will deal with the contributions one by one, reserving general comments for the conclusion.

But first a word about the poem's title: the editor has chosen as the text for these discussions the most recent edition, that of Valerie Krishna.[3] Krishna departs from all previous editions in applying the rather cumbersome title *The Alliterative Morte Arthure* to the poem, even though the manuscript itself twice calls it only "Morte Arthure," and this was probably the poet's own title.[4] We have managed for over a century to distinguish Malory's *Le Morte Darthur*, the stanzaic *Le Morte Arthur*, and the alliterative *Morte Arthure* by conventional spelling, and I see no reason to change now. In the following, I will use the brief reference *MA* in my own discussion, but Göller's preferred *AMA* appears in direct quotations from the book.

The first item in the collection is a translation by Kevin Crossley-Holland of lines 3218-3455 of the poem, titled "The Dream of the Wheel of Fortune" (p. 1-6). The translation of Middle English alliterative verse into modern English is always difficult; somehow rhymes are easier to find than modern alliterating synonyms, and the characteristic variation techniques of the alliterative style (including rare or difficult words) can create difficulties of interpretation. Crossley-Holland overcomes the first problem by giving meaning priority over verse-structure, and the result is somewhat more lightly alliterated than the original, while rhythms in a few lines lose the characteristic movement of the verse. The translation is therefore a little less poetic than Gardner's, but perhaps clearer and more accurate.[5] The second difficulty is not entirely overcome, however, and some misinterpretations of image and idea result: where Crossley-Holland has the lions of the opening scene licking their lips in "Longing to lap up the blood of my loyal knights" (line 3235), the poet showed lions "licking their tusks" (washing their faces in the manner of cats) *after* they had lapped up the blood of the knights; *þe froytez are theyn awen* in line 3403 means, not "you will reap the benefit," but "the revenues (of conquered France) are yours" to do with as you like; *that Gode schall reuenge* in line 3431 means, not "God will take revenge on him" (Godfrey of Bouillon), but "who will revenge God" in his conquest of Jerusalem.

There follows the first essay, Göller's "A Summary of Research" (pp. 7-14). The usefulness of this survey is limited; Göller's report of others' work is in most cases the briefest of references, which occasionally do not fairly report the arguments under discussion, and several important omissions demonstrate that, in spite of the number of unpublished dissertations cited, the survey is not comprehensive even of recent work. Thus, although Göller scolds "Anglo-Saxon critics" for overlooking "important research articles written in German" (pp. 8-9), he himself does not cite Hanspeter Schelp's detailed and informative explication of the poem's opening scenes.[6] Though Göller acknowledges that the question of Arthur's characterization and its relationship to the poem's structure is "particularly controversial" (p. 8), he cites neither the important 1975 study of George R. Keiser nor John Finlayson's earlier article on Arthur's battle with the giant of Mont-Saint-Michel, an important clue to the poet's intentions in the earlier part of the poem.[7]

Such weaknesses can perhaps be attributed in part to the writer's own thesis in this and the next article, his view that the poem's greatest importance is as a source "of historical facts . . . and . . . interpretations of the course of contemporary events" (pp. 13-14), whose "message" is a sermon against the French war. George R. Keiser's valuable criticism of the supposed specific parallels in the poem to events in the reign of Edward III is dismissed as "lopsided" (p. 13), and in the same paragraph Göller accuses John Barnie of inconsistency (on what grounds it is unclear) in expressing "doubts as to the historical source value" of the poem.[8] Yet Göller's discussion of the closely connected controversy over date reaches no explicit conclusion, and the vagueness about date in the following article suggests that this vital question is of no interest to him.

For the most part, indeed, this collection of brief references reaches no particular conclusions, and even the writer's attempts to define current major issues are lost amid the welter of lesser disputes. Nor are these issues always accurately stated: "Whereas the epic-heroic character of the *AMA* was emphasised by the older generation of critics, it is now, in concordance with Matthews, considered a medieval tragedy of fortune" (p. 8). Aside from the fact that John Finlayson, the current proponent of the "epic-heroic" view, is hardly of a generation older than Matthews, the implication that these two views are in conflict is an oversimplification.[9] Other important questions are simply ignored: though Göller cites the discovery of the Winchester Malory manuscript as making a new edition of *MA* "imperative" (p. 7), he mentions no reasons, and fails to notice that the Krishna edition, his chosen text, makes no use at all of this important textual information.

The article is less than coherent in structure; so far as I can determine, the sequence of topics runs something like this: editions, literary historians' evaluations, source studies, genre, characterization and structure, the two dreams, the figures Gawain and Mordred, humor and ambiguity, the theory of common authorship, meter, formulaic techniques, and date and historical allusions. The incoherence of the discussion is troublesome enough; a further irritation is the use of endnotes for references. This is a practice I am ordinarily comfortable with, but not when nearly every sentence ends with a reference number, and the names of the critics holding the views mentioned are all too often not included in the text. On the whole, both beginning and advanced students of *MA* are better served by Michael Foley's comprehensive bibliography for 1950–1975 in the *Chaucer Review*: Foley's annotations are clear, accurate, and objective.[10]

In view of the deficiencies of this initial survey chapter, one hesitates to suggest that the present collection might have been better served by an introduction that dealt with its actual contents. The preface tells us that the contributions form "an integrated whole," but it is difficult to discern the integration without the editor's guidance; all he tells us in this first essay is that he himself is more interested in the history the poem supposedly illustrates than in the poem itself as a work of art. No attempt is made to show the relevance of the essays that follow to the issues defined here, and one is left with the impression that the editor's view of the poem is shared by all contributors. Fortunately this is not true.

The second essay is "Reality versus Romance: A Reassessment of the *Alliterative Morte Arthure*" (pp. 15–29), written by Göller in cooperation with Reinhard Gleissner and Mary Mennicken. The fault of incoherence noted in the opening essay is redoubled here; the reason may be that this piece combines the two separate Arthurian Congress papers of Göller and Gleissner (the contribution of Mennicken is perhaps as research assistant or translator).[11] One can for this reason attempt only the most general of summaries: the first section appears to deal with genre, the second with historical allusions in the poem, the third with style, and the fourth with the poet's criticism of war. The first section opens with the most extraordinary definition of the poem's genre I have yet encountered: it runs roughly, "The poem is not like a romance; therefore it is an anti-romance." In Göller's words: "If it could at all be called a romance, it is one with a very peculiar twist to it. The *AMA* has outgrown its genre historically. While still clinging to its traditional framework, stock characters, and themes, it has become its own opposite. This is particularly evident in the light of its contemporary near relation, the so-called stanzaic *Morte Arthur*, with its love story and pure romance character. When compared with works of this kind, the *AMA* can and should be called an anti-romance"

(p. 15). The writer never tells *why* we should compare *MA* with "works of this kind"; he is apparently misled by the similarity of the titles to suppose a closer relationship between the two works than in fact exists. Later, "In the *AMA*, the opening boudoir scene of the stanzaic *Morte Arthur* (Arthur and Guinevere lie in bed, chatting about bygone adventures) has been replaced by the battlefield" (p. 16). Quite aside from the fact that *MA* opens, not on the battlefield, but on a splendid feasting scene, the writer seems to be unaware of what the poet's sources actually were (the Arthurian chronicles of Geoffrey of Monmouth, Robert Wace, and the latter's English translators).[12] Although the OF Vulgate prose romance *Mort Artu* (the source of the English stanzaic poem) had a considerable influence on certain details in the last third of *MA*, that influence is supplementary to the basic narrative structure derived from the chronicles; and that structure has no relationship to the "traditional framework, stock characters, and themes" of stereotyped romance.

John Finlayson has recently pointed out "the difficulties implicit in the ambiguity of the word 'romance,'" which can lead unwary critics to "the paradoxical position of stating that the work under discussion as 'romance' is not, in fact, a romance or 'romantic.' . . . To continue to take *romance* both as a comprehensive literary categorization *and* as a closely defined genre incorporating precise values and literary motifs is to invite continuing confusion in critical discussion of Middle English chivalric narratives."[13] It would appear that this is the trap into which Professor Göller has fallen.

In the second section Göller provides another kind of definition of the poem's genre: it is "a literary work which illustrates parallels and analogies to historical persons and events by means of an imaginary story (parable)" (p. 17). No previous critic, however historically oriented, has gone so far in reducing the poem's value entirely to its external references. Yet the rather random "historical analogies" Göller identifies do not begin to provide the focused commentary that the word *parable* implies. We are told, first, that Edward III founded a chivalric order but was accused by a hostile French chronicler of raping the Countess of Salisbury (an accusation which no other evidence supports); this apparently proves that chivalry was a sham. Then, Arthur has a council of war before deciding to confront the Romans on the field "just as English kings were accustomed to do" (p. 18). Because the Roman conquerors of Britain wrested tribute from the *com[m]ons* (line 274, quoted out of the context that emphasizes that the tribute was gained by force "in the absence of all men of arms"), Göller sees a reference to conflicts between the lower house of Parliament and the king over taxation and calls Arthur's remark "incriminating" (p. 18). I know of no medieval session of Parliament where the Commons insisted on paying tribute to a foreign power against the king's wishes. Then the writer refers to the often canvassed association of various royal ladies with Wallingford Castle in the fourteenth century—"a place which is not mentioned anywhere else in Arthurian literature" (p. 18); apparently he is not familiar with Chrétien's *Cligès*.[14] The lack of focus on a date in this assortment of references is perhaps due to Gleissner's rather broad concentration on "the late 14th and/or early 15th century" in his Arthurian Congress paper; the "historical allusions" cited range from the 1320s to 1400.[15]

Having dismissed Keiser's criticisms of George Neilson's "historical analogies" as "lopsided" in his first essay in the book, Göller now proceeds to ignore them. Great significance is seen in the fact that Charles of Blois (the *French* king's candidate for the Duchy of Brittany) was a distant cousin of Philippa of Hainault (whose husband Edward III supported Jean de Montfort); the writer makes no attempt to explain what this has to do with the rape-murder of the poem's young duchess of Brittany.[16] Göller then goes on to insist that the "revolutionary" use of bowmen at Crécy and the poem's battle of "Sessoyne" is key to their identification (as Keiser points out, *MA*'s bowmen are from Wace's *Brut*).[17] This sequence is then capped by the writer's transformation of William Matthews's report of a *rumored* Danish invasion in 1363 to actual "Danish plunderers who ravaged the English coast during the Hundred Years War" (p. 19); the Danes in *MA* are also taken from Wace.[18] Historical accuracy is evidently not among the writer's concerns.

In the next paragraph, Arthur's granting of a dower to the duchess of Lorraine after her husband's capture is seen as "a common practice of the time" (p. 20). This may well be true.[19] But the "evidence" Göller adduces is the granting to Isabella de Coucy of her husband's estates after he "went over to the French king in 1379" (p. 20). Isabella de Coucy was Edward III's daughter and Richard II's aunt—hardly a comparable case.

Apparently Göller's purpose up to this point is merely to show that "there is a close relationship between historical persons and events and their reflections in the poem" (p. 20). Since the writer disclaims any attempt to read the poem "as a *roman à clef*" (p. 17), the reflection remains murky; no one would deny, after all, that *MA* in some sort reflects its times. Contemporary criticism of wasteful feasting and showy dress, for example, is found at the end of the century as well as earlier (see Chaucer's *Parson's Tale*), yet nobles and royals continued to feast and dress richly.

Göller's real point is found at the beginning of the third section: "In spite of what has been said by Benson concerning the relationship of romance and reality in the fifteenth century, it is safe to say that the idea of warfare based on chivalric laws was recognized as outdated by the fourteenth century" (p. 21). This flat denial of a reputable scholar's carefully marshaled evidence also implicitly dismisses John Barnie's discussion of the real force of chivalry in the fourteenth-century wars and shows no knowledge of M. H. Keen's standard work on the laws of war as they operated throughout the Hundred Years' War.[20] One is forced to conclude that not only is Göller not much interested in poetry, he is not much interested in history either.

The writer then turns to *MA*'s style, in an apparent attempt to show that the poet used several aspects of style as a vehicle for war-criticism. Unfortunately, Göller seems as little interested in the poem's stylistic tradition as he is in poetry or history. Some of his pronouncements: the *MA*-poet's "use of the alliterative long line . . . differs from that found in other *Arthurian* works of the alliterative revival" (p. 22); how it differs he leaves us to guess. In any case, "The alliterative long line is an unsuitable vehicle for the gentler tone of the typical romance" (so much for *Gawain and the Green Knight*). "The author has abandoned the *aventure* structure which is an essential feature of other Arthurian prose and verse romances" (p. 22) — but which is not found in the poet's Arthurian-chronicle sources. "Obscenity was taboo in medieval courtly literature" (p. 22) — so much for Jean de Meun or Chaucer. But in any case, no one has ever called *MA* a "courtly" poem in the sense Göller seems to mean.

One may well ask how obscenity enters the picture. Göller characterizes a brutal rape (of the duchess of Brittany) and genital mutilation (of the giant-rapist) as "bawdy" (p. 22), and then goes on to tell us that "the author seems to have been mildly obsessed with wounds below the belt" (p. 23). For, in addition to the giant's wound, the viscount of Rome is killed by a wound nine inches *above* the breeches-opening (the belt-buckle, as it were), and a purely scribal error in line 2112 gives us a "Sir Ienitall." The obsession is not the poet's.

This is not to say that the more serious obscenity of violence does not enter the poem. Yet to say that "the terrible descriptions of death are not to be found in the sources or forerunners of the *AMA*" (p. 24) is to misstate the facts. If a blow spilling the guts of "Feraunt's kinsman" is "revolting and disgusting" (p. 23), the guts of Sir Ferumbras had earlier been spilled by Oliver in one direct source; if the vertical or horizontal sundering of the human torso seems "farcical" to Göller (p. 24), it is nevertheless paralleled in Layamon and the alliterative *Destruction of Troy* (not to mention chansons de geste); and the devastation of Metz in lines 3036-43 ought to be compared to the effect of the siege engines on the people of Jerusalem in the alliterative *Siege of Jerusalem*, another direct source and one far more gruesome in its gory details.[21] The writer simply seems to be unfamiliar with the conventions of late medieval war poems; again the problem of genre confusion appears.

In the fourth section of the paper Göller concludes, "There can be no doubt that the poet is saying that *every* war is unjust" (p. 26). Yet the example he gives, Gawain's accusation that the Romans have murdered noncombatants and clergy in their invasion of France (lines 1316-17), demonstrates the opposite — Arthur's responsibility as king to protect his people from such injury, and by war if necessary. There were indeed principled total pacifists among the Lollards at the end of the century, but the *MA*-poet was not among them (nor was Gower, whose war criticism is often cited in this sort of argument). Göller is finally reduced to a rather plaintive puzzlement that the poet, in spite of his condemnation of all war, still demonstrates "enthusiasm for the description of war" (p. 28). The poem has simply escaped him, as a historical document even more than as a work of art.

The third essay in the collection, Maureen Fries's "The Poem in the Tradition of Arthurian Literature" (pp. 30-43), is a valuable corrective to Göller's confusion over the poem's sources and place in literary tradition. Beginning with the earliest references to Arthur in Celtic sources, Fries sketches in rapidly the "chronicle tradition" as embodied in Geoffrey of Monmouth's *Historia Regum Britanniae*, Robert Wace's *Roman de Brut*, and Layamon's *Brut*, with particular emphasis on aspects of these works that were influential for *MA*, which derived its plot-structure from this tradition. Fries then turns to possible influences from the prose romances of the OF Vulgate Cycle, particularly the *Mort Artu*. She concludes with a discussion of the poet's "most admirable innovation in the Arthurian tradition *per se*," his "handling of characterization" (p. 39). Recognizing that the themes and structures of the Vulgate romance tradition were "part of a very different story which the *AMA* poet knew but did not choose to tell" (p. 40), Fries notes the poet's treatment of Lancelot as a minor character and his development of the chronicle rather than the romance characterization of Guinevere. More important innovations are the sympathetic treatment of Mordred, the emphasis on Gawain as "warrior-nephew" (p. 41), and the unique characterization of the central hero as "the most human of Arthurs" (p. 42) in his quick anger, his deep grief, his humor, and his believable drive for power. Thus Fries's emphasis finally is on the poet's originality and creative freedom in dealing with a wide variety of often incompatible sources.

Fries does not attempt to present a complete account of the poet's sources, a task beyond the scope of a brief essay; many of these were in any case non-Arthurian and beyond her intended focus. But within these limitations, her essay is a reliable and enlightening guide to the place of *MA* within the Arthurian tradition — or rather between the two traditions of chronicle and romance. Thus if one notes that her emphasis lies perhaps too heavily on the romance side (*Mort Artu* having been a supplementary rather than central source) and that, perhaps as a result, she tends to overstate the poet's sympathy for Mordred (see the variety of terms of abuse he uses in the last thousand lines of the poem), these are relatively minor matters.

The next essay, Jutta Wurster's "The Audience" (pp. 44-56), is a painstaking, scholarly, and well-balanced account of the current consensus regarding the audience for Alliterative Revival poetry generally and *MA* in particular. Wurster begins her discussion with a summary of the "extrinsic" evidence for audience: the arguments of Hulbert, Salter, and Turville-Petre as to whether those of noble status were interested in alliterative verse;[22] the evidence of the manuscript and the poem's language (as well as of other alliterative manuscripts and texts); and the evidence of surviving booklists and noble manuscripts. A well-balanced account of the poet as revealed in his work ("intrinsic evidence") follows — his sympathies, his education and experience, his "commitment to Christian values" and "awareness of the difficulties involved in being a knight in the war-torn world of the fourteenth century" (p. 55). Although the article breaks no really new ground, it provides a lucid, intelligent, and comprehensive view of a still controversial question.

There follows Manfred Markus's "The Language and Style: The

Paradox of Heroic Poetry" (pp. 57–69). This essay does not begin reassuringly: "Whereas the London area had experienced smooth cultural development during the Middle English period and had had more time to come to terms with the foreign *superstratum*, particularly the language, the 'provinces' in the Midlands and the North must have been under the impact of culture shock in the fourteenth century, realising that their English, influenced by Norse, was quite different from the Gallicised southern standard" (p. 57). Thus we are given notice not only that Markus has done no actual research into the linguistic situation in England in the fourteenth century but that he is unfamiliar with the heavily "Gallicised" lexicon of Alliterative Revival verse in general and *MA* in particular. Indeed, the *MA*-poet's unique or rare borrowings from the French are so notable that William Matthews was once led to suppose his lexicon was evidence of a "lost French source."[23]

There is no substitute in stylistic study for the intimate acquaintance with the actual text in question; but Markus's generalizations about *MA* reveal little about the peculiar characteristics of this poem's style as distinguished from that of other poems of the Revival, and his primary research appears to have been done in previous writers' studies of *Sir Gawain*, with dependence on the generalizations of Boroff, Benson and others about late medieval alliterative style.[24] Thus there is little that is new in the discovery that the *MA*-poet used synonyms and periphrases for variation, as all Revival poets did, or that many of these synonyms were taken from a traditional stock lexicon, or that like other alliterative poets he often turned adjectives into substantives (these topics form the substance of Markus's examination of "lexis"). One might be surprised to find, however, that because Arthur is not called "the Conqueror" in the last thousand lines of the poem he gradually "loses his identity" (p. 59), an entirely modern concept, and one is surprised to be told that "the periphrastic designation of God, though common in the alliterative tradition . . . is totally avoided in the *AMA*" (p. 59). This is simply not true; see lines 1303, 3217, 3806, and 3808.

When Markus turns briefly to metrical and formulaic style, he shows again that he has not studied the poem itself but rather has depended on the generalizations of others: "What urged the author of the *AMA* to be particularly conservative in his use of the alliterative pattern may well have been a strong sense of a normative structure needed to bring home his art of subtle variation" (p. 62). The generalization about the poet's conservatism is taken from Krishna, who means by it that the poem has a greater number of traditional *variations* from the standard *a a : a x* line than other poems of its time.[25] A much smaller proportion of the poem's lines, then, have a "normative structure" than truly conservative poems like *The Destruction of Troy*.[26] Neither Krishna nor Markus takes into account the poet's extraordinary use of lines grouped by the same alliterating sound (a topic Markus dismisses in a phrase as one among a number of variations).

Further detailed discussion of a critic who takes it "for granted that many of the second half-lines do not make semantic sense in their contexts" (p. 63), who thinks the "brutality" of Arthur's fight with the giant of Mont-Saint-Michel "throw[s] a rather negative light on Arthur" instead of the giant (p. 64), or who finds irony in the poet's references to "our men" and "our king" in the final, tragic battles seems unnecessary. Markus's thesis that the poem expresses "late medieval relativism" by means of verbal ambiguity, contextual irony, and similar devices may well be true; but it will take a critic more familiar with the actual text to demonstrate these devices in *MA*.

A much better essay, Jean Ritzke-Rutherford's "Formulaic Microstructure: The Cluster" (pp. 70–82), systematizes concepts and formulaic elements more loosely dealt with (or dealt with without clear distinctions) in earlier writing on *MA* and fourteenth-century formulaic techniques. Ritzke-Rutherford provides clear definitions with examples for the *formula*, the (almost) unvarying half-line, the *formulaic system*, the half-line with some unvarying elements and one stressed element that varies with the alliteration of the line, and the *cluster*, the stock collocation (without fixed form) of certain alliterating words, formulas, and formulaic systems by means of which the long line is constructed. The last is a rather new concept (based in part on the earlier work of Finlayson and others), and Ritzke-Rutherford devotes most of the article to its definition and exemplification, partly by comparison to clusters found in Old English verse and Layamon. The provision of clear and related but distinct terms that results should prove of great value in future discussions of formulaic techniques, not only in *MA* but in other Middle English alliterative poems. In addition, the suggestion of continuity in the persistence of certain clusters from Old English is an important contribution to that debate and may help explain the "archaic" synonyms for which the Revival lexicon is famous.

But there are provisos. The most remarkable feature of the *MA*-poet's style is his use of the same alliterating sound through two, three, or more consecutive lines; the great majority of his verses are so grouped. Ritzke-Rutherford attempts to explain this as a result of "clusters that have grown in the course of their use within a particular tradition," with *MA* "one of the late products of such a development" (p. 79). One could wish that some attempt had been made within the article to *place MA* within its own Middle English tradition; a valuable model is Finlayson's comparison of the poem's stock collections with those of *Destruction of Troy* and *Wars of Alexander*.[27] Such comparisons suggest that the use of grouped lines in *MA* is the result of a conscious stylistic choice, one that, rather than drawing on a *previous* expansion of traditional clusters, required the poet's own deliberate expansion of them by the addition of new words and the invention of new formulas, as well as by the occasional combination of previously independent clusters from different notion-spheres. The examples Ritzke-Rutherford presents on pp. 78-79 involving "the essential idea of battle with a giant" provide useful evidence. Among them we find the new formula *on a jamby stede* (lines 373, 2894), with the key word *jamby* a unique borrowing from the French; the collocation, unparalleled elsewhere, of "giant" with "Genoa / Genoese" and "jag" v.; and the core cluster "joust, jolly, gentle," etc., as evidenced by other Revival texts — "Justed full jolilé þise gentyle knyʒtes" (*Sir Gawain*, line 42), "So iolilé þes gentil iusted on were" (*Awntyrs of Arthure*, line 502), "For-justes þe jolieste: with joyn[yng] of werr'" (*Seige Jerus.*, line 538), "And alle hise gentyle forjusted on Jerico playnes" (*Cleanness*, line 1216)[28] — combined with the stock collocation of "giant" and "engender" in nonbattle contexts (*Cleanness*, line 272, *Piers Plowman A* 7.219; cf. *MA*, lines 612, 843, 2111). The *MA*-poet's grouped lines, in short, provide an unparalleled opportunity for the study of the extended cluster, but — as Finlayson recognized — the extension must be acknowledged as the poet's own.

According to Ritzke-Rutherford, "The words for 'giant,' 'jolly,' 'gentle,' 'jagged,' and 'genital' recur as a group some fourteen times in the poem" (p. 78). This is a very misleading way of stating the case; "giant" occurs in alliterating position some fourteen times (including three lines not cited here, 559, 825, and 843) and is collocated with "jolly" three times, with "gentle" seven times, with "jagged" five times, and with "genitals" *once* (line 1123). Yet she goes on to say, "The force of word association is so strong that it even leads to the coining of a highly unusual and hitherto unexplained name — that of Sir Ienitalle in [line 2112]" (p. 78); thus "Krishna's emendation to

Sir Ionathal is unnecessary" (p. 79n.). This, I submit, is utter nonsense. Ritzke-Rutherford's previous work is in Old English.[29] Perhaps for this reason one could not expect her to be aware of the close similarity between *o* and *e* in fifteenth-century cursive script, or perhaps even of the well-attested scribal tendency to corruption of spelling by the attraction of neighboring words (*gentill* in the second half-line). Nor, since she has not studied the poet's use of sources, ought one perhaps to expect her to acknowledge the presence of a "Ionathal dorocestrensis" in this battle in Geoffrey's *Historia*.[30] But surely a student of formulaic techniques must be aware that not all words that alliterate on the same sound are *ipso facto* members of a cluster (see "Jerico" in the line from *Cleanness* quoted above). *Genitales* occurs in line 1123 for a specific contextual reason: as the giant, in raping the young Duchess, had "slit her to the navel" (line 979), so Arthur, splitting the giant's genitals with his blow, enacts precise retributive justice. The scribal error *Ienitall* in line 2112 is quite unrelated.

The next article is also by Ritzke-Rutherford: "Formulaic Macrostructure: The Theme of Battle" (pp. 83-95). Her attempt to systematize the discussion of larger formulaic elements is not so successful as for "microstructure"; definitions of the *motif*, the *type-scene* and the *theme* are set forth in the previous article (p.75), but are assumed here without real exemplification, and the relationships between them remain unclear. Her focus in the first part of this article is on the "mass battle" type-scene as it appears in *MA*, which she breaks down into twelve more or less consecutive elements, beginning with "challenge or message" and ending with "victory and aftermath" (p. 85). No attempt is made, however, to prove its applicability to all such battles in the poem. The categories are very broadly defined, but even so not every category appears in every mass battle in *MA*; there is no formal array of troops in the suddenly provoked first battle with the Romans (line 1352 ff.), no "dawn or a flashing light or a *locus amoenus*" in the poem's last battle by the Tamar, nor in the forayers' battle with the duke of Lorraine, no "challenge or message" to begin the Battle of "Sessoyne" (lines 1973 ff.), unless one counts the initial challenge at Arthur's New Year's feast of which the battle is the culmination. If such variations are possible without weakening the concept of the "type-scene," then Ritzke-Rutherford's comment that "the pattern found in *AMA* . . . differs widely from that found in other Middle English alliterative poems" (p. 85) is simply untrue, as examples from *Destruction of Troy, Siege of Jerusalem*, and the like would amply demonstrate. Indeed, comparison of these categories to Froissart's account of the battle of Poitiers or Nájera shows the same general pattern. What is in question, perhaps, is not a formulaic pattern unique to traditional heroic verse, but, first, a reflection of real wars (which involved actual messages or challenges, councils, battle preparations, dawns, exhortations, blows, wounds, etc.) and, second, a recognized rhetorical topos based on this reality. The rhetorical (rather than traditional-alliterative) basis of *MA*'s battle scenes is confirmed by the simple fact that most or all of these elements are found in battle descriptions in Geoffrey of Monmouth and the poet's other chronicle sources. Larry D. Benson has pointed out the close alliance between Middle English alliterative style and formal rhetoric, and this alliance is constantly exemplified in *MA*.[31]

If the type-scene "mass battle" arises from the rhetorical rather than the specifically alliterative tradition, it is nonetheless a valuable concept as a key to the poem's larger structures, as Ritzke-Rutherford demonstrates in the later pages of her paper (pp. 91–95). Her discovery of symmetrical "doubling and parallelism" at a number of points illuminates the poet's structural artistry, and though her analysis only begins to scratch the surface of the poem's elaborate patterning, it is a surface that has long needed to be scratched. Ritzke-Rutherford's conclusion that *MA* in this respect "recalls the intricate structures of the best poems of the Ricardian era" (p. 95) is a vital step forward in the understanding of *MA*'s place in the Alliterative Revival. Also intriguing and plausible is the suggestion that the structure of the whole may have been influenced by the poet's acquaintance with Seneca, possibly in Italian translation.

Nevertheless, this essay is again marred by some perverse readings and a number of inaccuracies. Corresponding to the "genital" nonsense of the previous piece, for example, is Ritzke-Rutherford's contention that the manuscript reading *slaughte of þe pople* in line 2675 must be translated "slaughter of the people" (and of course not emended), for it describes knights that are "weary and sated" with this activity (p. 89). Since the knights in question have been doing nothing more than riding all night across country, and the "people" in question are those "that sang . . . in the bright groves" (line 2676)—that is, the birds—this argument can hold no force.[32] There is a certain insistence here as elsewhere in the collection on seeing criticism of Arthur and his knights in every aspect and detail of the poem. Thus the grotesquely evil giant of Saint Michael's Mount becomes grotesquely comic instead, the battle with him a piece of "buffoonery" (p. 87), and Arthur's stature is thereby lessened. It is perhaps significant that none among the four critics who write about this episode in this volume mentions the three girls who are the giant's captives, who are doomed to die from the giant's attentions, and who pray for Christ's help for their only hope of rescue when Arthur appears to be defeated (see lines 1029-32, 1132-39). John Finlayson's article on this battle, largely neglected by these contributors, remains with certain qualifications the most reliable guide to this episode.[33]

Karl Lippe's "Armorial Bearings and Their Meaning" (pp. 96-105) begins with a sometimes inaccurate quotation and translation of all passages in the poem that refer to or describe shields of arms. Noting that the poet often adds descriptive terms to the technical language of blazon, Lippe remarks, "The literary critic is, of course, prepared to overlook this neglect of the rules and to grant a good deal of license to the poet, who is forced by the alliterative long line to observe the necessary number of staves and stresses. The fact that descriptions of many of the shields of arms . . . are incomplete or inexact causes graver problems, and casts doubt on the heraldic competence of the author" (p. 99). Clearly we must not expect anything remarkable from Lippe in the way of literary criticism, in view of his disappointment that the poem is not a roll of arms; perhaps he shares Professor Göller's interest in the poem as a source of historical facts and finds it wanting in this respect. But Lippe's discussion is not even particularly good heraldic criticism, as demonstrated by his analysis of the false shield adopted by Mordred in the last battle—"thre lyons all of whitte siluyre / Passande in purpre" (lines 4183-84). Somehow or other in Lippe's account this becomes "a red shield with silver lions on it" (p. 102); one must hope that Lippe's change of the field's tincture from purple to red (in heraldic language *gules*) is the result of mere negligence, for a red shield fits his argument rather better.[34]

That argument is simply that this blazon is "an allusion to the English royal shield" in which a change of metal (silver rather than gold) indicates cadency—that is, that Mordred is related by blood to Arthur and in fact is Arthur's bastard as in the Vulgate tradition; by adopting the shield, Mordred "openly declares his claim to the English throne" (p. 102). Other "evidence" for this persistent but perverse idea will be dealt with later, but first the heraldry.[35]

The "English royal shield" from 1340 on showed the "lions of England" only in the second and third quarters, Edward III having quartered his mother's royal French arms as part of his claim to the French throne. "England" itself (gules, three lions passant gardant in pale or) differs in more than one way from Mordred's blazon; not only in the change of *two* tinctures, but in the absence in the latter of the term *gardant* (facing the viewer), which in normal blazon means that the lions are facing forward. Nor are we told that Mordred's lions are "in pale" (arrayed in a vertical row); they might equally have been arrayed "two and one" (two side by side above a single lion centered below).

In any case, cadency in the English royal arms was never signified by the change of tincture; not only was that method of differencing relatively rare in England, but the royal arms were "a law unto themselves," and royal marks of cadency are well documented from the thirteenth century on, consisting of a label or a bordure (or in one case a bend).[36] Even the arms of royal bastards (e.g., the Beauforts) are well documented; none shows a change of tincture. Even if this were not so, the very "differencing" in Mordred's change of tinctures indicates an acknowledgement that he has *no* "claim to the throne"; such marks were the means of distinguishing cadet branches from senior branches, or the younger generation from the current holder of the title.[37]

All this is fun for the heraldry buff but finally irrelevant for *MA*. The royal arms *within the poem* are "gules, [three] crowns or, on a chief the Virgin and Child" (lines 3646-51), a blazon to which Mordred's false shield has no resemblance whatsoever, and thus cannot be seen as claiming either blood relationship or sovereignty.

Lippe presents other "evidence" that the poet means us to see Mordred as Arthur's bastard: the epithet "Malebranche," the phrase "fals fosterde foode," and Gawain's reference to "engendure" (p. 102). As Jan Jönsjö's recent *Middle English Nicknames* shows, the name "the Malebranche" applied to Mordred in lines 4062 and 4174 has nothing to do with illegitimacy (though this has been a common guess).[38] Jönsjö's gloss "bad or wicked child" is fully supported by parallel nicknames such as "Malenfaunt, Badson, Yvelcild," and the like, and the obverse "Bonenfaunt, Derson, Godsone," and the like. Among the classes whose nicknames Jönsjö records, there seems to have been little or no tendency to mark illegitimacy by nickname, and among the royalty and nobility there was little tendency to euphemism in these matters, "bastard" being nearly a title of honor when the father was of sufficient rank. Interpretation of "Malebranche" as "bastard" in fact blurs the poet's point: Mordred, as traitor, rebel, and oathbreaker, has betrayed his noble heritage and turned against the man who brought him up *as if* he were his own child (see lines 689-90). As I suggested in an earlier article, there may well be an overtone from Dante's *Inferno* here as well, since the Italian poet coincidentally calls the devils in his eighth circle *Malebranche*, "Evil-claws."[39]

"Fals fosterde foode" in line 3776 does not mean "perfidious bastard" but "false foster child." Krishna's gloss on *foode*, "bastard," is entirely unsupported by any definition or citation in the *MED* or *OED*; *foode* means simply "child" and is equivalent in root-meaning to the *nurree* of line 689. Gawain refers, in other words, not to Mordred's parentage but to his nurture and education in Arthur's court, which he has now betrayed.

"Engendure" is used in line 3743 with the extended meaning "creation, origination," and refers to the "treason" that Mordred has "timbered" (constructed, brought into being) in line 3742: "from such a begetting (of treason) little joy arises"; the sense is derived from the verb.[40] It is of course possible that on another level Gawain is referring to Mordred's own begetting; as Mordred's brother he would naturally wish heartily to deny relationship to the traitor, even if it meant slandering his mother's chastity. But if bastardy is implied, nothing is said *or* implied about who Mordred's father might have been; that is left for the poet himself, who calls him the "son of a churl" in line 4181, as the traitor shows his lack of nobility by his cowardly disguise in the change of arms.

I have gone on at some length on this question in an effort to scotch this apparently unkillable snake once again. Mordred's relationship to Arthur in the poem, as in the poet's chronicle sources, is nothing more — and nothing less — than that of sister's son (line 689), the one among several in this nephew-crowded work whom Arthur made the mistake of trusting most. As for Mordred's false blazon, elsewhere in this collection Renate Haas shows considerably more insight when she associates its lions with those of Arthur's dream (p. 127), of which they are a fulfillment.

Jörg O. Fichte's "The Figure of Sir Gawain" (pp. 106-16) is the best piece in the collection, and I do not mean this as faint praise. Fichte focuses on Gawain's "greatly expanded role" (p. 106) in comparison to the poet's sources and the problem of interpretation that results, since two opposed valuations of the character are possible — the "Gawain enthusiasts," who praise his nobility and Christ-like sacrifice, and the "Gawain critics," who see him as a type of reckless and destructive *desmesure*. In attempting to resolve the opposition, Fichte turns first to the characterization presented by the poem, in which there is an evident discrepancy between the opinions and valuations expressed by other characters and Gawain's actual behavior as judged by common medieval norms. The behavior shows an incremental pattern of pride and anger, one which indeed attributes to Gawain "a superabundance of fortitude" but which also progressively demonstrates his lack of "any degree of prudence" (p. 109). The destructive effects of *fortitudo* without *sapientia* are most tellingly demonstrated by Gawain's failure of leadership responsibility both in the "Foray" battle near Metz and in his landing to face Mordred's vast army at Southampton with only his personal retinue. The culmination of this development is seen in Gawain's "berserker" behavior shortly before his death, in which we see "*ira* turning into *furor*" (p. 111); this progressive "fall from reason" (p. 112) results in the character's victimization by his own sins of arrogance and wrath. Thus even the "limited praise" voiced by the poet in the first lament for Gawain is undercut, and the eulogies of Mordred and Arthur that follow "are projections rather than statements of fact and should not be taken as the poet's sentiments" (p. 112).

Fichte next traces the structural parallel between the gradual corruption of Arthur's character in the course of his rise to power and "the ascendancy of Gawain" (p. 113). In particular, after Gawain's death we see Arthur's motives and actions exactly paralleling the hero's—but only to a certain point. Each character has a moment when he recognizes that he has led his men to destruction by his own actions, but whereas this realization drives Gawain to madness as he "sinks to the level of an irrational beast," the king "rises in moral stature" as he expiates his guilt in the destruction of Mordred, and ends his life reconciled with God (p. 114).

Fichte concludes with a brief overview of the poem's religious frame and "central moral argument" (p. 115), the overcoming of reason and grace by pride which leads inevitably to "temporal fall," while still leaving open the possibility of salvation by confession and atonement. Almost alone among the contributors to this book, Fichte seems to realize that the poet's purpose in this work lies deeper than the simple condemnation of war in and for itself. His admirable grasp of structure and character development, his informed and balanced awareness of the moral framework within which the poet was working, and his close attention to the text (with only a few minor errors, e.g., the all-too-common supposition that the speaker of lines 3049-53 is the countess of Crasyn, not the duchess of Lorraine, p. 113) make this essay an essential one for future students of *MA*.

Next is Renate Haas, "Laments for the Dead" (pp. 117-29). The essay's focus on "laments" is broadly interpreted, since Haas treats even messages bearing bad news as laments (e.g., the Templar's news of the giant, lines 852-67), as well as short expressions of concern over injuries (e.g., line 2685). Thus one finds a "complex of death laments" surrounding the episode of the giant of Mont-Saint-Michel which corresponds structurally to the "collection at the end" (p. 126). Arthur's rise and fall are thus set within a framework of laments for the dead, and in the similarities and differences between the two groups of laments can be seen some of the moral dimensions of that structure. Although Haas's concentration on laments is rather too narrow to provide a reliable guide to the poem's meaning, her discussion helps illuminate the poet's structural artistry. In addition, there is some fine, detailed analysis of the sequence and structure of the laments at the end of the poem (pp. 120-29).

Like Ritzke-Rutherford (and Göller and Markus) Haas gives concentrated attention to the episode of the Mont-Saint-Michel giant, and like them tends to distort the episode in an attempt to belittle Arthur's stature as Christian defender of the oppressed. Some stress is laid here, for example, on the old widow's brusqueness as she greets the king as a "mere messenger" (p. 120); in fact she greets him as a young knight who has come through mere bravado to win glory by fighting the giant (lines 961-69), and whom she half scorns for his vanity and half pities for his nobility and youth (lines 970-71). Ensuing events show her to have been mistaken in her judgment (cf. lines 966-69 to 1042, for example), and the thrust of her speech is to identify Arthur as an ordinary human being undertaking a heroic task rather than a legendary hero like "Wade or Wawayn" (line 964). In spite of the poet's half-joking irony in the reference to the "legendary" Gawain, this treatment is consonant with his insistence on the human reality of his hero. If the match with the giant is ultimately "unchivalrous" (p. 120), that fact may say more about the inadequacy of mere formal chivalry to overcome full-blown evil than about Arthur's own inadequacy as a knight.

There follows yet another essay by Karl Heinz Göller, "The Dream of the Dragon and Bear" (pp. 130-39). This essay may tell you more than you wanted to know about the folklore and traditional symbolism of the dragon and the bear; only five of the paper's ten pages actually deal with *MA*. A good deal of the material is simply irrelevant (e.g., the Babylonians and Chaldeans).[41] Also irrelevant, but nevertheless central to Göller's argument, is his certainty that Geoffrey of Monmouth "knew the Celtic word Arthur = 'bear' " (p. 134), "which was evidently common knowledge at the time" (p. 135). Whether or not this is true, it has nothing to do with the interpretation of the dream in *MA*, written over 250 years later. Though Geoffrey's *Historia* was one of the poet's principal sources, Arthur in that work is repeatedly and explicitly associated only with the dragon, Geoffrey apparently having decided to ignore the linguistic association if it was known to him. The Welsh *Brut Tysilio*, to which some prominence is also given, was unknown to the *MA*-poet.

Thus Göller's conclusion that "Arthur is, at one and the same time, the dragon *and* bear" in *MA* (p. 137) must rely on verbal correspondences separated by over two thousand lines (824 and 3253, 785 and 3172); and meanwhile more exact correspondences have intervened (lines 824 and 842, 785 and 1276, 1969, etc.). Even if the correspondences were more remarkable, a distance of over two thousand lines (and several narrative months) is not "at one and the same time." Though there is indeed a complex connection between the dream bear and Arthur's later behavior, it can only be understood through the structure of the poem and the development of Arthur's character over time, from giant killer immediately after his dream to giant's alter ego at the height of his success. "At one and the same time" simply muddles this development.

The poet, it is true, creates some confusion in the interpretation of these dream figures, but through the dragon rather than the bear. Late in the composition of the poem he decided, under the influence of the alliterative *Siege of Jerusalem*, to transfer Arthur's traditional dragon standard from his hero to the Emperor Lucius and his lieutenant the viscount of Rome. Thus Göller's assertion that "Arthur's ensign is also the Golden Dragon which he inherited from his father Uther" (p. 138, repeated also in his earlier essay, p. 28), while true enough of Geoffrey of Monmouth's version of the story, is not true of *MA*. A further such casual misstatement of the facts of the text is found in the following paragraph, where we are told that, Lucius having murdered the commons, clergy, and others of France, "Arthur does exactly the same thing after the capture of Metz" (p. 138). This change entirely ignores Arthur's explicit mercy to the inhabitants of Metz, including the "chase men" or clergy (lines 3057-59).

Göller's final paragraph, arguing that Arthur dies unredeemed, has no apparent relationship to the rest of the essay and again shows little attention to the actual text; no passages are cited to support his view. Since this collection is supposed to form an integrated whole, one must wonder at the total absence of dialogue with Fichte's diametrically opposed (and well-supported) view.

Finally, there is Anke Janssen's "The Dream of the Wheel of Fortune" (pp. 140-52), an essay focusing only on the core of Arthur's second dream, the image of the Wheel of Fortune and the Nine Worthies. Janssen begins with the "Boethian conception of Fortune" (p. 140), defined in terms of the subjection of Fortune to divine Providence, a concept well attested in the poem. But almost immediately we are told that, since God rules Fortune, Arthur's "fatal end cannot be attributed to Dame Fortune's fickleness but to God's just punishment for his evil deeds" (p. 141). This judgment rather begs the question. When Lady Philosophy instructs Boethius that all fortune is good since it always has a moral purpose, she attributes three purposes to the fortune that appears bad: to exercise virtue in the good man, to lead the wicked man to leave the path of vice and take to virtue, or to punish the wicked who do not heed the lesson.[42] Assuming (as Janssen does) that Arthur's "evil deeds" lead to his fall, it remains to be determined whether he is punished, or merely chastised.

Janssen turns next to Petrarch's discussion of Fortune, particularly his emphasis on the baleful effect of *good* fortune, which leads the fortunate into the sin of pride and the abandonment of reason. This is an idea of great interest for the rising structure of the poem — the gradual deterioration of the hero's character as success follows success — but Janssen does not pursue it, for reasons to be mentioned shortly. The specific concept of *fortuna belli*, "fortune-in-war," is next cited from other writers who emphasize the unpredictability of battle, and thus the perilousness of entering into war.

Janssen's discussion of the Nine Worthies is briefer and breaks no new ground; it is when she approaches the unique combination of these two themes in the *MA* dream that the central point of her essay is discernible. Citing previous critics who have seen the dream as "the turning point of Arthur's fate" (p. 144) and who thus identify the poem's genre as tragedy, Janssen says, "The fact that the Dream of Fortune has been examined almost exclusively in terms of genre has definitely influenced, if not prejudiced, the interpretation of the *AMA* as a whole" (p. 144). Since it is simply nonsense to say that George Keiser's important study, which she cites as example, is concerned only with "genre," this somewhat cryptic remark needs interpretation which she does not provide.[43] The rest of the essay indicates that Janssen's concern is not with the identification of the poem as a "tragedy" but rather with the rising and falling structure (with its "turning point") implied by that genre. For her there is evidently neither rise nor fall, neither deterioration of the hero's character nor rehabilitation after his fall: Arthur is alike wicked from beginning to end, his wars all alike unjust, the dream thus no turning point but rather the poet's admonition to "the princes of his time" to abandon the war with France (p. 151).

To support this interpretation, Janssen resorts to selective quotation, subtle (and not-so-subtle) distortion of the evidence, and loaded language. Among other things, the poet's praise of Arthur and his knights and his identification with them throughout ("our king, our folk") is simply ignored, as is his definition of a number of battles as conflicts between Christians and pagans or apostates; Lucius' depredations in the invasion of France (lines 1235-54) are dismissed as "no worse" than Arthur's in his previous conquests. Significantly, there is no reference to Arthur's battle with the giant except citation in a footnote of lines 1176-77, a reference to fortune; Arthur's later ascription of his victory over that embodied evil to God is ignored. Meanwhile, no attention is given to what may be the central problem in the poet's treatment of war: the definition of the "just war" and the judgment of Arthur's wars with respect to that definition.

The issues in the poem are more complex than Janssen will allow, and I would argue that they can be understood only within the framework of the poem's tragic structure. Since I have dealt with this question elsewhere,[44] I will for the rest merely point out two or three particularly egregious distortions. On page 146 Arthur is condemned for "indulg[ing] in the very pursuits [hawking] that the Worthies have come to regret bitterly," citing his deer hunt of line 58; yet what the Worthies regret is not that they have "reuaye[d]" (line 3275), as if hawking for waterbirds were a sin in itself, but rather the heedlessness with which they have devoted their lives to such activities (line 3274); in any case, Arthur renounces them in lines 3997-4004. On page 147: "The reader has an uneasy feeling that the conqueror-king was just waiting for something like the challenge of the Roman emperor in order to have a good excuse for continuing his briefly interrupted wars of conquest"—a feeling that ignores Arthur's rebuke to Cador in lines 259-64. On page 148 Fortune gives Arthur the sword, "requesting him explicitly to use it in battle" (there is no such request, explicit or implicit) and to "brandish it threateningly" (there is no reference to threat). On page 151 Arthur "clos[es] his ears" to the philosopher's "admonition that he will be condemned for his feats of arms on Doomsday (lines 3440-45)"; what the philosopher says is that the Nine Worthies will be "demyd on Domesdaye, for dedis of armes,/For þe doughtyeste þat euer was duelland in erthe" (lines 3442-43). On the same page: "By succumbing to the sin of *superbia*, with all its ugly aspects, [Arthur] foregoes salvation"; aside from begging the question of Arthur's rehabilitation—Janssen ignores the last thousand lines of the poem—this is a radical misstatement of orthodox Christian doctrine. No man, however sinful, "foregoes salvation" while the breath to repent and the possibility of atonement remain in him.

If "the Dream of Fortune contains the message of the poem *in nuce*" (p. 151), then the poem's last thousand lines seem to be pointlessly elaborated; the poet's treatment of the final war with Mordred is many times longer than what he found in his chronicle sources. Janssen's only reference to this ending is the suggestion that Arthur himself is responsible for Mordred's rebellion and the suffering it brings to his people (p. 147)—a judgment with which Arthur himself would agree and which drives him (as Fichte suggests on pp. 114-15) to self-sacrificing expiation. One has only to compare Arthur's final understanding of his fall (lines 4296-4306) to the Worthies' lament from the Wheel (lines 3272-77) to understand that the poet's identification of Arthur with the Worthies of the dream is not his final word on the subject.

In conclusion, one can only praise the editors of D. S. Brewer's "Arthurian Studies" series for including a book on *Morte Arthure* early in the series—and yet wish they had modeled it more closely on the varied and stimulating Malory volume.[45] One could not wish *not* to have this volume, in view of the important and useful contributions of Fries, Wurster, Ritzke-Rutherford, and especially Fichte, which do advance our understanding of this text. Yet the volume is dominated in more senses than one by the views of Karl Heinz Göller, and it is in these that the "reassessment" of the title seems to consist. What is the nature of this reassessment? Göller's insistence on viewing the poem as a political document intended to admonish the English king (which one is never made clear, in view of the vagueness about date) to give over the French war all too often simply ignores the evidence and arguments offered by some of his own contributors, not to mention those of previous scholars. Because this reductive view of the poem doesn't really fit the text, ironies are sought where none has been seen before, so that where there is no direct criticism of Arthur and his knights ironic criticism is found — and in this is the poet's "art." It is difficult to see in what way this "reassessment" represents an advance over the views of Matthews, presented over twenty years ago and often criticized since.[46] One is disturbed above all by the absence of scholarly dialogue in these interpretations — the tendency of too many of these contributors simply to ignore or dismiss opposing views rather than to make a reasoned effort to refute them.

I would not wish to suggest, however, either that the poem has no historical relevance or that its purposes are not in some measure didactic, even though *Fürstenspiegel* ("mirror for princes") is to some extent a misnomer if it implies any expectation that reigning English monarchs of the fourteenth and early fifteenth centuries would read or hear the poem. Nor do I by any means take the position that there is no criticism of imperial war in the poem. Reassessment on these points is precisely what *is* needed in future criticism of the poem, particularly since we now can be fairly certain that it was composed, not in 1365 or 1375, but between 1399 and 1403.[47] Yet one must join the chorus of warnings against treating *MA* as a roman à clef, against seeing Mordred "as" Richard II or Arthur "as" Henry IV, or vice versa. Though there are indeed a number of "historical allusions" to events and personages in these few years, the poem is only in part a commentary on the fall of a particular king, just as it is only in part a commentary on the wasteful and destructive wars of his predecessor. Perhaps we should see the poet's theme as not war in and of itself, nor yet the betrayal of kinsman by kinsman, but rather human pride which draws man away from God and toward conquest and betrayal, and the humbling of pride by Fortune as a servant of Providence, which can lead man back to God. Some of this I have learned from Fichte.

As for the poet's art, I would like to issue a heartfelt plea that future students of formulaic techniques and other aspects of style in *MA* take time to aquaint themselves with these aspects of the poem's immediate predecessors and contemporaries, particularly in those poems which

MA is most like — *The Destruction of Troy*, *The Siege of Jerusalem*, and *The Wars of Alexander* — as well as with the formal elements of medieval rhetoric.[48] In this age of computers, perhaps the time has come to build on and advance J. P. Oakden's seminal work on Middle English alliterative style, necessarily impressionistic owing to the volume of the material and the limitations of merely human counting and sorting techniques.[49] Ritzke-Rutherford's definition and distinction of terms — formula, formulaic system, cluster — seem to me to offer real aid to such a project, and the continually expanding resources offered by the *Middle English Dictionary* keep offering further insights into the lexicon. But there is no substitute finally for the close study, word by word, phrase by phrase, clause by clause, of the specific text in question. This is especially true of *Morte Arthure*, a work in which we have only begun to understand the complexities of language, of style, of structure, and of meaning.

Notes

1. See the abstracts in the "Courrier" section of the *Bulletin bibliographique de la Société Internationale Arthurienne* (hereafter *BBSIA*), 31 (1979), 275, 276, 278, and 301-2.

2. Only the name of Jörg O. Fichte is not included in the list of participants in the Congress, "Le Douzième Congrès International Arthurien," *BBSIA*, 31 (1979), 249-54.

3. Krishna, ed., *The Alliterative Morte Arthure* (New York: Burt Franklin, 1976). Since this text is used by all contributors, in what follows I also quote from it in my own discussion, with one or two corrections of Krishna's transcriptions enclosed in brackets. My own edition of the poem is shortly to appear in the Garland Medieval Texts series.

4. See the facsimile, *The Thornton Manuscript*, rev. ed. (London: Scolar Press, 1977), fols. 54 and 98v. All three Middle English texts cited in the following sentence derived their titles from the Old French romance *Mort Artu*.

5. John Gardner, trans., *The Alliterative Morte Arthure, The Owl and the Nightingale, and Five Other Middle English Poems* (Carbondale and Edwardsville: Southern Illinois Univ. Press, 1973), pp. 85-91.

6. Schelp, "Gestalt und Funktion des Auftakts in der mittelenglischen alliterierenden *Morte Arthure*," *Archiv für das Studium der Neueren Sprachen und Literaturen* 207 (1971), 420-38.

7. Keiser, "The Theme of Justice in the Alliterative *Morte Arthure*," *Annuale Mediaevale*, 16 (1975), 94-109; Finlayson, "Arthur and the Giant of St. Michael's Mount," *Medium Ævum*, 33 (1964), 112-20.

8. Keiser, "Edward III and the Alliterative *Morte Arthure*," *Speculum*, 48 (1973), 37-51; Barnie, *War in Medieval English Society* (Ithaca: Cornell Univ. Press, 1974), pp. 147-50.

9. William Matthews, *The Tragedy of Arthur: A Study of the Alliterative "Morte Arthure"* (Berkeley and Los Angeles: Univ. of California Press, 1960); John Finlayson, ed., *Morte Arthure*, York Medieval Texts (Evanston: Northwestern Univ. Press, 1967), pp. 11-13.

10. Foley, "The Alliterative *Morte Arthure*: An Annotated Bibliography, 1950-1975," *Chaucer Review*, 14 (1979), 166-87.

11. Gleissner, "Der alliterierende *Morte Arthure*: ein politisches Gedicht in seiner Zeit," and Göller, "Der Allitterierende [*sic*] *Morte Arthure* als Anti-Romance," *BBSIA*, 31 (1979), 275-76.

12. My forthcoming edition will contain a detailed account of the poet's sources; meanwhile, see Paul Branscheid, "Über die Quellen des stabreimenden *Morte Arthure*," *Anglia*, 8 (1885), Anzeiger, 179-236.

13. Finlayson, "Definitions of Middle English Romance, I," *Chaucer Review*, 15 (1980), 50. Speaking later of the "difference sharply evident in the two *Mortes*," he adds, "To classify them together and define their common characteristics is an exercise of very limited usefulness" (p. 53).

14. Branscheid, however, points out Chrétien's mention of "Galinguefort" in the *Cligès* ("Quellen," pp. 225-26).

15. Gleissner, "Ein politisches Gedicht," p. 275.

16. The poem's duchess of Brittany was first linked with the wife of Jean de Montfort by George Neilson, " 'Morte Arthure' and the War of Brittany," *Notes and Queries*, 9th ser., 10 (1902), 163, a link refuted by Keiser, "Edward III," pp. 42-43.

17. Keiser, "Edward III," p. 40.

18. Matthews, *Tragedy*, pp. 184, 212-13. Though Matthews asserts that "the Danes who aid Mordred do not appear in the chronicles" (p. 184), they are found both in Wace and Robert Manning: see *La Partie arthurienne du Roman de Brut*, ed. I. D. O. Arnold and M. M. Pelan (Paris: Librairie C. Klincksieck, 1962), p. 155, line 4660, and *The Chronicle of Robert Manning of Brunne*, ed. F. J. Furnivall, RS 87 (London, 1887), II, 493, line 14,236.

19. After the execution of participants in the assassination plot against Henry IV in early 1400, the king distributed the traitors' confiscated estates to his own followers, but not before he had made provision from them for the widows and children of the executed men—and even for the mothers of the two priests involved. See James H. Wylie, *History of England under Henry IV* (London: Longmans, Green, 1884), I, 118.

20. See Larry D. Benson, *Malory's* Morte Darthur (Cambridge: Harvard Univ. Press, 1976), pp. 137-201; Barnie, "Aristocracy, Knighthood, and Chivalry," Chapter 3 of *War in Medieval Society*; M. H. Keen, *The Laws of War in the Late Middle Ages* (London: Routledge & Kegan Paul, 1965).

21. See Sidney J. Herrtage, ed., *Sir Ferumbras,* EETS e.s. 34 (London, 1879), lines 746-48; Layamon, *Brut,* ed. G. L. Brook and R. F. Leslie, EETS 277 (London, 1978), lines 10,669-91; G. A. Panton and D. Donaldson, eds., *The Destruction of Troy,* EETS 39 and 56 (London, 1869, 1874), lines 5936-40, 7508-9, 7014-16, 7325-26, etc.; E. Kölbing and Mabel Day, eds., *The Siege of Jerusalem,* EETS 188 (London, 1932), lines 819-32. This is a small selection from a large number of such passages.

22. J. R. Hulbert, "A Hypothesis concerning the Alliterative Revival," *Modern Philology,* 28 (1931), 405-22; Elizabeth Salter, "The Alliterative Revival, *Modern Philology,* 64 (1966), Part I, pp. 146-50, Part II, pp. 233-37; Thorlac Turville-Petre, *The Alliterative Revival* (Cambridge: D. S. Brewer, 1977), pp. 40-47.

23. Matthews, *Tragedy,* pp. 181-82, 211-12.

24. Marie Boroff, Sir Gawain and the Green Knight: *A Stylistic and Metrical Study* (1962; repr. Hamden, Conn.: Archon Books, 1973); Larry D. Benson, *Art and Tradition in* Sir Gawain and the Green Knight (New Brunswick: Rutgers Univ. Press, 1965), pp. 110-66.

25. Krishna, *Morte Arthure,* pp. 23-24.

26. See J. P. Oakden, *Alliterative Poetry in Middle English: The Dialectal and Metrical Survey* (1930; repr. Hamden, Conn.: Archon Books, 1968), pp. 167-70, 181-200.

27. John Finlayson, "Formulaic Technique in 'Morte Arthure,' " *Anglia,* 81 (1963), 372-93.

28. *Sir Gawain and the Green Knight,* ed. J. R. R. Tolkien, E. V. Gordon, and Norman Davis, 2d ed. (Oxford: Clarendon Press, 1968); *The Awntyrs off Arthure at the Terne Wathelyn,* ed. Ralph Hanna III (Manchester: Manchester Univ. Press, 1974); *The Siege of Jerusalem,* ed. Kölbing and Day (note 21 above); *Cleanness,* in *The Poems of the Pearl Manuscript,* ed. Malcolm Andrew and Ronald Waldron (Berkeley: Univ. of California Press, 1979).

29. Jean Ritzke-Rutherford, *Light and Darkness in Anglo-Saxon Thought and Writing,* Sprache und Literatur: Regensburger Arbeiten zur Anglistik und Amerikanistik 17 (Frankfurt: Lang, 1979).

30. See Krishna's note, *Morte Arthure,* p. 185.

31. Benson, *Art and Tradition,* pp. 124-25.

32. Line 2675 in full reads, "And some was sleghte one slepe with slaughte of þe pople / þat sange." In my edition I interpret the line as meaning, "And some had relaxed into sleep with a sudden onset, (because) of the folk that sang" and do not emend. The interpretation relies on *Pearl,* line 59, "I slode vpon a slepyng-slaȝte."

33. Finlayson, "Arthur and the Giant."

34. Lippe might perhaps have argued that *purpure* in the Middle Ages denoted a deep crimson or scarlet rather than the modern blue-red (see *OED,* s.v. "purpur" *sb.,* 3, and "purple" *sb.,* 1) and thus could legitimately be translated "red." But the

contrast between heraldic "purpure" and "gules" remains, and the translation "red" is at the least misleading.

35. Lippe simply dismisses the cogent arguments of Charles Lionel Regan, "The Paternity of Mordred in the Alliterative *Morte Arthure*," *BBSIA*, 25 (1973), 153-54. Thus one is forced to cover much of the same ground again.

36. Arthur Charles Fox-Davies, *A Complete Guide to Heraldry* (1909; repr. New York: Bonanza Books, 1978), pp. 478, 481, 491-96; Charles Boutell, *Heraldry, Historical and Popular*, 3d ed. (London: Richard Bentley, 1864), pp. 230-49.

37. See Fox-Davies, *Heraldry*, pp. 478-79, 481-82, 494.

38. Jönsjö, *Studies in Middle English Nicknames: I. Compounds*, Lund Studies in English 55 (Lund, 1979), p. 127. Lippe cites this study but dismisses Jönsjö's gloss (p. 172).

39. Mary Hamel, "The Dream of a King: The Alliterative *Morte Arthure* and Dante," *Chaucer Review*, 14 (1980), 304.

40. See the *Middle English Dictionary*, ed. Hans Kurath and Sherman M. Kuhn (Ann Arbor: Univ. of Michigan Press, 1952—), s.v. "engendren" v., sense 4.

41. A more useful and better-documented guide to the purely medieval lore of the dragon, with particular emphasis on battle standards, is J. S. P. Tatlock's "The Dragons of Wessex and Wales," *Speculum*, 8 (1933), 223-35.

42. Boethius, *The Consolation of Philosophy*, trans. Richard Green (Indianapolis: Bobbs-Merrill, 1962), Book IV, Prose 7 (pp. 97-99).

43. Keiser, "The Theme of Justice" (note 7 above).

44. Hamel, "The Dream of a King."

45. Toshiyuki Takamiya and Derek Brewer, eds., *Aspects of Malory*, Arthurian Studies I (Cambridge: D. S. Brewer, 1981).

46. Matthews, *Tragedy*, pp. 178-92.

47. See Larry D. Benson, "The Date of the Alliterative *Morte Arthure*," in *Medieval Studies in Honor of Lillian Herlands Hornstein*, ed. Jess. B. Bessinger, Jr., and Robert K. Raymo (New York: New York Univ. Press, 1976), pp. 19-40. My own researches, to be published in my forthcoming edition, confirm the date proposed by Benson.

48. The recent article of Valerie Krishna, "Parataxis, Formulaic Density, and Thrift in the Alliterative *Morte Arthure*," *Speculum*, 57 (1982), 63-83, makes no reference to other Alliterative Revival poems.

49. J. P. Oakden, *Alliterative Poetry in Middle English: A Survey of the Traditions* (1935; repr. Hamden, Conn.: Archon Books, 1968).

The Deterioration of Early Nineteenth-Century Book Paper

Paul S. Koda

John Murray. *Practical Remarks on Modern Paper.* North Hills, Pa.: Bird & Bull Press, 1981. 120 pp.

Every scholar and reader has had the unsettling experience of opening a book published in the nineteenth century only to find himself holding a handful of leaves broken away from the binding. With the application of the slightest pressure he sees that same sheaf of leaves crumble to dust. This dismaying experience has become more and more commonplace as the twentieth century has drawn to a close. Consequently, there has been an increase in the number of alarms sounded on the deteriorating state of paper in books, magazines, manuscripts, and journals. Even though the epidemic proportions of the problem have been universally recognized only during the past decade, warnings about unstable paper have been voiced for over a century and a half. Certainly a long, loud, and early—if not the earliest—warning was given by John Murray in the July 1823 issue of the *Gentleman's Magazine*, where he complains about a copy of the Bible which is *"crumbling literally into dust."*[1] The complaint caused enough of a sensation to encourage Murray to publish a pamphlet on the subject that same year (with a reprint in 1824), and then in 1829 to publish a longer work called *Practical Remarks on Modern Paper*. The 1981 reprint of that work is reviewed here.[2]

Reviews of reprints pose special problems. For the most part they are not worth reviewing (or reviewing for the second time, assuming they were reviewed when they were first published) unless they meet one or more criteria. These criteria include the rediscovery of useful or interesting information for today's readers; the revaluation of a person's work so that it becomes more or less historically significant than was thought before; the production of an attractive, even outstanding, piece of book art; the drawing of a new portrait of a person who is interesting in his own right; the adoption of the occasion to reexamine old assumptions and to publish new observations on a subject of contemporary interest; or the "improvement" of the work by making it more accessible through scholarly additions such as indexes or annotations.

Before determining to what extent Murray's *Modern Paper* and the Bird and Bull Press meet these criteria, one needs to understand Murray as a person living and working in the context of early nineteenth-century England. Such understanding may be reached by examining Murray's biography and the writings that led up to the publication of *Modern Paper*.

Most of what is known about Murray is published in two columns of the *Dictionary of National Biography*. His dates are 1786?–1851, and he is described as a "scientific writer and lecturer." His interests were numerous and eclectic, for he published prolifically in such diverse areas as poetry, chemistry, medicine, and inventions. This diversity prompted Richard Bissell Prosser to remark that Murray's "wide range of subjects . . . prevented him from attaining eminence in any" single field.[3] In spite of his superficial treatment of some subjects, however, the man has an attraction that arouses a sympathetic curiousity well expressed by Henry Morris in his "Note from the Publisher" in the 1981 edition: "What sort of person was this who had so many interests, researched and wrote on so many varied subjects and was a practical inventor as well?" (p. 27).

Although Morris's question is impossible to answer with certainty, one can ask whether Murray was that typical turn-of-the-century man: one who had an eighteenth-century sensibility, one who tried to understand and master all there was to know, but also one who was caught in the intensifying specializations of the nineteenth century when attempts to attain universality prevented eminence. As wide as his interests were, Murray must, in the end, be called a scientist, but a socially aware scientist with an eye toward immediate events. These traits are evident in his *Minor Poems* published in 1816.[4] There are thirty-nine short poems, with short lines, spread with much spacing over fifty-two pages. The poems' titles reflect the common romantic themes of Murray's day: "The Lily" and "To the Lark" and "The Eolian Harp" and "To the Cuckoo." In contrast to these poems is one entitled "The Glow-Worm," a creature about which Murray wrote several scientific treatises. This poem's twenty-nine lines are buttressed with three Latin footnotes identifying the flora and fauna in the glowworm's habitat. Another poem, "The Comet, Sept. 1811," also reflects Murray's scientific bent by taking the occasion of the appearance of an especially bright comet in 1811 for its subject. Poems about natural phenomena or contemporary events are certainly not unheard of, even when accompanied by scientific footnotes. What is unusual about *Minor Poems* are the forty-five pages of scientific essays about the subjects of the poems which conclude the book. The number of pages devoted to these treatises nearly matches the number of pages for the poems themselves. Murray devotes seven-and-one-half pages of notes to glowworms and four-and-one-half to comets.

Murray's *Minor Poems* shows a mind with a vigorous rhetorical imagination, a keen awareness of the events occurring around him, and a scientific discursiveness. All of these elements, along with a strong dose of moral indignation, are also present in his writings about paper. For if Murray's writings about paper are anything at all, they are polemics designed to move the public to action, to do something about books and manuscripts "crumbling literally to dust," as did the Bible he writes of in his 1823 letter. "Our beautiful Religion, our Literature, our Science, all are threatened," says Murray, deploring "the present state of that wretched compound called *Paper*." Apparently Murray's indignant outburst was prompted by two personal experiences. The first was with a paper called "Bath wove Post," which was used for writing letters and, "being folded up, crack at the edges, and fall asunder" or whose ink faded, rendering the page "*carte blanche*." The second was with a "large copy of the Bible printed in Oxford, 1816 (never used), and issued by the British and Foreign Bible Society." Murray names two "causes of [the] destruction" of paper: the "*material*, and the mode of bleaching the rags."[5] He goes on to elaborate on the instability of ink, the harmful effects of chlorine bleachings on rags for paper, and the various substitutes that may be used in place of rags. He concludes with a list of chemical tests he made on the 1816 Bible.

There was much public approval of his letter because, in the same year, he issued a twenty-three-page pamphlet on the subject.[6] In it he describes the ready acceptance of the 1823 letter: "What immediately succeeds appeared in the *Gentleman's Magazine*, and it was copied from that respectable publication into almost all the journals whether metropolitan or provincial. This is proof of the general and intense interest excited" (p. v). At the beginning of the pamphlet Murray quotes the entire 1823 letter. There are over sixty variants between the first and second publication of the letter. Most of them are changes in emphasis where Murray rearranges word order or, more frequently, italicizes key words so that he can better underscore his dismay about the deleterious state of paper.

Partly because of the wide approval of his letter, Murray also received new information about papermaking in the 1820s. This is readily seen in the two-and-one-half page letter he prints from an anonymous correspondent who discusses paper manufacturing at length and with seeming authority, for his correspondent had "some idea of paper making" (p. 12). The correspondent claims that the main cause of bad paper is the kind of pulp required by the papermaking machine in order to produce paper. Unlike the long-fibered pulp, which has a greater cohesion, used in making handmade papers, the rag for the machine is "required to be ground to a complete powder" (p. 12). The correspondent lists other machine-related processes for making paper that result in an inferior product. They include a change from surface to internal sizing, the machine's inability to shake the fibers together as well as that operation can be done by hand, and the use of cold rather than warm water, which does not provide an adequate suspension of fibers. The correspondent dismisses bleaching and the mixture of linen and cotton fibers as major causes in the manufacture of poor paper—two causes that Murray places very high on his own list—and concludes with an impassioned plea "to prevent this growing and serious evil" because "one of these [papermaking] machines will throw off as much paper in twelve hours, as fifteen men can do in the same period of time," thereby throwing men out of work (p. 14). The loss of work by hand papermakers is certainly at the heart of the correspondent's denigration of machine-made paper: given this concern, it is understandable why he stresses machine-related causes for bad paper.

Murray's reaction to his correspondent's letter is curious. On the one hand he agrees with his correspondent by giving "him ample credit for his intelligence and information," but on the other hand he rejects the same intelligence and information for being impractical and out of date (p. 15). A specific example is useful in showing Murray's ambiguity on the issue. It has to do with the fact that making paper with short-fibered pulp will produce a weak paper—the very kind of paper that Murray wanted to abolish. Murray admits short-fibered pulp produces a weak paper. Yet when it comes to a choice between manufacturing a strong paper by hand or a weak paper by machine, Murray chooses the latter. He does not see it as a choice of one kind of paper over another: rather, he sees it as a choice for the mechanical inventions of the Machine Age with the implication that technology has finally struck off centuries-old fetters that once bound imagination and opportunity. He also sees it as a choice for the political power and wealth the Industrial Revolution was bringing to Britain. Murray's assumptions and arguments for his position are worth quoting in full:

> I am, however, inclined to doubt the *impracticability* of the construction of a machine, that shall preserve the fibre so essential to its cohesion, in an age of such splendid mechanical atchievements [*sic*]; — that can even boast of a *machine for mathematical calculations*, and which in the improvements of the steam engine and its subserviency, has revealed more wonders than ever rose obedient to the want of Abdallah.
>
> It is entirely to the superiority of our mechanical skill, conjoined with our perseverance and industry, aided and extended by insular and local advantages, as navigable canals, fuel, &c. that we can compete with the rest of Europe, where manual labour is of such cheap attainment. The senseless destruction of machinery, which in former times disgraced this country, must have been ever lamented and pitied by all who pride themselves on the name of BRITON — the richest title — the proudest inheritance on earth. [p. 15][7]

By feeling he has to reject the political and economic views of his correspondent, Murray must perforce dismiss his good technical knowledge about paper. He does not dismiss it outright but continues his pamphlet by once again assigning to bleaching, ink, and cotton the major blame for bad paper.

Murray's position against his correspondent's evaluation of the causes leading to paper deterioration had turned around by the time his book was published in 1829. It reversed so completely, in fact, that in words echoing his correspondent Murray expresses his "favour of hand-made paper, over that manufactured by machinery," but with the proviso that machinery has an important role to play in future papermaking.

> In process of time [machinery] may certainly, in this inventive and ingenious age, receive improvements that may obviate all objections, and the vast quantity of work done by the machine, compared with that effected by manual labour, will raise its value in the estimation of the paper-makers, as one machine will throw off as much paper as fifteen men can make in a similar period. I should be sorry that any opinion of mine should be construed into a sentiment hostile to the diffusion of mechanical aids: it is only by such ingenious applications of mental prowess that we can compete with the pro-

gressive demand which our literature claims from us. It is by the ingenuity of our mechanical arts, conjoined with our local advantages of insular situation, and our canals, and our coal-mines, that we can withstand our continental neighbors, and compete for the prize of superiority. We would, therefore, suffer mind to bring its full stores to the contest, and avail ourselves of its wonderful and varied resources. On the Continent of Europe, manual labor is of much cheaper obtainment than with us, and a substitute must therefore be found in British genius, less we be worsted in the struggle. [pp. 79–80]

Murray was so convinced by this time that "machinery," or the papermaking machine, had been a leading cause in making poor paper that he included it in *Modern Paper* as one of the five major causes for poor paper. The other four were the "mechanical consistency of the pulp," the "adventitious mixture of earthy substances in the pulp," the "*alum* which is used in the size," and the "process of bleaching" (pp. 80–82). Citing these five causes, Murray offers an accurate, comprehensive summary of the main technological, physical, and chemical substances and processes resulting in the deterioration of early nineteenth-century machine-made paper. For the level of scientific investigation that was possible in Murray's day, his causes can legitimately be called causes. Today, I suspect, we are more likely to say they describe paper deterioration but do not explain the how and why of paper deterioration; we are more inclined to say that his causes describe manufacturing rather than scientific causes. A good example of the difference may be seen in Murray's identification of the use of alum and bleaching in paper manufacturing as leading causes of deterioration. He was right. But scientific analysis of the time was not sophisticated enough to permit him to discover the basic fiber of paper, which is cellulose, and the acid attacks made upon it by both alum and bleaching.

This inability to discover the "root" causes of paper deterioration locked Murray into a course of action that is ultimately unsatisfying for us and must have been frustrating for him. That course is reiteration. Given the finite number of substances in paper, the state of science in the 1820s, and Murray's strong belief in the exclusiveness of his findings, it became apparent that his experiments with paper would have to come to a conclusion and that, consequently, he would have to turn to new areas of investigation. By 1824 Murray had finished most of the important possible experiments on paper. The book is simply a tying together of loose ends, a tidying up of evidence and ideas, a softening of the urgency and immediacy.

From our point of view in the twentieth century, both the pamphlet and the book are useful: the pamphlet for social history and the book for science. Yet those who are interested in how science was done at that time or, more important, how Murray conducted his experiments on paper, will have to read the pamphlet as well as the book. In several instances the pamphlet is not only more vivid and concrete but it also provides details of experiments as well as whole experiments not found in the book. A good example of both Murray's experimentation and his style may be seen in the following excerpt:

> I have lately examined by chemical re-agents, a specimen of *"thick* laid post," the *weight* of which struck me as remarkable; for *three sheets*, the size of common letter paper, (weighed at the post office,) subjected me to *five postages*, being 1 ¼ oz. when I conceived I had only *treble* postage to pay.
>
> The paper being macerated in distilled water, and the fluid passed through a filter, (previously washed with distilled water,) afforded *no indications* of a *muriate*, by *nitrate*, or *acetate of silver*.
>
> With *nitrate of baryta,* a copious white cloud was formed, — the index of a *sulfate*.
>
> Tested, subsequently, with *oxalate of ammonia*, a dense white cloud was immediately announced; the presence of *lime* was therefore evident.
>
> As the most delicate tests, such as *litmus*, &c. remained unchanged, I conclude *alum* to have been either absent, or too small in quantity to be detected.
>
> The thickness and weight were therefore entirely owing to *sulfate of lime* or *gypsum*. It was a paper chiefly composed of ALABASTER! [p. 18][8]

If Murray's twenty-three-page pamphlet contains the bulk of the experimentation and information he had on paper, what are the other one hundred pages of *Modern Paper* about? The first chapter is a history of the materials used for transmitting information in the ancient world. Murray delves into the past uses of metal, stone, wood, skin, and papyrus. None of this information had been earlier published by Murray. Chapter two continues his discussion of skins and parchment, but its major subject is the history of papermaking thoughout the world, including the methods and materials of making paper by hand and by machine. Once again, much of the information is new to Murray's writings. The third chapter presents a summary of his findings on paper, and although Murray has written about them earlier, this is the first time he organizes the information with some care. The chapter concludes with discussions of paper fiber substitutes, with an extended commentary on bleaching and on inks used for forgery documents. In the last chapter Murray talks about restoring faded manuscripts. This information expands his earlier writings. Most of Murray's additions are not about paper analysis or paper deterioration but about subjects like early writing materials and substitutes for cotton and linen fibers.

Is Murray's *Modern Paper* useful today, or is it simply a historical curiosity? And is the Bird and Bull reprint the best vehicle for making the book available again after 150 years?[9] As shown above, Murray's writings have a certain interest for the picture he gives of the conflict between an old, established craft and a new, highly technological manufacturing process which challenged it. And perhaps interest is heightened because the broad social and economic implications of the conflict are revealed sharply and at a personal level. But interesting as these issues are, they are not new; many histories of early nineteenth-century England treat them exhaustively with equal if not better examples, although not specifically about the papermaking industry. Murray's history of writing materials and of papermaking fibers has also been superseded by modern scholars, and his description of paper manufacturing is only moderately successful.

Even though one would not now use *Modern Paper* for information about the history of writing materials or about the way paper was manufactured, there is one area in which Murray can still be useful: for the identification and description of the materials used for making the machine-made papers of his time. No detailed manual or textbook for making machine paper was published before the 1860s. Descriptions of the papermaking machine and how the machine manufactured the web of paper had been published during the early decades of the century, but very little information about specific chemicals used in making paper had appeared. Such information would be useful today for the manufacturing history of machine-made papers, a study yet to be undertaken; more importantly, it would be useful for paper conservators working on early machine-made paper to know what chemicals they would expect to find in paper from that period. Modern chemical analysis of older materials is only partially reliable for determining the makeup of early paper; it should not be forgotten that *Modern Paper* is a contemporary document that records the materials in use at the time. The combination of present-day analysis and contemporary documentation provides the most reliable information for conservators.

It is not easy, however, to obtain specific information about manufacturing materials from *Modern Paper*. Murray's prose is often awkward and difficult, and his book had no index. This is an especially critical omission because Murray usually does not confine his discussion of a given topic to only one place in the book. On the subject of bleaching in the manufacturing process, for example, the reader will find relevant information on pages 70-71, 82-83, and 92. And even though Murray does have an analytical table of contents, which is matched to his chapter headings and which was a common way to access information in books in his period, it is not detailed enough to lead the reader to all Murray's observations on a single subject like bleaching. One would not expect to find an index in the 1829 edition of *Modern Paper* because indexes were not a usual feature in books published at the time. If such a book as *Modern Paper* is to be useful to readers today, an index is necessary. Unfortunately, Bird and Bull does not provide one. Equally important—perhaps even more important—would have been the inclusion of a detailed glossary of papermaking chemicals.

The publisher has, on the other hand, asked Leonard Schlosser to write an introduction to the book. Schlosser is a knowledgeable paper historian, and his introduction performs two important services. The first is to explain the chemistry of papermaking by machine in the 1820s. He does not go into every detail, for that story still has to be researched and told, but he does draw the broad outlines so that the reader sees what papermaking was like at the time and what it is generally today. Schlosser also evaluates Murray's contribution to paper testing and analysis. Schlosser also gives a succinct history of the paper manufacturing processes and materials that have contributed to the deterioration of paper. It is, if this is an appropriate term, a history of paper deterioration. No complete history of deterioration exists (admittedly, it would be a species of "negative" history, a record of failure, yet a history useful for librarians and conservators), for it first requires a thorough study of papermaking in the nineteenth century, which has also not been written. Yet Schlosser's explication of *Modern Paper* contributes to our understanding of why paper has been deteriorating at an accelerating rate ever since the end of the eighteenth century.

Schlosser's introduction is good to have, but what about the Bird and Bull reprint itself? The press has been publishing works on papermaking and on the history of papermaking for many years. Often they reprint classic documents of the craft, and Murray's *Modern Paper* is typical of their publications with its excellent typography, paper, and printing. Limited to 300 copies and priced at $125, the book is very much a private press publication, one produced for collectors. On the other hand, the text of the book is an important document in the history of paper deterioration and conservation because it is the first extended discussion of the subject. For its place in history and as a beautiful piece of craftsmanship, the Bird and Bull *Modern Paper* is worth having; but for research purposes only Schlosser's introduction makes it worth having. Adding to the historical stock of a library is the obligation of all librarians, but when it is a matter of "unimproved" stock, the inexpensive offset reprints or microfilm copies will suffice. Publishers who "improve" earlier texts with scholarly additions can and should command higher prices. It is regrettable that Bird and Bull did not take this opportunity to publish a scholarly edition of *Modern Paper*. Such an edition, it can be imagined, would have won the hearty approbation of John Murray.

Notes

1. John Murray, July 1823, p. 22. The italics are Murray's.

2. It is worth noting that a similar complaint about poor paper, entitled "Frauds and Imperfections in Paper-making," appeared in the same month in the *Annals of Philosophy* (London: Baldwin, Craddock and Joy, 1823, p. 68). Lee E. Grove mentions the reference in his "John Murray and Paper Deterioration" *Libri*, 16:3 (1966), 194–204, where he summarizes Murray's book and discusses the importance to librarians of his warnings about paper deterioration.

3. Richard Bissell Prosser, "John Murray," *DNB* (1894), 13, 1291.

4. John Murray, *Minor Poems* (Dumfries: Printed by C. Monro, 1816).

5. John Murray, *Gentleman's Magazine*, pp. 21–22. Because of the importance of this 1816 edition of the Bible to Murray's research on and writing about bad paper, a fuller citation to the Bible is worth recording: *The Holy Bible, Containing the Old and New Testaments, Appointed to Be Read in Churches, Stereotype Edition* (London: Printed by George Eyre and Andrew Strahan, for the British and Foreign Bible Society, 1816). The reader may like to know the paper in the copy I examined (New York Public Library copy *YCD/+ 1816) is nearly as brittle as Murray's copy. A single and careful turn of a leaf would often cause a tear or a corner to break off.

6. *Observations and Experiments on the Bad Composition of Modern Paper; With the Description of a Permanent Writing Ink, Which Cannot be Discharged* (London: G. and W. B. Whittaker, 1823). I take the title and quotations from the 1824 publication of the pamphlet. The 1823 publication is recorded in *BMC*, 16:384. Because the publisher, format, and number of pages are identical for the two publications, it seems likely that the 1824 publication is a reprint of the 1823 publication. It is the one to which I refer parenthetically in the rest of this paper.

7. The machine for mathematical calculations Murray talks about is undoubtedly that of Charles Babbage, who is often called the Father of the Computer and whose work aroused great scientific interest in the early decades of the nineteenth century.

8. There are also differences in the accounts of the identical experiment described in the letter, the pamphlet, and the book. In his analysis of the 1816 Bible, Murray says in the letter, "Litmus paper was reddened in a solution of the leaves in distilled water" (*Gentleman's Magazine*, p. 22); in the pamphlet, "The leaves were macerated in distilled water, and the liquid filtered, *litmus* paper was *reddened*" (*Observations*, p. 9); and in the book, "The leaves were macerated in water, and the solution passed through bibulous paper. *Litmus* paper was reddened" (*Modern Paper*, p. 86).

9. In bibliographical terms the book is not a reprint but a completely reset edition, making it the second edition. It is a relatively error-free resetting. Although the two original copies of *Modern Paper* I examined (NjP EX TS1090.M8 and NN *KF 1829 80-246) have been washed and rebound, it seems clear that the paper would have held up well without restoration. I found collateral evidence for the stability and longevity of the paper in a copy of Murray's *A Glance at Some of the Beauties and Sublimities of Switzerland* (London: Longman/NcU RBC DQ23.M87), which was published the same year and printed on identical paper by the same printer, P. Neill of Edinburgh. In the preface to the Bird and Bull edition Henry Morris describes the paper in the original 1829 edition as machine-made, but he expresses some doubt when he says it is "probably machine-made" (p. 28). His uncertainty is understandable because the ribbed surface of the paper prevents us from seeing the pattern made by the wire of the papermaking machine. However, both the Princeton and New York Public Library copies of *Modern Paper* as well as the copy of the University of North Carolina's *Beauties of Switzerland* contain sheets with seam marks, which is evidence that the paper was made by machine.

Emily Dickinson's Workshop

Jerome Loving

> *The Manuscript Books of Emily Dickinson.* Ed. R. W. Franklin. Cambridge: Harvard University Press, 1981. 2 vols. xxii, 1442 pp. total.

In *The Editing of Emily Dickinson* (1967), R. W. Franklin concluded his criticism of the 1955 variorum edition by addressing the problem of editing a poet who did not (as far as we know) prepare her poems for publication. Any approach, he argued, that is exclusively author-oriented will fail editorially because of the large number of variants in the Dickinson canon of approximately 1,775 poems. To drive home his point, he noted that a draft of "Those fair — fictitious People" (no. 499 in the variorum) contained twenty-six suggestions that fit eleven places in the poem. "From this, 7680 poems are possible — not versions but, according to our critical principles, poems."[1] Ignoring for the nonce his belief that a version constitutes another poem, we can appreciate the quandary in which the editor of Emily Dickinson finds himself. He must fill not only the role of editor but of critic and philosopher as well. He must choose between two, three, or more different versions, or in the case of no. 499 become, as it were, a structuralist before a number painting whose possibilities are legion.

Apparently this belief led Professor Franklin to edit in two volumes *The Manuscript Books of Emily Dickinson.* In doing so, Franklin has succeeded where other editors have failed. Unable to coax the poet downstairs, Franklin's predecessors have left the Amherst homestead with poems that are, in the textual sense, poems written by Dickinson *and* themselves. Franklin, on the other hand, has proceeded upstairs, into the poet's corner room, and seized the actual poems from the locked box that had secured them. The result is his facsimile edition of the poetry, or most of it. The edition contains the original forty fascicles, arranged chronologically and renumbered, as well as the unbound fascicle sheets. Regarding the second group of manuscripts or packets, the word *set* is used to distinguish them from the poet's forty completed "books" of poetry — packets sewn together mainly between 1858 and 1863. The manuscripts that her sister Lavinia found, along with fair copies of poems sent to friends, are excluded from the edition; for the intention is to present only the manuscripts Dickinson included, or copied as if for inclusion, in her manuscript books.

Franklin's real achievement lies not only in renumbering the sequence of packets which Mabel Loomis Todd, the poet's first editor, numbered arbitrarily, but in establishing the sequence of poems within the original forty packets (a term now abandoned for *fascicle* or *set*). This is accomplished through the use of editorial notes from the 1890s as well as through evidence gathered from the examination of stain offsets, matching smudge patterns, pin impressions, and anything else that establishes the original order of the sheets of poetry. Thus, the critic gains admission to Dickinson's workshop, or to a fair semblance of its original order. The next logical step is to publish a reader's edition following Franklin's arrangement in *The Manuscript Books*. In the meantime we can take a closer look, certainly a more comprehensive one, at the manuscripts. Here the infamous dash is found to exist in great variety (as if the poet were searching for a symbol her lexicon lacked), variant lines look as final (but no more final) than the ones they might replace, calligraphic figures that could be considered either lower- or upper-case abound, and so on. In short, we see enough to praise again the work Franklin's edition challenges: *The Complete Poems of Emily Dickinson* (1955), edited by Thomas H. Johnson.

The facsimile edition takes us a step or two beyond Johnson's edition in the endeavor to read the poems as Dickinson left them. Indeed, it takes us also backward, or full circle back to the dilemma faced by Dickinson's first editors, Mrs. Todd and Thomas Wentworth Higginson. And that is, we continue to stare at her ambiguity, especially with regard to variant lines. As potential editors we have to admit our defeat. By forcing the critic to help "write" the poem he explicates, Dickinson continues in her second life, as it were, to defy those who would auction off "the mind of man." If the facsimile edition were to serve no other useful purpose, it succeeds splendidly in showing us that Dickinson will always continue as a fugitive of the so-called eclectic text. This is her legacy, or her joke on the literary establishment that — as it endeavored in the nineteenth century — continues in the twentieth to edit Dickinson to its liking, or according to its textual standards. In Higginson's time, a poem had to rhyme, it had to parse and spell right, and above all it had to make sense. In our time, a poem can do anything it pleases but it must first be itself. Entering the Dickinson workshop, however, is like entering a funhouse that is truly haunted, full of the doppelganger and the confidence man. One need only teach the usual anthology selections to find Dickinson contradicting herself

Emily Dickinson's Workshop

with the ease of Emerson and Whitman, certainly her partners in the making of the American muse. With Emerson's and Whitman's hieroglyphs, though, we have at least the wording they seem finally to have intended. With Dickinson we must choose between similar vagaries. We must judge for ourselves the better version. Perhaps "poem" *is* a safer term, for it keeps us from dismissing the other "version." It allows us to consider equally the alternate version (a choice that Thomas H. Johnson allows himself frequently between his three-volume variorum and the one-volume edition of 1960).

It might be said that the true poem is published only in *The Manuscript Books*. For where else other than in the manuscripts themselves is variant material allowed to function as Dickinson apparently intended? In other words, her final intention is represented in the way she left the poems—indeed, left most of them for more than twenty years. In making this observation, we should distinguish between single-version poems, that is, slightly different versions of the same poem sent to friends and poems that carry the variants with them. In the first group we have whole and separate poems, but in the second we find poems that are purposely unfinished. Unfortunately, this purpose has been hidden by editions that print only one version or another. Even the Johnson variorum makes the variant version subordinate by placing it in the notes. Consider, for example, "I'm Nobody! Who are you?" (no. 288). Johnson chose for his primary text in the variorum the original version, but in his 1960 edition he selected the variant version instead. In the Franklin facsimile, however, we have both versions and hence the true poem:

> I'm Nobody! Who are you?
> Are you — Nobody — too?
> Then there's a pair of us!
> Dont tell! they'd banish us — you know
>   *advertise*
> How dreary — to be — Somebody!
> How public — like a Frog —
> To tell your name — the livelong June
>   *one's*
> To an admiring Bog!

One might argue in Johnson's behalf, as Franklin did in his 1967 book, that the variant version is more appropriate to the sense of the poem. Since to a nobody who wants to remain a nobody, being advertised is worse than being banished. But the fact remains that Dickinson never canceled the original version. The facsimile, therefore, invites us to reconsider the poem. In doing so, we discover that each version constitutes a different level of cosmic consciousness, so to speak. In the original the possibility of a colloquy suggested by the first two lines is extended in the choice of "your" in the penultimate line. It is a dialogue between the self and its alter ego, the ego and the id, or whatever allegorical means we choose to dramatize the process of thought. And using the Socratic method the self and its other confront the unpleasant fact that the sum of their identities is perhaps even less than one—or nobody in the vast cosmos.

In the 1960 version the same truth is approached from another direction. The key is found in the shift from "banish" to "advertise" (its opposite in this context). Here the same belief in the hypothetical life is threatened by the *advertisement* that such a life consists of what Emerson called the Lords of Life, that long string of illusions whose sum is zero—or nobody. "Nothing is left us now but death," Emerson wrote in "Experience." "We look to that with a grim satisfaction, saying There at least is reality that will not dodge us."[2] In "I'm Nobody! Who are you?" we have Dickinson's confrontation with the final circle. Also, in the second version the loneliness that results from the discovery of the single self is underscored by the fact that the poem becomes less dialectical and more rhetorical. In both versions, to insist that one's identity is more than the sum of its illusions is as "dreary" an occupation as that of a frog telling its name "to an admiring Bog!" But with the shift from "your" to "one's," illusion of a conversation is swept away. Now the poem becomes a dramatic monologue which accentuates the inevitable state of being alone.

The theme is the same in both the 1955 and 1960 Johnson versions, merely approached from two different angles to demonstrate the paradox of going full circle with oneself. The paradox is that one can claim neither victory nor defeat in his pursuit of identity. It is both banished and advertised. The real truth—like the poet who tells it—is forever illusive, forever incomplete with the message. Hence, in this case the real Dickinson is available only in *The Manuscript Books*. Whether this is true with other variant poems remains to be seen. A similar examination of, say, "I taste a liquor never brewed" might well reveal significant nuances.

Suffice to say that Franklin presents the poetry in a new and stimulating manner. For this reason, publication of the edition is as important to us as was the Johnson variorum to the generation that was forced to depend on the erroneous editions issued variously from the houses of Todd-Higginson-Bingham and Dickinson-Bianchi-Hampson. Furthermore, the edition is presented as simply as possible for so complex an editorial operation. In an introduction in which the more burdensome jargon of textual editors is avoided, Franklin provides a brief history of the problems encountered in editing Dickinson's manuscripts and a general summary of how his edition corrects the Johnson edition. Because the variorum was arranged chronologically, it obscured Dickinson's fascicle structure. In a sense, Johnson's edition both corrected and compounded previous editorial errors. While truthful to the manuscript version (or variant), it also followed the example of the earlier editors in their ignorance of the fascicle arrangement. With Franklin's arrangement we have not only the possibility of multi-versioned poems but the possibility that Dickinson intended the fascicles themselves as artistic gatherings—"gatherings intrarelated by theme, imagery, emotional movement" (p. ix). Testing the validity of such a hypothesis is naturally beyond the scope of this review, but the question of why the poet went into the manuscript book business has not been answered with any satisfaction. We learn in the introduction that Dickinson stopped copying fascicle sheets for a time in the later 1860s as her poetic drive began to wane. She resumed the practice (on sets 8–15) in the 1870s but gradually abandoned it again as she did the writing of new poems. It has been suggested that she arranged the fascicles and sets so that a particular poem could be located easily. Yet Dickinson never numbered the packets or established any kind of index to them.

True to the penultimate nature of Dickinson's poetry, this edition presents as many questions as it does answers. Why, for example, do the earliest fascicles show no alternate readings, the first such unresolved choice appearing in Fascicle 5 and only five others through Fascicle 10? Apparently she originally set out to establish a systematic record of her poems, but variants developed as she made copies for friends. Yet it was not until about 1861 that the poet returned to the fascicles to record variants. Does this mark a point at which Dickinson began to view her work as important? And if so, what then caused her to stop this self-publication? Such questions are implicit in Franklin's edition. Generally, he sees the fascicle process as an evolutionary one that started out "as a comprehensive record of completed poems" but "became in a sense a continuing workshop." Here she would produce a new copy for friends, or in reading among the poems "enter the specific poetic process again" (p. x). With this as a possibility, we might consider the packets as a form of journal from which she composed "original" work in the same way Emerson found his "savings bank" in his journals (many of which were also sewn together by the author). Indeed, in the spirit of the multiversioned poems themselves, her method of composition may have taken the form of thematic revision. Visions and revisions.

Yet we have to stop and ask ourselves if what we might perceive as Dickinson's thematic restatements are in fact revisions of our own. That is, while the Franklin facsimile doubtless brings us closer to the original order (or disorder), it is also selective. It omits, for example, versions of the poems sent to friends and not copied into a fascicle. Even one of the seven published in the poet's lifetime ("Sic transit gloria mundi") is missing from the edition. An early poem and one of occasion (Valentine's Week), it is nevertheless part of the Dickinson canon. Missing too are poems sent next door to Susan Gilbert, the poet's sister-in-law, and poems found in Dickinson's room after her death but not part of a fascicle or set. Once again the poet has forced the editor into the role of author. Having devised a way to simplify this mass of poetic contradictions and repetitions, Franklin now points the way to a structure that has meaning. But whose meaning is it?

To say it another way, this edition seduces us into finishing the poems because it is not a variorum but a workshop. It is a laboratory of our own making, equipped with such modern conveniences as eleven appendixes and three indexes. It might be said that the editor has become a Todd to our Higginson. Like Mabel Loomis Todd, R. W. Franklin has copied out the poems for our selection and interpretation. Indeed, as potential "coeditors" we might follow Higginson's example in the 1890 edition and assign headings for the fascicles or groups of fascicles. Instead of such nineteenth-century headings as "Life," "Love," "Nature," and "Time and Eternity," we might choose headings that reflect our own anxieties. The point is that Franklin's arrangement (though certainly more scientifically arrived at) brings us no closer to the poet's *meaning* than did the first edition by Todd and Higginson. It is a selection whose purpose continues to elude us. Like the batch of poems Higginson received from Mrs. Todd, this one awaits our giving meaning to Franklin's arrangement. And yet in terms of what Dickinson's final intention really was, we haven't a clue.

We have to ask the question that Stanley Fish asks in the title of his recent book: "Is There a Text in This Class?" Never mind the current debate over the definitions and dangers of such new critical approaches as structuralism, poststructuralism, reader reponse technique, and deconstruction. In the case of Dickinson there is no one final text to deconstruct, to strip of meaning. The final meaning has already been stripped away for us by the poet herself. Walt Whitman once described himself as "furtive" as a hen, and yet the editors of the twentieth century finally tracked him down and, in an editorial undertaking that is properly described as one of the most problem-haunted in the history of American letters, forced him into a variorum.[3] But it was—alas—a variorum of the *printed* poems during the poet's lifetime. Dickinson made sure that the same for her would be brief indeed.

Furthermore, these seven poems were copy edited to contemporary literary standards. The only other poems (and there were many) that Dickinson "published" were those that she sent to friends. Here and only here do we find Dickinson in the act of final intention because she permitted them to leave the locked box. And yet with the exception of poems fortuitously duplicated in the fascicles, these "poems" (using Franklin's 1967 definition now) are excluded from the facsimile edition. Franklin was well advised to choose the title he did for his work. He demonstrates extraordinary skill and precision in carrying out the task. As archivist of the collection, he takes us on a most careful tour of the workshop of 1886. The more we see, though, the more we realize the impossibility of a variorum edition. The penultimate nature of both the arrangement and the poems themselves suggests how truly modern this poet was. Her poetry has been called the poetry of absence or silence, but it is really the poetry of choice. It has to be because a finished poem is rather like an explicated one. The counterstatement that animates all modern poetry beginning with Emerson and Whitman is gone. It no longer shimmers with the duality of truth that we find in "I'm Nobody! Who are you?" In another poem Dickinson says that the Truth "must dazzle gradually." Her poems do this best in *The Manuscript Books*.

Notes

1. *The Editing of Emily Dickinson: A Reconsideration*, ed. R. W. Franklin (Madison: Univ. of Wisconsin Press, 1967), p. 142.

2. *The Complete Works of Ralph Waldo Emerson*, ed. Waldo Emerson (Boston: Houghton-Mifflin, 1903-4), III, 49.

3. I refer to *Walt Whitman, Leaves of Grass: A Textual Variorum of the Printed Poems*, ed. Sculley Bradley et al. (New York: New York Univ. Press, 1980), 3 vols.

Biographical Decoding: Gissing's Life and Work

Robert L. Selig

John Halperin. *Gissing: A Life in Books.* Oxford: Oxford University Press, 1982. 426 pp.

John Halperin's new critical biography of Gissing has much to offer in its updated life but somewhat less in its interspersed analyses of George Gissing's works. Halperin does make a major contribution to our knowledge of the man and fills many gaps within the public record. Most attractively, the biographer approaches this gentle but troubled late-Victorian writer with sympathy and even affection. Halperin's account illuminates many shadows left by previous biographers but leaves intact our basic image of Gissing: a courageous man who overcame his youthful disgrace at college to become an important writer, yet one who always tended toward depression and who showed poor judgment in the women he chose to share his bed and board. Halperin's literary criticism, however, takes the somewhat reductive form of biographical decoding, as he attempts to show that every effective Gissing character stands as a mere projection of the writer's own attitudes and experiences.

Four earlier biographies of Gissing exist. Morley Roberts's highly unreliable and semifictionalized account, *The Private Life of Henry Maitland* (1912), mingles actual memories of Gissing's own reminiscences with erroneous details and outright inventions. Mabel Collins Donnelly's *George Gissing: Grave Comedian* (1954) provides the broad outlines of his life but displays spotty research. Jacob Korg's *George Gissing: A Critical Biography* (1963) remains the best introduction to the man and his works, though Korg lacked access to much important information discovered since 1963. Michael Collie's *George Gissing: A Biography* (1977) tries to challenge the earlier accounts but offers an undependable blend of fact, error, and fanciful speculation. Even for those quite familiar with all four previous biographies, Halperin's accurate narrative of Gissing's life provides valuable new details. Thus, in describing the eighteen-year-old Gissing's disastrous relationship with the Manchester prostitute Nell Harrison, Halperin labels the venereal disease that the young man caught from Nell as gonorrhea rather than syphilis (p. 17) — an important distinction for interpreting Gissing's later sex life.[1] Treating his 1877 year of exile in the United States, Halperin recounts his abrupt departure from a temporary teaching job in Waltham, Massachusetts, disclosing that Gissing "failed without explanation to meet his classes" and that he returned without warning to his disconcerted family in Wakefield that fall (p. 22). In recounting the novelist's erotic adventures after separating from his shrewish second wife, Halperin reveals previously unpublished details of a Gissing "affair" with one Mrs. Williams just before he began courting Gabrielle Fleury, his future third "wife" in all but name (pp. 273, 275). And toward the book's close, some poignant and hitherto unpublished quotations from Mlle. Fleury describe the last moments of the novelist's life: "He had 'no thought of horror, but of mere bewilderment.' He spoke of having 'done . . . nothing . . . How I wasted the golden days! How strong I was!' He told her: 'Life is meaningless' " (p. 348).

I must point out, however, that all the fresh material I have thus far mentioned (except, perhaps, the diagnosis of gonorrhea) comes from an as yet unpublished Gissing biography by Pierre Coustillas, who allowed Halperin use of a typed early draft. One inevitably feels a certain frustration at Halperin's frequent use of a private, though trustworthy, source, often without the accompaniment of Coustillas's documentation. Such procedure can impede fellow scholars from pursuing fresh clues or even from weighing evidence for some of Halperin's own conclusions. Also I must note Halperin's rather sparing use of unpublished Gissing letters and documents: just some twenty-nine references, with only a smattering of short direct quotations. But I have experienced quirky objections from Gissing's present heirs myself, and permission denials may in part explain Halperin's modest use of primary sources, as well as his decision to enrich his own study with materials from Coustillas's unpublished work.[2]

In addition to new material, Halperin offers many intelligent speculations about the novelist's life. Thus he argues for the likelihood of an active sex life between the novelist's first and second marriages, and he assumes that Gissing and Edith Underwood had sex together before their unwise marriage. Halperin also expresses righteous indignation at the niggardly treatment of Gissing by the publishers Smith, Elder — a "firm of cut-throats" (pp. 87–88, 113–14, 121, 139,

156-58). Perhaps most convincingly, Halperin argues that Gissing's final novels are less impressive than those from the late 1880s and mid 1890s precisely because he had become rather less unhappy: to write at his best, Halperin believes, Gissing needed the goad of depression (p. 217). Unless Coustillas's biography sees publication, *Gissing: A Life in Books* will likely remain the single fullest account of Gissing the man.

In contrast to the biographical merits of Halperin's book, its interspersed sections of critical analysis are disappointing. With a surprising lack of subtlety or caution, Halperin goes through each individual work to pick out biographical elements, like a chemist decanting a very simple mixture. Admittedly, Gissing put more of himself into his fiction than most writers do, but Halperin tends to deprive each text of an artistic existence apart from the author's life. In *The Born Exile: George Gissing*, Gillian Tindall took a somewhat similar approach but with more circumspection and also with an important caveat: "Even when such a writer does set out to put chunks of his own life straight into a book . . . the writing-mechanism inevitably proceeds of its own volition, subtly altering, transforming, sharpening, making the fictional account different in a number of ways from the reality."[3] In a contrasting and typical passage, Halperin takes a reductive approach to one of the writer's most objectified and richly imagined novels, *Born in Exile*. Halperin calls it "one of Gissing's most sustained pieces of fictional autobiography" and asserts that "the stories of Peak and Gissing are virtually identical" (pp. 159-60). He then gives a simple list of resemblances between the novel's hero, Godwin Peak, and his creator. Each has left college under embarrassing circumstances, each yearns to marry a rich and cultivated woman, each feels himself in a state of social exile, and each displays acute shame about his lower-middle-class origins (pp. 159-60). Yet Halperin ignores the obvious differences between Peak's behavior and that of George Gissing. Peak woos Sidwell Warricombe, the gracious daughter of wealthy country folk, but Gissing, when he wrote *Born in Exile*, had just married an ignorant London slattern. In order to impress Sidwell, Peak commits the intellectual fraud of a skeptic who masquerades as a candidate for the clergy, but Gissing persisted in writing depressive works of fiction in spite of his wish to win the approval of a British reading public that craved moral uplift. Most importantly, Peak has a harsh virility, a sternness, and a decisiveness that his gentle and self-abnegating creator always lacked. And Gissing judges the hypocritical Peak with a cool and unsentimental objectivity. If this is autobiography, then what is fiction?

In addition to finding autobiography where there is none, Halperin tries, inappropriately, to convert it into an instrument for evaluating the merit of each of Gissing's works. At least Gillian Tindall handles the art-life relationship in a thematic way, but Halperin marches through every single book with a heavy biographical tread and then ranks each along a scale of excellence on the basis of one criterion: how well the book projects an effective self-portrait of Gissing. For example, he dismisses *Our Friend the Charlatan* as Gissing's third poorest novel (in my opinion, an above average though not a major work) because the protagonist "is not a 'Gissing-*persona*' " and because "Gissing could only successfully write about himself" (p. 307). On the other hand, Halperin calls *In the Year of Jubilee* (in my opinion, a flawed though culturally interesting novel) "one of Gissing's greatest achievements" and concludes that its "immense power . . . lies in its autobiographical content" (pp. 198, 202). Halperin asserts that both the male and female protagonists are projections of Gissing himself: "The result of their marriage is an oddity among the novels: two 'Gissings' wedded to one another" (p. 204). But, in fact, all that the heroine has in common with her creator is a nagging uncertainty about her "social position" (pp. 203-4)—an uncertainty caused by a pseudoeducation which has nothing in common with Gissing's own solid training in the classics and English literature: "Miss Lord represented a type; to study her as a sample of the pretentious half-educated class was interesting; this sort of girl was turned out in thousands every year, from so-called High Schools; if they managed to pass some examination or other, their conceit grew boundless. Craftily, he [Lionel Tarrant—the hero] had tested her knowledge; it seemed all sham."[4] In short, Nancy Lord hardly has Gissing's basic attributes, not even in feminine disguise. In contrast to the heroine, Lionel Tarrant is all too much a wish-fulfilling projection of Gissing's own desire to escape from the obligations of his hateful second marriage. However, the novelist's failure to judge with any adequacy Tarrant's desertion of his pregnant wife, Nancy, stands as a weakness—not as a sign of "greatness."

Halperin blurs the distinction between well-objectified characters who share some of Gissing's traits and those who appear as daydream self-projections. In discussing *New Grub Street*, that masterful portrayal of numerous struggling writers, Halperin notes that the one with the temperament closest to Gissing's, the novelist Edwin Reardon, has a "self-destructive, impractical side . . . insisted upon with a vehemence approaching self-mockery" (p. 143). In this context the term "self-mockery" oversimplifies Gissing's fictional achievement of creating, weighing, and judging a character who may well be based on certain aspects of himself. But in discussing *Sleeping Fires* and proclaiming it "one of the greatest short novels ever written" (p. 220), Halperin ignores the lack of fictional objectivity in this minor little silver-fork romance. The hero, Langley, represents Gissing's fondest dreams of wealth and endless leisure for perpetual world tourism: "The nobleman's death enriched him with a legacy of which he stood in no need whatever, and murmuring to himself, 'To him that hath shall be given,' he wandered off to spend a year or two abroad."[5] Even more damagingly, *Sleeping Fires* becomes a piece of fictional special pleading for Gissing's own sexual disasters and mistakes. Long before the story begins, the heroine has jilted Langley because he had fathered an illegitimate son. Although the protagonist loses track of his boy, the heroine finds him and brings him up herself but conceals his existence from Langley. When she finally reveals the boy's identity to him, this long-lost child dies suddenly, and Langley blames her for having kept the boy away from him. Finally she admits her narrow-minded errors and agrees to marry Langley and live happily ever after. For Halperin to call such a self-indulgent daydream a "neglected masterpiece" does injustice to Gissing's genuine masterworks—*New Grub Street* and *Born in Exile*—in which he transforms aspects of his own private experience into objectified narrative art.

Other unconvincing judgments result from Halperin's insistence upon evaluating each work by biographical standards. Two more examples stand out. *The Emancipated*, a grossly neglected novel, is dismissed as "a disappointment." Inaccurately, he makes the book sound like the far-inferior *Sleeping Fires*: "The 'emancipation' at issue is that from narrow prejudice, mostly female, in social and religious matters" (p. 123). Halperin mistakes the rantings against "Puritan morality" by the second-rate Reuben Elgar for Gissing's own polemics and unfairly concludes that "the commentary on religion is not subtle" (pp. 123-24). With equal imprecision, he takes as Gissing's own credo Cecily Doran's inexperienced belief that "an artist is privileged" (p. 125), though she quickly learns her mistake when the pseudoartist Elgar brutally mistreats her and the genuine one, Mallard, behaves with scrupulous decency. Subtlety in *The Emancipated* arises, in fact, from an essentially Arnoldian position: although enlightened human beings should reject puritanical dogmas, they must still live ethically, especially if they aim to produce great art.

A similar critical distortion occurs when Halperin curtly dismisses Gissing's large body of very fine short stories: "Yet Gissing never really mastered the short story: only a few of the hundred or so he wrote are first-rate" (p. 191). One's confidence in this judgment is undermined as Halperin goes through selected examples in search of biographical traces. In actuality the typical short story from Gissing's mature period achieves greater detachment and narrative objectivity than many of his full-length novels. But consider Halperin's complete remarks on one of Gissing's most delightful short pieces, "Comrades in Arms":

> Among the stories written for Shorter's *English Illustrated Magazine* in December 1893 is "Comrades in Arms," which extols the virtues of having as few attachments and dependants as possible, especially when young. The protagonist is another writer, this one contemptuous of public taste and fearful of accidentally writing a best-seller. He lives in lodging and relishes his isolation. When you are poor it is better to be lonely and free than attached to someone and thus responsible for his welfare, the story tells us. Here is Gissing unmarrying himself again in imagination. [p. 193]

But "Comrades in Arms" deals with a relationship between a male dissatisfied with loneliness and a perky newspaperwoman who loves her independence. With good-humored firmness, she rejects the man's advances in order to keep her womanly freedom and to avoid the cultural stereotype of feminine homemaker. "Dear boy," she tells her suitor, "I don't want to marry. Look at this room, dirty and disorderly. This is all the home I care for."[6] From Halperin's account of this piece as simple autobiography, who could tell that it contains one of Gissing's most appealing portraits of a liberated woman, a late-Victorian heroine in the feminist mode?

Halperin attacks those critics who believe that Gissing's fiction might sometimes refer to movements in the social world around him — feminism, say, or socialism — rather than to Gissing's private life and his own private feelings. Thus Halperin rebukes social critics of *Demos* (a book he overrates): "Modern criticism has often attempted—perversely, I think—to assess the accuracy of his account of English socialism in the eighties instead of dealing with it as fiction. *Demos* is not a historical novel; it is a discussion of social behavior and class. Gissing made no real attempt to write contemporary history, though certainly he wanted to cash in on current social and political unease. As always, his object was to create a work of art. And in this he succeeded, for *Demos* is his first great "art." Halperin's position might seem a logical outgrowth of the "contemporary history" and "social behavior and class," one wonders if a work that reflects its own times really does exclude itself from "art." Halperin's position might seem a logical outgrowth of the poststructuralist credo—that the written word cannot refer to the nonwritten world—except that he also asserts that most of Gissing's fiction refers to external events from the novelist's own life. In any case, throughout his study Halperin often appears to contradict his own stated objections to critical readings of Gissing that take account of "contemporary history." Thus he praises the judiciousness of *The Private Papers of Henry Ryecroft* in attacking modern science for creating hideous military weapons (p. vii). He admires *In the Year of Jubilee* for its "vision" of mass advertising "as the most visible sign of modern triviality and decay" (pp. 206-7). He commends *The Whirlpool* and also *The Crown of Life* for describing English imperialism as a threat to world peace (pp. 246, 294). And most insistently of all, Halperin points to Gissing's perceptive "environmentalism"—his defense of green countryside against industrial blight—in *A Life's Morning* (p. 70), *Demos* (pp. 81-82), *Denzil Quarrier* (p. 169), and *In the Year of Jubilee* (pp. 205-6). Presumably Halperin cares more about such matters than he cares about English socialism, but how can he evaluate the accuracy of these fictional warnings against scientific warfare, mass culture, imperialism, or ecological rot without examining the world in which Gissing lived as well as our own world?

All the same, one can in some measure sympathize with Halperin's critical inconsistencies, for he clearly wishes to do more in his interspersed analyses than biographical decoding can readily permit. However inappropriate his method seems, one must respect his efforts to evaluate anew Gissing's many books and to question fixed opinions about their relative worth. Gissing's critics have often failed to take sufficient account of the unusually wide gap between his finest works and his failures. Although one often disagrees with

Halperin's reassessments and often feels dissatisfied with his stated critical reasons, one can frequently applaud isolated judgments: that *The Nether World*, *Born in Exile*, and *The Private Papers of Henry Ryecroft* are first-rate Gissing achievements (p. 2); that *The Paying Guest* is an underrated comic novella (p. 223); that *By the Ionian Sea*—a now neglected travel memoir—is a showcase of "some of Gissing's best writing" (p. 299). Above all, one can endorse Halperin's strong praise of *New Grub Street*: "*New Grub Street* . . . is in my opinion an unqualified masterpiece. Certainly it is better than any novel by Disraeli, Collins, Reade, Kingsley, or George Moore, better than any of Mrs. Gaskell's novels with the possible exception of *Wives and Daughters*, better than any of Charlotte Brontë's novels with the possible exception of *Jane Eyre*, better than any of Meredith's novels with the possible exceptions of *The Ordeal of Richard Feverel* and *The Egoist*; indeed, it may well be a greater novel than any of those I have named" (p. 2). If Halperin's method had allowed him to give relevant critical reasons for his high opinion of these and other Gissing chefs-d'oeuvre, one could recommend *George Gissing: A Life in Books* for its critical arguments as well as its biography. But Halperin succeeds far better in telling the story of George Gissing's life than in analyzing the work of this major and still neglected storyteller.

Notes

1. Regrettably, Halperin's documentation fails to make clear the evidence for this diagnosis. Is it based on a medical doctor's opinion concerning the "salmon-coloured" and spotted inside of the "swollen" prepuce, graphically described by Gissing's Owen College friend, John George Black—who had caught the same venereal disease from Nell? See P. Coustillas, "George Gissing à Manchester," *Etudes Anglaises*, 16 (July–September 1963), 258-59.

2. In recognition of his large debt, Halperin dedicates *Gissing: A Biography* to Coustillas.

3. Gillian Tindall, *The Born Exile: George Gissing* (London: Temple Smith, 1974), p. 24.

4. George Gissing, *In the Year of Jubilee*, 3 vols. (London: Lawrence and Bullen, 1894), II, 21.

5. George Gissing, *Sleeping Fires* (New York: D. Appleton, 1896), p. 29.

6. George Gissing, "Comrades in Arms," in his *Human Odds and Ends: Stories and Sketches* (London: Lawrence and Bullen, 1898), p. 16.

and their work is marked by a charm and passion that too seldom appear in more professional approaches to the field.

The two books under consideration serve quite respectably to represent the mixture of professional and amateur study that seems to characterize the history of detective fiction criticism. They also represent, both separately and together, the continuing difficulties that beset such criticism. If one can apply Bacon's notions of delicate learning, contentious learning, and fantastical learning to research on the thriller, even a slight familiarity with its history demonstrates that delicate learning has dominated the field, though fantastical learning is rapidly overtaking it. The traditional criticism of the genre has been done by slumming intellectuals, dabbling with their left hands in the style of the amateurs, without committing themselves to any genuine engagement. They were often serious scholars in other, more acceptable kinds of literature who wrote about a favorite book or two, an author that pleased them, or confessed with a delighted shame that they enjoyed reading Dorothy Sayers or Agatha Christie. In recent years, such criticism has been pushed aside by explorers returned from exotic climes—myth studies, structuralism, Russian Formalist criticism, semiotics, the works of all those difficult Frenchmen with the hyphenated names—eager to try out their newly acquired skills on a field ripe for harvesting. Many of the pioneers in those sorts of studies have dealt with popular culture in richly suggestive ways, and detective fiction often turns out to be especially fertile ground for their methods and purposes.

Like just about everyone else who has ventured into the tricky business of examining detective fiction, Dennis Porter and Robin Winks seek to discover exactly why people read it in the first place. This is always the starting point, partly because all of us believe we have the answer that has eluded everyone else. Oddly, I can think of no other kind of literary analysis that compels its practitioner to initiate his work with that question, which indicates the peculiar difficulties of the subject; nobody, after all, needs to explain why people read epics or sonnets or has to justify an interest in the poetry of Samuel Johnson or songs from the plays of Henry James. Every critic of the genre, however, must respond to the notorious questions, posed by Edmund Wilson in two more or less curmudgeonly essays: "Why Do People Read Detective Stories?" and "Who Cares Who Killed Roger Ackroyd?"

The second question, of course, is much easier to answer than the first. As Wilson surely knew, millions of readers enjoy detective fiction—I have always felt he intended to be deliberately provocative in those essays anyway—including those who write about it. The ways that Porter and Robin Winks choose to answer the first question very neatly delineate their differences as well as the two major paths of detective fiction criticism. Although both are academics, only Porter approaches his topic with something of the familiar methodology of the professional student of literature; a professor of French, Porter employs the theories of a number of those sexy Europeans who are so fashionable in literary study today. Even though Winks, a professor of history, is the mystery reviewer for the *New Republic*, he consciously assumes the stance of the amateur in manner and matter. Appropriately, Porter's book is a "pursuit," while Winks's is subtitled "an excursion." The former is a serious scholarly-critical effort, the latter an extended personal essay. One can properly be called an analysis, the other an appreciation: each displays the mixture of virtues and defects typical of its approach.

Dennis Porter begins his study by citing briefly the major objections to detective fiction—"predictable problems of no intrinsic interest, stereotyped characterizations, and undistinguished writing. . . . a literature for puzzle addicts and thrill seekers produced at best by ingenious purveyors of commodities" (p. 3). To these objections he proposes two main lines of defense, which also indicate some of the directions of his inquiry. He points out that such recent schools as Russian Formalism, French structuralism, and American myth criticism have all shown the pervasiveness and importance of formula at all levels of literature, suggesting that "it is no longer possible simply to dismiss a work on the grounds that it involves the application of formula" (p. 3). Beyond the problem for formula, however, Porter's real interest lies in the peculiar qualities of relaxation and escape offered by detective fiction and apparently desired by its readers: "Why . . . do a great many people escape into detective novel reading as opposed, say, to other recreational activities such as making love, watching football, vacationing, buying clothes, listening to music, or simply walking the dog?" (pp. 3-4). He concentrates, therefore, on "readability," those aspects of form and content peculiar to detective fiction that entice a reader, sustain the attraction over the length of a book, and resolve themselves into a satisfactory conclusion. He proposes to examine the "relationship of complicity between an author and a reader, involving the acknowledgement of shared community values as well as of fixed narrative forms" (p. 6). His discussion of narrative gives us the "art" of his subtitle, while his discussion of theme what he chooses to call "ideology."

Dividing his book into two parts, each devoted to one of those concerns, Porter aligns himself with those critics, mostly European, who have studied such matters as folklore, fairy tales, and other formulaic literature, narrativity, and reader-centered analysis. The names he most often drops are now familiar: Claude Lévi-Strauss, Tzvetan Todorov, Viktor Shklovsky, Vladimir Propp, and above all, Roland Barthes. His investigations, like theirs, lead him to some often interesting conclusions, though many of them do not differ except in density of language from more traditional study. Studying a surprisingly few authors and books, he believes that the suspenseful narrative of all sorts of detective fiction has as its goal not completion but retardation, that readers enjoy most of all the impediment of progress through a book, which neatly reverses many previous assumptions about keeping the pages turning and hurtling relentlessly toward a conclusion. Suspense becomes, for Porter, an assortment of devices and digressions that create resistance in the form of enjoyable obstacles to the movement of the tale.

This unusual premise, stated with some care and some attention to a few specific texts, enables Porter to devote much of the rest of his book to some generally old-fashioned literary-historical work. He rehashes a quantity of familiar facts about the development of police forces and pertinent information about some authors' lives, going over quite well traveled territory. Then he settles down to straightforward, traditional, orthodox study of specific works of fiction, particular passages in them, and common elements of the form. One of his best chapters, "The Language of Detection," is simply an intelligent close analysis of distinctive passages from a few memorable books, not very much different from the sort of thing any close reader, especially an unreconstructed (should that be deconstructed?) old New Critic, would do. He focuses on such matters as sentence structure, diction, imagery, phrases, punctuation, and so forth, a procedure that strikes me as a useful and not at all unusual method of analysis. In dealing with narrative and its interruptions, he can't quite bring himself to write of structure and texture, but apparently that is exactly what he is studying, despite the fancy gift wrapping of flashy vocabulary. In a short chapter entitled "The Landscape of Detection" he again shows that he can do a perfectly good job on an important and specific element of form without recourse to the obscure abstractions of some of the theories he professes. When he does examine the specifications of structure and texture, items of dialogue, character, and description and their relationship to the progress of the story, he finds that these conventional devices come to be entertaining, informative, even enriching ways of making the narrative pause. They then somehow cause in the reader a pleasurable postponement of his final gratification.

Porter discovers in both the peculiar techniques of narrative delay and the reassuring ideology of detective fiction an important example of readability and how it works; he further suggests that the real basis for narrative, ideology, and everything else that constitutes readability resides in sexuality. All pleasures, he suggests, are essentially sexual and the pleasures of narrative follow the model of the sexual act. Narrative delayed is pleasure postponed—pauses excite and intensify reader engagement, becoming a kind of intrinsically enjoyable foreplay ("forepleasure" is his word) that impedes and thus contributes to the orgasmic completion. The detective story, he concludes, presents more nakedly than other literary genres an intellectual version of the classic pattern of sexual engagement, an erotics of narrative. This is all very fine, of course, but seems to have several things wrong with it, beyond reminding us that intellectuals always end up talking dirty. For one thing, it is very familiar, far too much like the stuff we've all been hearing since high school about rising and falling action, climaxes, and so forth. For another, any narrative, perhaps even any action that forms itself into a discernible series or sequence, can no doubt be seen to possess not only a beginning, middle, and end, but an excitation, a foreplay, a tumescence, climax, and detumescene. Mr. Porter, oddly, only admits the possibility of a verbal narrative— entirely forgetting about the visual and the auditory narratives we are all familiar with—and he never seems to realize the reductive nature of his sexual reading of a normal and ordinary sequence. I think his notion of sex a bit naive as well, but that's also characteristic of intellectuals.

The rest of Porter's book offers little that is new. Like most academic critics of the genre, Porter really knows very few detective novelists and prefers to work with a very few examples. His extensive discussions of Conan Doyle, Fleming, Hammett, and Chandler demonstrate no knowledge of the best work on those writers and, consequently, repeat a great deal that has already been done. His chapter on

Simenon, curiously for a professor of French, is one of the weakest in the book. He has a perfunctory concluding section, "Beyond Detection," which does not advance his thesis very far, though it ties things together neatly. In it he takes seriously the silly argument about detective fiction presenting us with a disguised version of the Primal Scene, an even more reductive interpretation than anything he himself has proposed, and even spends time on the frivolous and, frankly, foolish ideas of Marjorie Nicolson in her essay "The Professor and the Detective."[1]

One important truth about the new wave of literary studies from which Porter derives some of his ideas must not go unremarked. Whenever a formalist, structuralist, phenomenologist, deconstructionist, semiotician, or practitioner of whatever the latest -ology or -ism may be — whenever he feels constrained to state his ideas at their most intense point of summary, or whenever he seems headed for uncertainty, the first sign is a stagnant cloud of impenetrable terminology. When in doubt, throw words at the unsuspecting reader. My favorite example of this tendency in Porter's book is a sentence that for opacity alone suits his definition of narrative impediment but, alas, provides no joy at all. It occurs on page 94 in his chapter, ironically, on "The Detective Novel as Readable Text": "Up to this point in my discussion of readability I have concentrated on the syntagmatic axis of narrative — on the way in which it is structured by the combined hermeneutic and proairetic codes, so that it forms itself into a logico-temporal whole — and on rhetorical devices employed to facilitate the reader's task by ordering and signposting the abundance of verbal material to be processed." Not only do I not feel an orgasm coming on, I can't even work up the ghost of a tingle. Perhaps he's not my type.

Whatever my objections to Porter's warmed-over insights and banal conclusions, and to his occasionally opaque prose, *The Pursuit of Crime* is undoubtedly a serious, careful, and sometimes successful attempt at dealing with an interesting and difficult subject. Though narrow, derivative, and often reductive, it systematically confronts its central problem and suggests some useful solutions. If Porter's windup is usually more substantial than his delivery, he does manage to get the ball over the plate now and then.

In contrast with *The Pursuit of Crime,* Robin Winks's *Modus Operandi* stakes out an almost invulnerable position for itself and constantly returns to that position throughout the course of its "excursion." Winks wanders casually through a great many books, authors, and ideas, seldom bothering to prove his assertions or to extend his really outrageous statements into logical argument or specific analysis. Thus, he recurrently reminds his readers that he is, after all, only an amateur and only conducting an excursion. Who could be so unkind, so solemn, so pedantic, so stuffy as to demand some intellectual responsibility from a man gaily proffering charming little bouquets of personal opinion in a highly self-regarding style? Well, it's a thankless job, but someone has to do it: it might as well be me. Whatever its virtues, one of the most irritating qualities of Winks's book is its tone of ironic self-deprecation, a pose that enables an author to get away with a lot without being called to account; it is a characteristic of a great deal of traditional criticism of detective fiction, as Winks himself hints, and is probably as pedantic a method of defense as a battery of turgid footnotes or a whole bibliography translated from the original Hungarian. It is also typical of the nosegay school of criticism in general — all nudges in the ribs, raised eyebrows, and delicate sniffs.

After his first long paragraph, wry in tone, allusive in method, relaxed in attitude, Winks follows with another paragraph commenting on the first, talking of just how much the "Low Brow," the "Middle Brow," and the "High Brow" will have derived from his introduction. He makes it quite clear that he is aiming to furrow the higher sort of brow but will not take the trouble of "several German doctoral dissertations" to draw fine lines and make subtle distinctions between categories. (Even if they deserve it, it seems to me that the poor Germans do get blamed for rather a lot in literary scholarship.) As he tells us, "This is an intensely personal essay; it does not seek to 'cover' the field, 'fill a gap,' 'survey a scene,' or provide a theory of literary criticism. It is precisely as advertised: an excursion" (p. 5). Yet despite all these modest disclaimers and sporadic dabblings, and his insistence on "the intensely personal" quality of his book, Winks, often rather offhandedly, lays down quite a lot of dogma in his stroll through detective literature. On two facing pages, chosen (honestly) at random, I find "Except in rare instances — the Australian film *Breaker Morant* is one such instance — visual modes no longer successfully carry pure narrative" (p. 44), which not only denies the fact of hundreds of recent films, good and bad, but also characteristically cites an "approved" film, which just happens to be a slow, talky example of a stage play turned into a movie, a rather unsuccessful piece of narrative. On the next page he remarks in passing on "John Dickson Carr's sterile exercises in sophistry, sometimes called 'locked-room puzzles.'" But isn't Carr one of the great practitioners of the classic detective novel? Like him or not, he deserves at least equal consideration with Agatha Christie, whom Winks admires.

Both quotations demonstrate certain qualities about Winks's style and tone. He has a clever way of dismissing or praising certain works, writers, or notions in an aside, as if to avoid the necessity of proving or illustrating his remarks. On the other hand, though he claims to love the form, he always reminds his reader of the excellence of his taste in other matters; in those instances, he invariably alludes to something acceptably highbrow, protecting his judgements with received opinion. In both style and content his book, whatever its personal scope and intent, seems to me therefore a great deal more academic in the worst senses of the word than the serious scholarly effort of someone like Dennis Porter.

Winks has a certain perhaps unnameable quality in his prose that reminds me very much of the writing of William F. Buckley, another writer he admires. It has just that terribly smug and falsely sophisticated tone, that embarassing failure to achieve its effects entirely, that pretense that one shares the writer's assumptions about everything but must admit his superiority in all respects: it always reminds me of some runner who is terrific at the ninety-yard dash. It is a prose honed by years of reading the right books for the right reasons among the right people at the right schools: at bottom, as Winks's beloved Henry James would say, it is dead wrong in every way.

Although his taste is often bad, Winks, unlike Porter, has read a great many mysteries by a great many writers; though his book is about a third the length of *The Pursuit of Crime,* it displays a much greater familiarity with the whole genre and with some of its better-known critics than Porter's book. Porter, for example, devotes an entire chapter—a well organized, clearly written, intelligently reasoned one at that—to "The Landscape of Detection," in which, if he says nothing new, he succeeds at least in fitting that subject into the entirety of his study. He cites only a few writers but quotes a handful of relevant passages and compresses a wide range or reference into a coherent statement. In *Modus Operadi,* on the other hand, we find in three or four pages almost three dozen writers and books mentioned in a discussion of landscape. This particular section, by the way, demonstrates so precisely the nature of Winks's approach and the special qualities of his experience that it demands at least some quotation. After telling us of walking the landscape of John Buchan's *The Thirty-Nine Steps,* Winks goes on to recall reading Hardy in Winchester, Lawrence in Australia, Edith Wharton at some place called the Mount, Maugham in Singapore, and so on. He then tells firsthand of the vividness of certain books in capturing other places he has been— Tanganyika ("in 1954 when still a colony"—I believe that's what Kingsley Amis called postgraduate one-upmanship), South Africa, northern Holland, Spain, Armidale, New South Wales (a nice touch), and, "though I have not been to Tibet, I have been up and over that part of the Himalayas by which one drops down from Darjeeling into Gangtok, in Sikkim, and Lionel Davidson's *Rose of Tibet* seemed right there" (p. 61). There's more, but this should be enough to show just what kind of excursion we are being taken on. Winks's rapid-fire namedropping and placedropping make one feel as if he were flipping through several issues of *National Geographic,* ending up with that dizzying drop into Gangtok, in Sikkim. The whole thing would be even more offensive, I suppose, if it weren't so unintentionally funny.

Like most dabblers in the great amateur tradition, Winks is a snob. He has the right opinions for the right time of year—feminism is in, so it's okay, but William Haggard, the quiet fascist of the spy novel, is also okay because his racism is of the gentlemanly sort. I would have bet the mortgage that Winks, like most academics, loves Sayers's *Gaudy Night,* a long, dreary, self-indulgent, sentimental falsification of academic life, full of poisonous class hatred and the sort of writing that reminds us of what a Joyce character calls the "opal hush boys." And of course Winks does love it. His book is full of all sorts of examples of fashionable academic choices, mostly conditioned by the context of gentility and breeding that surround his preferences: if anti-Catholicism is the anti-Semitism of the intellectual, then feminism and Anglophilia are the badges of his hatred of the lower classes.

In some manner sad to contemplate, the usual choice of the serious student of detective fiction is represented in these two books and their several contrasts. Surely there must be a middle way—a love of the genre, a knowledge of mysteries, of the secondary work they have engendered, and of literature in general. These would seem to be the best foundations for such a mediating approach. Perhaps too many students of the genre feel impelled to give us the true and, therefore, last word on it, rather than learning to coexist with a variety of differing theories and interpretations. There has to be a way to study detective fiction that works literarily, without recourse to occasionally bizarre structures and premises; there must also be a way to do so with wit and clarity instead of archness and withered whimsy. Both books possess a certain value, but unfortunately do not possess it in common. One is solid, as they say, but deeply flawed by its singleminded commitment to a rather tenuous thesis; the other has superficial charm and great readability, but underneath seems specious and perhaps even corrupt. Porter's book seems wrong in many places but well worth knowing; although there is probably more common sense in Winks's book, it seems to me forgettable. Porter is provocative, Winks merely provoking. I can disagree wholeheartedly with the former but still learn from him; I can share many of the tastes of the latter but find his book unsatisfying. *The Pursuit of Crime* is a useful book on detective fiction; *Modus Operandi* is a lightweight ramble through the same territory. In general I have to prefer the professional job over the amateur, the critic over the fan, wishing each had perhaps a little of the other.

Notes

1. Marjorie Hope Nicolson, "The Professor and the Detective," in *The Art of the Mystery Story*, ed. Howard Haycraft (New York: Grosset and Dunlap, 1947), pp. 110-27.

Contributors

Gary L. Aho is Associate Professor of English at the University of Massachusetts, Amherst.

Quentin Anderson is Levi Professor in the Humanities, Emeritus, at Columbia University.

Scott Donaldson is Professor of English at the College of William and Mary.

Maurice English is Director of the University of Pennsylvania Press.

Richard J. Finneran is Professor of English at Newcomb College.

Melvin J. Friedman is Professor of Comparative Literature and English at the University of Wisconsin, Milwaukee.

George Grella is Associate Professor of English at the University of Rochester.

Mary Hamel is Associate Professor of English at Mount Saint Mary's College.

Paul S. Koda is Curator of Rare Books at the University of North Carolina, Chapel Hill.

Jacob Korg is Professor of English at the University of Washington.

Michael Kramer is Assistant Professor of English, University of California, Davis.

Ian Lancashire is Professor of English at the University of Toronto, Mississauga.

Kent Ljungquist is Associate Professor of English at Worcester Polytechnic Institute.

Jerome Loving is Professor of English at Texas A & M University.

Christian K. Messenger is Associate Professor of English at the University of Illinois, Chicago.

Robert L. Selig is Professor of English at Purdue University, Calumet.

JOHN A. WILLIAMS is Professor of English at Rutgers University, Newark College of Arts and Sciences.

JOSEPH WITTREICH is Professor of English at the University of Maryland.